second edition

the
social psychology
of organizing

KARL E. WEICK
Cornell University

McGraw-Hill, Inc.
New York St. Louis San Francisco Auckland Bogotá
Caracas Lisbon London Madrid Mexico City Milan
Montreal New Delhi San Juan Singapore
Sydney Tokyo Toronto

THE SOCIAL PSYCHOLOGY OF ORGANIZING

Library of Congress Cataloging in Publication Data

Weick, Karl E.
   The social psychology of organizing.

   (Topics in social psychology)
   Bibliography: p.
   Includes index.
   1. Organization-Psychological aspects.
1. Title.
HM131. W39 1979   301.18'32   79-10015
ISBN 0-07-554808-9

Second Edition
24 25 26 27 28 QSR QSR 0 9 8 7 6 5 4

This book is printed on acid-free paper.

foreword

This series *Topics in Social Psychology* is directed toward the student with no prior background in social psychology. Taken as a whole, the series covers the ever-expanding field of social psychology reasonably well, but a major advantage of the series is that each individual book was written by well-known scholars in the area. The instructor can select a subset of the books to make up the course in social psychology, the particular subset depending on the instructor's own definition of our field. The original purpose of this series was to provide such freedom for the instructor while maintaining a thoughtful and expert treatment of each topic. In addition, the first editions of the series have been widely used in a variety of other ways: such as supplementary reading in nonpsychology courses; to introduce more advanced courses in psychology, or for the sheer fun of peeking at recent developments in social psychology.

We have developed second editions that serve much the same purpose. Each book is somewhat longer and more open in design, uses updated materials, and in general takes advantage of constructive feedback from colleagues and students across the country. So many people found the first editions of the individual books useful that we have tried to make the second editions even more thorough and complete, and therefore more easily separated from the rest of the series.

Karl Weick's contribution to this series centers on the psychology of organizing—when and why people do it. Weick's fresh and innovative approach to this classic problem provides an intriguing introduction for the beginning student. Indeed, Weick's creativity is so evident in this volume that more advanced students will find it very stimulating.

Charles A. Kiesler

acknowledgments

Initially I wish to acknowledge the National Science Foundation (BNS 75-09864) for their support of the theoretical development summarized in this volume.

Piet Hein delights in defining man as that animal who himself draws lines that he himself stumbles over. I delight in the fact that my world has a few people who understand line drawing and stumbling, people who gloss the stumbling artfully and who are tolerant patrons of those artists in everyday life who insist on drawing still more lines. These rare and wondrous people made this book possible. This is as much a book by Ellen Berscheid, Michel Bougon, Justin Davidson, Craig Lundberg, James March, Marge Marquis, Fritz Mulhauser, Lou Pondy, Gerald Salancik, Milton Trapold, Peter Vaill, Caroline Violette, Gene Webb, and our Swedish son Björn Lorentzon, as it is a book by me. From close in, our three sons, Kirk, Kyle, and Kris, live line drawing rather than write about it, which makes it a fleshy, human, often gentle world. Finally, Karen's artlessness, sense of humor, and patience stitch the whole thing together so that occasionally it makes sense, which is why we all dedicate this book to her with love.

v

contents

interlocked behaviors and organizing   89

natural selection and organizing   119

enactment and organizing   147

selection and organizing   171

retention and organizing 205

implications of organizing 233

This book is about organizational appreciation. To understand organizing is to appreciate events such as these:

an introduction to organizing

A professor, named Alex Bavelas, often plays golf with other professors. "Once, he took the foursome down to the golf course, and they were going to draw straws for partners. He said, 'Let's do this *after* the game' " (Brand 1975, p. 47).

"The story goes that three umpires disagreed about the task of calling balls and strikes. The first one said, 'I calls them as they is.' The second one said, 'I calls them as I sees them.' The third and cleverest umpire said, 'They ain't nothin' till I calls them' " (Simons 1976, p. 29).

"A police officer with a special ability for resolving sticky situations in unusual ways, often involving a disarming use of humor, was in the process of issuing a citation for a minor traffic violation when a hostile crowd began to gather around him. By the time he had given the offender his ticket, the mood of the crowd was ugly and the sergeant was not certain he would be able to get back to the relative safety of his patrol car. It then occurred to him to announce in a loud voice: 'You have just witnessed the issuance of a traffic ticket by a member of your Oakland Police Department.' And while the bystanders were busy trying to fathom the deeper meaning of this all too obvious communique, he got into his cruiser and drove off" (Watzlawick, Weakland, and Fisch 1974, pp. 108-9).

In 1938 the Ford Motor Car Co. tried to reach a new group of customers by introducing a car that was smaller than their V8 in size and power. After several years of development they produced a car (dubbed 92A) that was narrower, shorter, and 600 pounds lighter than the regular Ford. However, the small motor cost only $3 less to manufacture and the entire car could be built for only $36 less than the big car. By mid-April the project was abandoned, signifying that the company would not expand the range of its models downward (Nevins and Hill 1963, p. 118).

Farmers have been buying heavier and more advanced machinery to save labor. The heavier machines have caused problems. "They pack the soil and sometimes harden the subsoil and keep water from penetrating to the plant's roots. The subsoil then must be tilled with an even larger, deeper plow which, of course, requires a more powerful tractor to pull it" (Reed 1975).

"Uruguayan conductor Jose Serebrier stabbed himself through the hand with his baton when he became 'over-passionate' while leading 180 members of a brass-percussion ensemble and chorus through a special Easter musical festival in Mexico City recently. 'The baton broke into pieces,' Serebrier said. 'One piece was sticking through my hand. I guess I was more surprised than anybody. Ironically I never use a baton. But I decided to use one for this performance because I thought it would help achieve greater musical control. That was a mistake because I got over-passionate. All of a sudden I had stabbed myself. But I didn't stop conducting. I managed to pull the piece of baton out of my hand without stopping the music.' The band played on and the chorus sang for another 20 minutes until the finale. Afterwards Serebrier was taken to a local hospital for treatment" ("Suicide attempts?" April 10, 1975).

"Time-motion and eye-movement studies confirm my observation that conductors are able to fix visually different performers at precisely defined times and then make sweeping gestures in their direction. In a previous study I found that successful quarterbacks do the same thing, singling one player out of many after a precise number of counts and, with a precise overhand motion, projecting a score object in that player's direction. Since plots of quarterback and conductor ages show little overlap, it is evident that one could quite successfully become the other. This concept, called Sequential Career Commonality Utilization, is now being applied in many other fields, and the Sequential Career Commonality Utilization Branch is slated to achieve bureau status in a few years. The greatest breakthrough achieved by this branch was the finding of politician-night watchman commonalities, such as random walking, peering into darkness, and lack of a requirement for intelligent conversation suggesting that either could serve as the other" (Anderson 1974, p. 727).

"Secretary of the Army Howard H. Callaway is asking that his 'Glad You Asked' policy be considered throughout the Army. Secretary Callaway explained the 'Glad You Asked' concept this way: suppose that tomorrow morning someone calls you and asks about your stickiest problem—the last thing in the world you wanted anyone to call about. You answer, 'Glad You Asked,' and mean it. This is possible when your attitude and actions result from an open, candid, honest evaluation of the facts at hand" ("Glad you asked," 1975).

"If the National Hockey League has been wondering why it cannot keep expanding indiscriminately, the final round of the Stanley Cup playoffs between the Buffalo Sabers and the Philadelphia Flyers may have provided one big reason: fog. . . . Last night the temperature was about 76 degrees at game time, but near the 90 mark inside the rink. For the last 33 minutes, including 18½ minutes of overtime, the contest was halted 12 times by referee Lloyd Gilmour when the clouds of steam made it impossible to see the puck. . . . Rene Roberts of Buffalo burst out of one fogbank in sudden death to tally the gamewinning goal" (Keese 1975).

"Computer simulations (of organizations) have a propensity for luring researchers into Bonini's paradox—the more realistic and detailed one's model, the more the model resembles the modeled organization, including resemblance in the directions of incomprehensibility and indescribability" (Starbuck 1976, p. 1101).

All ten of those episodes illustrate *organizing*, which is defined as a *consensually validated grammar for reducing equivocality by means of sensible interlocked behaviors*. To organize is to assemble ongoing interdependent actions into sensible sequences that generate sensible outcomes.

Two contrasting definitions will help the reader understand what is being asserted:

1 Organizations are "structures of mutual expectation, attached to roles which define what each of its members shall expect from others and from himself" (Vickers 1967, pp. 109-10).

2 An organization is "an identifiable social entity pursuing multiple objectives through the coordinated activities and relations among members and objects. Such a social system is open-ended and dependent for survival on other individuals and sub-systems in the larger entity—society (Hunt 1972, p. 4).

Organizing is first of all grounded in agreements concerning what is real and illusory, a grounding that is called *consensual validation*. This term was coined by Harry Stack Sullivan; Ruth Munroe, in describing Sullivan's work, captures the phrase's nuance that we wish to incorporate into organizing:

In my glossary of Sullivanese, consensual validation seems to be "common sense" of a high order—the things people agree upon because their common sensual apparatus and deeply common interpersonal experiences make them seem objectively so. It is a critical and cautious term for the "reality" so often used by other psychological schools (Munroe 1955, p. 356, f.n.).

The important issues of consensus in organizing concern rules for building social processes out of behaviors and interpretations that can be imposed on the puzzling inputs to these processes.

Organizing is like a grammar in the sense that it is a systematic account of some rules and conventions by which sets of interlocked behaviors are assembled to form social processes that are intelligible to actors. It is also a grammar in the sense that it consists of rules for forming variables and causal linkages into meaningful structures (later called cause maps) that summarize the recent experience of the people who are organized. The grammar consists of recipes for getting things done when one person alone can't do them and recipes for interpreting what has been done.

Organizing is directed initially at any input that is not self-evident. Happenings that represent a change, a difference, or a discontinuity from what has been going on, happenings that seem to have more than one meaning (they are equivocal) are the occasion for sizable collective activity. Once these inputs have become less equivocal, there is a decrease in the amount of collective activity directed at them.

Finally, the substance of organizing, the raw material that supplies the stable elements for the grammar, is interlocked behaviors (Buckley 1967, chap. 4). This interlocking is circular and was described by Allport:

> When individuals respond to one another in a direct, face-to-face manner, a social stimulus, given, for example, by the behavior of individual A, is likely to evoke from individual B a response which serves in turn as a stimulus to A causing him to react further. The direction of the stimuli and of their effects is thus *circular*, the response of each person being reevoked or increased by the reactions which his own responses called forth from others" (1924, pp. 148-49).

The sequence Allport describes is called a double-interact throughout this book and is analyzed in Chapter 4.

For the moment, it is sufficient to say that Bavelas's golfers, Callaway's colonels, Serebrier's musicians, and the other characters depicted in the initial examples are all engaged in the same organizing that we associate with General Motors, NASA, IBM, and McDonald's. In every case there is a shared sense of appropriate procedures and appropriate interpretations, an assemblage of behaviors distributed among two or more people, and a puzzle to be worked on. The conjunction of these procedures, interpretations, behaviors, and puzzles describes what organizing does and what an organization is (see Fig. 1.1).

With this preliminary understanding in hand we can review the relevance of each example for the arguments to be presented.

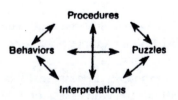

Figure 1.1

BAVELAS AND RETROSPECT

Bavelas's crazy foursome is interesting because for 18 holes they participate in a puzzle. What they've been doing for those 18 holes won't be known until the match is finished and they find who their partner is (was?). For example, the putt that I worry about on the 16th hole is worth the worry if my partner turns out to be Professor Bavelas, but if my partner is either Professor Webb or Professor Leavitt, then my worry is inappropriate.

But chronic and enduring puzzles like this aren't confined to the golf course. Organizations run into them all the time. But organizations are often reluctant to admit that a good deal of their activity consists of reconstructing plausible histories after-the-fact to explain where they are now, even though no such history actually got them to precisely this place. "How can I know how I've played until I see who my partner was?" On the 18th green that's the puzzle that has to be managed within Bavelas's foursome. But in the form of the related assertion, "How can I know what I think until I see what I say?" that puzzle has to be managed day after day by everybody who deals with organizations. The consequences of that reality will unfold as we proceed.

With a touch of regret we also note that Bavelas's world gains relevance for organizations because he was unable to get any takers for his proposal. In the actual match where this innovation was proposed, people found the prospect so strange that they all refused to try it. Collectivities such as the ones we will explore in this book also have their aversions to risk. Thus, we become much more interested in the question of when they will take chances, foster mutations, become playful.

UMPIRES AND ENACTMENT

The umpire who correctly asserts "They ain't nothin' till I calls them" rather neatly fingers a key element in organizational life: the important role that people play in creating the environments that impose on them. Organizations, despite their apparent preoccupation with facts, numbers, objectivity, concreteness, and accountability, are in fact saturated with subjectivity, abstraction, guesses, making do, invention, and arbitrariness . . . just like the rest of us. Much of what troubles organizations is of their own making; before completion of this essay, the ways in which organizations figure prominently in their own landscapes will become more evident.

COPS AND EQUIVOCALITY

The puzzle posed by Bavelas and the puzzle that faces the umpire who creates the reality of baseball both pale in comparison to the equivocal puzzle posed for an unruly crowd by the Oakland policeman. In their attempts to get "behind" the meaning of the remarks about writing tickets and to discover what input produced that output, members of the crowd probably turned to one another, sought some kind of help in figuring out what was up, and in their mixture of puzzlement and social activity proceeded to inattend the sergeant long enough for him to leave.

The basic raw materials on which organizations operate are informational inputs that are ambiguous, uncertain, equivocal. Whether the information is embedded in tangible raw materials, recalcitrant customers, assigned tasks, or union demands, there are many possibilities or sets of outcomes that *might* occur. Organizing serves to narrow the range of possibilities, to reduce the number of "might occurs." The activities of organizing are directed toward the establishment of a workable level of certainty. An organization attempts to transform equivocal information into a degree of unequivocality with which it can work and to which it is accustomed. This means that absolute certainty is seldom required. It also means that there can be enormous differences among organizations and industries with respect to the level of clarity that they regard as sufficient for action.

Members of organizations spend considerable time negotiating among themselves an acceptable version of what is going on. The activity itself is preserved by the phrase *consensual validation* and the content of the activity is preserved by the phrase *reducing equivocality*. The policeman's utterance could be interpreted to have two or more meanings (he's giving a ticket, he's nuts, he's signaling an accomplice, he's acting on TV, he's a clown, it's a trick, etc), and the true meaning can't be determined. That's what makes the scene equivocal. As the cop might have said, "We aim to police." When any outcome, such as the word *police* in the preceding sentence, could have been produced by two or more inputs ("We aim to keep law and order," "We aim to please"), the display is equivocal and people turn to their similar associates for help in sorting through the meanings and for help in stabilizing one of them (Festinger 1954).

FORDS AND MEMORIES

The troubles that the Ford Motor Car Company had in the 1930s producing a compact car suggest that one of their problems resulted from the fact that they presumed small cars are made the same way as large cars: take a big car and shrink it. Since Ford knew how to make large cars, they thought there was no problem. Suppose, however, that the Ford people had entertained some doubts about their expertise. Suppose they said both "Yes, we know how to make small cars," and "No, we don't know how to make small cars." The latter doubt suggests that small cars might not be simply scaled-down large cars. After all, shrinking a clock into a watch is neither easy nor cheap. Furthermore, even the belief among watchmakers that they can make watches is proving troublesome as the electronic watches built by firms who never before made watches begin to grab a sizable share of the market ("Seiko's smash" 1978).

The expensive Ford compact provides a handy summary of the possibility we will explore later, namely, that an ambivalent stance toward past wisdom makes adaptive sense. Organizations that both believe and doubt their past experience retain more flexibility and adaptive capacity.

Repeatedly, we will look at organizational practices for their relevance to the theme that adaptation precludes adaptability. Specialization in the production of large cars with technology, tasks, and skills devoted solely toward this production makes the organization profitable and efficient in the short run, but vulnerable in the long run. The biological version of this point is described by Dunn:

> Environmental changes often transform earlier adaptive specializations into cruel traps. As a changing environment passes beyond the range of a gene pool narrowed and made less versatile through specialization, it often forces the extinction of whole species. Just as in species formation those individual organisms fail to survive whose genetic range is inadequate to match the requirements of a changing environment, a species that generates a narrower genetic range (genetic pool of the population) through specialization may, when faced with environmental change, fail to support a dynamic adaptation and thus bring about extinction of the biotype (1971, p. 45).

TRACTORS AND VICIOUS CIRCLES

The problem created when heavy machinery packed the soil and necessitated heavier machinery to break it up is an eloquent example of feedback loops that sometimes turn into vicious circles. The cause-effect relationships that exist in organizations are dense and often circular. Sometimes these causal circuits cancel the influences of one variable on another, and sometimes they amplify the effects of one variable on another. It is the network of these causal relationships that impose many of the controls in organizations and that stabilize or disrupt the organization. It is the patterns of these causal links that account for much of what happens in organizations. Though not directly visible, these causal patterns account for more of what happens in organizations than do some of the more visible elements such as machinery, time clocks, and pollution equipment.

CONDUCTORS AND CONTROL

A glimpse of misplaced beliefs about control is found in the tragically charming anecdote about the enthusiastic conductor. The problem of coordinating 180 musicians *is* immense, but the idea that a mere baton "would help achieve greater musical control" seems pathetically heroic. Under these circumstances, again it is the pattern of alliances, causal loops, and norms that exist *between* people that accomplish or defeat efforts at control. Mutual influence between pairs of people is at the root of most control observed in much larger aggregations. While the conductor may presume that he and the baton produce an ordered performance, in actuality they probably are minor contributors to the outcome. Of more importance are the bonds and mutually supportive relation- ships that have been built up among small subsets of the musicians. It is these interpersonal bonds that hold the organization together and that become activated in response to the conductor, whether he stabs himself in the process or not.

QUARTERBACKS AND INTERCHANGEABILITY

The quarterback-conductor episode illustrates some possible consequences that occur when activity becomes overrationalized, overmanaged, overorganized. A recurrent theme in this book is that managers often get in the way of activities that have their own self-regulation, form, and self-correction tendencies.

These natural control circuits frequently are disrupted by managerial meddling. Management intervenes in the mistaken belief that single individuals do the controlling and that control is not implicit in causal circuits and inter- personal influence processes. Failure to acknowledge these sources of control, coupled with interventions that actively disrupt them, are the occasions for much mismanagement in organizations.

Although the theme is introduced with tongue-in-cheek by Anderson (1974), the issue of interchangeability of persons and positions is also a crucial one within organizations, and we shall refer to it frequently. If making hand motions at people really is the core of conducting, and if this is the only crucial activity involved in conducting, then it *is* true that aged quarterbacks might be substitutable for conductors . . . Sonny Jurgenson conducts Bruckner.

CALLAWAY AND OPENNESS

"Glad you asked" is an uncommonly rich summary of much that goes on in large organizations. The necessity to invoke this slogan and to push for its acceptance suggests a prior history of nasty surprises when outsiders started poking around. Incidentally, at the time Callaway first enunciated this policy he also went on record as saying that women would never enter West Point. ("Why are women now at West Point? Glad you asked.")

If it worked the way it was supposed to, the "Glad you asked" campaign should lead to more openness, more willingness to admit poor judgment in prior decisions, and a more candid and honest evaluation of the facts at hand. These outcomes are valued by many organizational theorists who try to enhance the authenticity with which organizational actors deal with one another (e.g., Argyris 1964). "Glad you asked," followed up by honest answers, would certainly seem to be a way to enhance authenticity. If this policy really did have the effect of making people relax in the belief that there was nothing to hide, then it might be the case that confidence and pride in work would result and that dealings with the public would be less deceptive.

Whenever policies such as "Glad you asked" are introduced, it is valuable to examine the internal consequences of such policies. "Glad you asked" seems to be a policy designed to manage external dealings. Historically the "Glad you asked" policy was articulated soon after the Watergate revelations. But to view "Glad you asked" as a policy that is responsive to the public is to miss much of its potential for *internally* organizing the actions of organizational members.

Think, for example, of the internal implications of "We're only number two—we try harder." If customers who have been alerted by this advertising "send back" to Avis workers cues that allow the Avis workers to try harder or to demonstrate that they are trying harder, if those slogans help Avis workers to make their work activities more sensible (e.g., "I wasn't sure before what I was doing, but now I know: I'm trying harder so that we can become number one"), and if the recognition of that symbol by the public has the effect of making Avis workers feel more pride in their organization, then a policy that looks as if it is directed mainly outward may in fact have its largest effect on actions of those insiders about whom the policy comments.

In short, when "Glad you asked" is implemented effectively, organizations become more open, candid, and trusting. However, the felt need to introduce this policy in the first place suggests that organizations have other values that supercede openness—one of them being managing the indicators that the public is responsive to.

HOCKEY FOG AND CAUSAL CHAINS

The fog-clouded Stanley Cup playoffs in Buffalo are an excellent illustration of the point that causal chains within organizations are lengthy as well as dense (Reynolds 1974). It seems hard to imagine that expanding the number of teams would result in a controversial playoff due to fog. Nevertheless, there is a kind of inevitability once some of these small beginnings of expansion are set in motion. As you sign more teams, it takes a longer season for all teams to play all other teams; the playoffs also last longer. This means that hockey, normally a cold-weather sport, now spills over into the spring for the playoffs and into the early fall for exhibition games. Both of these encroachments on warmer seasons raise the odds that hot air will mix with cold air coming from the ice and that the mixture will form clouds of vapor on the surface.

Notice that this long chain of causes also has the potential for being self-defeating. Not only does the fog cut down visibility for spectators, television cameras, and news photographers, but it also contains the potential for some genuine feuds over whether scores should be allowed.

The presence of fog is even self-defeating for players because it lessens the quality of play:

> What made last night's action even more bizarre was the spectacle of nearly exhausted players being asked to skate around the rink to stir up air currents and make the fog rise, with the game tied 4-4, and at its tensest in the sudden death. . . . "It was brutal out there," said Jerry Korab, the big Buffalo defenseman. "Not only did I lose at least 10 pounds, but I couldn't breathe. The fog smelled like gas or ammonia and got in my eyes, too" (Keese 1975).

In analyzing organizations we will want to examine the density of causal linkages and their circular patterns, but we will also want to examine the length of these chains of interdependence. Immediate activities can have remote consequences.

The ludicrous playoff might also look like a classic case of poor planning. That may be. But it's not obvious that even more planning is the answer: plans have been overrated as a crucial component for accomplishment of effective actions.

Plans are important in organizations, but not for the reasons people think. Cohen and March (1974) argue that plans are symbols, advertisements, games, and excuses for interactions. They are *symbols* in the sense that when an organization does not know how it is doing or knows that it is failing, it can signal a different message to observers. If the organization does not have a compact car in its line, it can announce plans to have one. On the basis of this announcement the firm may be valued more highly than an organization that makes no such announcement. It is less crucial that the organization is actually planning to make the car than that all concerned imagine this to be the case. It is in this sense that plans are symbols and that they negotiate a portion of the reality that then comes back and rearranges the organization.

Plans are *advertisements* in the sense that they often are used to attract investors to the firm. Plans show the organization at its best; they are documents designed to persuade, but again, they are more valuable externally than internally. One earmark of a plan that advertises is that it lacks relevant information about the organization. "Real" plans, those that bind the energies and time of people, contain a maximum of relevant information; plans that pass as advertisements are deficient on information.

Plans are *games* because they often are used to test how serious people are about the programs they advocate. If departments want programs badly enough, then they should be willing to spend the effort necessary to justify the program and to embed it in a plan. "If an administrator wishes to avoid saying 'yes' to everything, but has no basis for saying 'no' to anything, he tests the commitment of the department by asking for a plan" (Cohen and March 1974, p. 115).

Finally, plans become *excuses for interaction* in the sense that they induce conversations among diverse populations about projects that may have been low-priority items. The interaction may yield immediate positive results, but such outcomes are usually incidental. Much of the power of planning is explained by the people that it puts into contact and the information that these people exchange about *current* circumstances. When people meet to plan for contingencies five years away, contingencies that seldom materialize, they may modify one another's ideas about what should be done today. But that is about all that can be accomplished.

Plans are a pretext under which several valuable activities take place in organizations, but one of those activities is not forecasting. As Ambrose Bierce said, to plan is to "bother about the best method of accomplishing an accidental result" (1946, p. 327).

STARBUCK AND CLUTTER

Starbuck's summarization of the dilemma faced by Bonini (1963) when he tried to simulate an organization holds true for a much bigger set of inquiry procedures than computer simulations. Thick descriptions (Geertz 1973) of organizations may well be disorganized because that's the way organizations are. Organizations deal with equivocality, but their ways of dealing are often themselves equivocal and subject to many interpretations.

Cohen and March (1974) have suggested, for example, that university organizations have *goals* that are inconsistent, ill-defined, and loosely coupled; *technology* that no one understands; and *participants* who vary in how much time and effort they invest in the organization. If that's partially what a university organization is like, then a thick description of that organization will be confusing when it starts to comment about goals (e.g., Friday they wanted to discourage graduate students, but Thursday they wanted to en-courage them), technology (e.g., they don't have the foggiest idea how people get educated), or participants (e.g., the president didn't realize her provost was on sabbatical for the year). The irony is that this confusion in the observer's report testifies to its authenticity and not to its sloppiness.

Confusion as a indicator of validity is a crucial nuance because many of the ways of thinking about organizing that will be introduced in this book will portray organizations as superimposed structures. This imagery implies that there is not an underlying "reality" waiting to be discovered. Rather, organizations are viewed as the inventions of people, inventions superimposed on flows of experience and momentarily imposing some order on these streams. Notice, however, that many portions of the streams of experience will remain unorganized, and those portions being temporarily organized by imposed ideologies will remain equivocal. These enduring equivocalities should be detected by scrupulous observers, but since that which is noticed is partially indescribable and partially incomprehensible, the efforts at description will appear flawed. Such are the dilemmas that face those who choose as their topic of interest phenomena that are complex, fluid, collective.

Summary

We stated at the outset that this was a book about organizing and about the appreciating of organizing. Through examination of a diverse set of events, the reader has been exposed to both appreciating and organizing.

The activity of appreciating was implicit in the approach taken to each incident. Brief attempts were made to embellish each example, to examine it from a variety of angles, and to add to its richness.

A significant portion of the existing organizational literature is steeped in criticism (Lumsden 1973). Less often do we see analyses patterned after those found in such fields as rhetoric, literary criticism, and aesthetics (Elbow 1973; March 1976; Wimsatt 1976; Gass 1975; Silverman 1975). I feel there is a need for a dialectic between criticism and affirmation as modes of apprehending organizations. At the moment we are heavily into criticism. A balancing of this with more emphasis on affirmation would lead to more activity of this kind:

> The critic (of poetry or art) more commonly looks for interpretations that discover aspects of an artistic expression making it more interesting or more beautiful than when first observed, or developing the uncertainties of simultaneous attraction and repulsion. Truly distinguished pieces of criticism are almost always ones in which a critic enlarges our appreciation of the beauties and complexities of art that is loved (March 1976, p. 18).

In the process of embellishing, reworking, and contemplating each prior example, we began to identify some elements associated with organizing. In each example some portion of a stream of experience was bracketed, and efforts were made to turn the stream into information and then to do something about the information that had been constructed. The raw data which people tried to make sensible consisted of such diverse displays as packed dirt, a moving baseball, a pierced hand, a fog-shrouded puck, opponentless golf, a cryptic policy, an even more cryptic traffic citation, and an expensive cheap car. In each case our interest was in the genesis of the puzzling raw data, attempts by groups of people to transform those puzzles into information, and what was done as a result of the momentary imposing of meaning on those puzzles (e.g., the car project was abandoned, skaters created a human fan, the conductor conducted for another 20 minutes).

This very general picture of organizing was supplemented by brief mention of some elements that compose it; those elements will be discussed further in subsequent chapters. These elements include suggestions such as these:

1 Equivocal information triggers organizing.

2 Efforts to stabilize meanings for equivocal displays typically involve the efforts of two or more people.

3 Most efforts at sensemaking involve interpretation of previous happenings and of writing plausible histories that link these previous happenings with current outcomes.

4 Interdependencies among people are the substance of organizations, but these interdependencies are fluid and shifting.

5 Organizations have a major hand in creating the realities which they then view as "facts" to which they must accommodate.

6 An ambivalent stance with respect to "lessons of experience" is a major way in which organizations preserve some adaptability to cope with changed contingencies.

7 Events in organizations are held together and regulated by dense, circular, lengthy strands of causality perceived by members.

8 Networks of self-regulating causal links are realized in the form of coordinated behaviors between two or more people.

9 Organizations frequently use only parts of persons, and those portions used vary in the ease with which they can be replaced.

10 Most policies within organizations have both internal and external consequences, whether intended or not, and these consequences may work in opposite directions.

11 There is ambivalence within organizations toward being open and closed and toward being suspicious and trusting.

Additional properties of organizations will be developed as we proceed. However, we have already hinted at some of the directions that will be taken. To gain some perspective on how these hints mesh with and play off existing ideas about organizations we can examine a stunning example of the organizing process *in vivo*.

Organizing: The Emergence of "Majority Rule"

Piet Hein's aphoristic poem (or *grook*) entitled "Majority Rule" tells us a great deal about how organizing occurs:

> *His party was the Brotherhood of Brothers, and*
> *there were more of them than of the others.*
> *That is, they constituted that minority*
> *which formed the greater part of the majority.*
> *Within the party, he was of the faction*
> *that was supported by the greater fraction.*
> *And in each group, within each group, he sought*
> *the group that could command the most support.*
> *The final group had finally elected*
> *a triumvirate whom they all respected.*
> *Now of these three, two had the final word,*
> *because the two could overrule the third.*
> *One of these two was relatively weak,*
> *so one alone stood at the final peak.*
> *He was THE GREATER NUMBER of the pair*
> *which formed the most part of the three that were*
> *elected by the most of those whose boast*
> *it was to represent the most of most*
> *of most of most of the entire state —*
> *or of the most of it at any rate.*
> *He never gave himself a moment's slumber*
> *but sought the welfare of the greatest number.*
> *And all the people, everywhere they went*
> *knew to their cost exactly what it meant*
> *to be dictated to by the majority.*
> *But that meant nothing—they were the minority.*

One way to understand the events portrayed in this poem is to transform them into an organizational chart (Stieglitz 1975). It is common practice to depict organizations graphically and to regard the lines in the chart as indicating such things as communication relationships, lines of authority, chain of command, levels within the organization, superior-subordinate relationships, etc. A simplified organization chart for "Majority Rule" is found in Fig. 1.2. The numbers attached to each level are arbitrary, and the labels at each level correspond to the labels used in the poem with three additions. "Other parties," those forming the lesser part of the majority, have been dubbed Sisterhood of Sisters (SOS), Sisterhood of Brothers (SOB), and Brotherhood of Sisters (BOS).

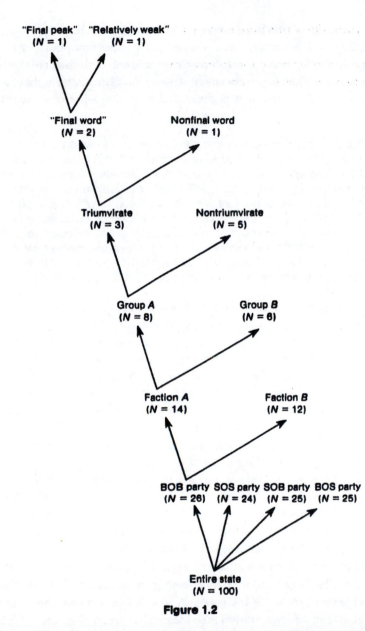

Figure 1.2

If we look at the chart, we can see several interesting features. For example, note the direction of the arrows. In most charts they would point from the top to the bottom, yet in this case they point in the reverse direction. This is partly because we are discussing the *process* of organizing and how organization emerges. Our discussion is consistent with the sizable literature (e.g., Partridge 1978) that talks about the emergence of leadership and demonstrates that this emergence is viewed as more or less legitimate—depending on the extent to which members participate in selecting the leader. The arrows in the chart, however, make an even more important point. They imply that subordinates ultimately determine the amount of influence exerted by those who lead. This is a prominent theme in organization theory (e.g., Mechanic 1964). The argument is presented in perhaps the clearest form by Barnard:

> If a directive communication is accepted by one to whom it is addressed, its authority for him is confirmed or established. It is admitted as the basis of action. Disobedience of such a communication is a denial of its authority for him. Therefore, under this definition the decision as to whether an order has authority or not lies with the persons to whom it is addressed, and does not reside in "persons of authority" or those who issue orders. In the last analysis the authority fails because the individuals in sufficient numbers regard the burden involved in accepting necessary order as changing the balance of advantage against their interest, and they withdraw or withhold the indispensable contributions (1938, pp. 163-65).

This quotation suggests several additional properties of the grook: (1) the person at the top can be in a vulnerable position; (2) subordinates often do not realize the amount of control they actually have—an observation that occurs repeatedly in experiments on coalition formation (e.g., Vinacke *et al.* 1966); (3) if the hierarchy is to be maintained, it must be continuously reestablished by the person above sending *acceptable* orders to the person below—in Barnard's language, orders must be within the "Zone of Indifference" for subordinates (1938, p. 167); (4) the acceptance of orders is always determined in part by self-interest—not only do orders vary in their acceptability, but subordinates vary in their interests and definitions of what is acceptable.

As a sidelight on the issue of authority, it is interesting to note that even though there are seven levels in our chart, the last three levels involve the *same* three people in different combinations. Three are picked to rule; of these three, two can override the third; and one of the two is weak, so one person winds up in actual control. The crucial property here is that effective influence in the large collectivity depends on alliances among a very few members. Several theorists describe organizational functioning in terms of alliances that are established (e.g., Caplow 1964; Cyert and March 1963). These theorists argue that to understand an organization is to locate the crucial alliances that control large numbers of people. This is precisely the point made by the grook. Despite the size of the original group ($N = 100$) and despite the fact that there are supposedly 100 different influential people, in reality the crucial decisions—those thought to be the *majority* decisions—are made by one person: the minority. The important point is not that one person rules; the important point is the fact that this control is made possible by the pattern of alliances that exists in the group. It is the pattern of relationships, *not* the fact that a "great man" sits on top of the heap, that makes it possible for influence to be concentrated.

Although control relationships are regarded by many as the key element for understanding the organization (e.g., Smith 1978; Scott *et al.* 1967; Tannenbaum 1968), there are other features commonly discussed in organization theory that are visible in the grook. For instance, the number of levels present in an organization (seven levels are depicted in the example) is regarded by many theorists as a crucial property that explains much of organizational functioning (e.g., Porter and Lawler 1965; Evan 1963). This property is commonly referred to as *flat versus tall organizations.*

There are several reasons why this dimension is judged important. Levels determine the number of subordinates that report to a given supervisor (Van Fleet and Bedeian 1977). If we hold the size of the organization constant, the fewer the number of levels, the greater the number of subordinates who report to a single supervisor, the less closely can the supervisor monitor his subordinates, and the more autonomy they have to make their own decisions. Thus the structural variable of *tall versus flat* has the important psychological consequence of determining the closeness and frequency with which any member can be supervised; this in turn affects the member's feelings of freedom vs. coercion. Generally, it is posited that the more self-determination allowed to the worker, the higher the worker's productivity and satisfaction (e.g., Blauner 1960; Katz 1964).

The distinction between tall and flat organizations also affects communication. In general, the flatter the organization, the less likely that communication will become distorted, since there are fewer decision points through which it passes before it reaches the unit that must take action. Phrased in a converse form, the rule is this: the greater the number of people through whom a communication must pass, the greater the likelihood that the communication will be transformed (Campbell 1958).

From another point of view, it is possible to interpret tall vs. flat in terms of another venerable concept in organization theory, the informal organization. Informal organization consists of the interaction patterns that develop in addition to those that are formally prescribed by lines of authority (Carzo and Yanouzas 1967, chap. 5). The relevance of the informal organization to the present discussion is that as organizations become flatter and as supervision becomes less direct, a greater number of informal contacts will probably be initiated and maintained, and these contacts will have a more substantial effect on performance (Cohen, Robinson, and Edwards 1969). When supervision is less frequent and less direct, informal contacts may be initiated for the purpose of getting work done (Blau 1954). In other words, assistance cannot be counted on from a supervisor to whom several persons report, so this support is sought at a parallel level from those who are engaged in similar activities. Added impetus for these informal alignments comes from the fact that in her role of helper the supervisor also sooner or later assumes the role of evaluator. She judges the output of the subordinates and bases her promotion and demotion decisions on these assessments. This means that the supervisor plays an extremely complicated role. Subordinates are hesitant to ask for assistance from the supervisor because they think it will reveal their incompetence and will affect subsequent decisions about their salary and promotion. The major point to be drawn from this is that organizations vary in their number of levels, and that the number of levels directly affects supervision, communication, and informal alliances and indirectly produces psychological consequences.

Most organizational theorists assume that organizing is done in order to promote goal attainment (e.g., Hauschildt and Hamel 1978; Etzioni 1964, pp. 5-19). This emphasis was apparent in Hunt's definition mentioned earlier (1972, p. 4). But a goal is not readily apparent in the grook unless we wish to speculate that something as nebulous as "survival," "attainment of welfare," or "attainment of control over the environment" is the "reason" why these people united. This would seem to stretch unduly the information contained in the grook. This point should not be dismissed, because in subsequent chapters it will be argued that organizing is *not* necessarily an attempt to attain some specified goal. The absence of a goal in the grook makes it *more*, rather than less, like an organization.

In the grook, one gets the impression that first organizing occurred; then, *after* it was concluded, the reason for the organizing became apparent. It is as if the persons acted so that they could eventually determine what it was that they had done. This sequence in which actions *precede* goal definition may well be a more accurate portrait of organizational functioning. The common assertion that goal consensus must occur prior to action obscures the fact that consensus is impossible unless there is something tangible around which it can occur. And this "something tangible" may well turn out to be actions *already completed*. Thus it is entirely possible that goal statements are retrospective rather than prospective.

Since any organization theory has to specify why members consent to join and remain in organizations, most theories discuss the "social contract" that is implicit in organizational membership (e.g., Barnard 1948, pp. 113-18; Thompson 1967, chap. 8; Levinson 1972, pp. 337-38). Schein designates this contract as a psychological contract and describes it this way:

> The notion of a psychological contract implies that the individual has a variety of expectations of the organization and that the organization has a variety of expectations of him. These expectations not only cover how

much work is to be performed for how much pay, but also involve the whole pattern of rights, privileges, and obligations between worker and organization (1965, p. 11).

It should be noted that implicit in the concept of the contract is the notion that there is an exchange of commodities, and it is this feature of the contract which has been given considerable prominence in writings about organization (e.g., Whyte 1959; Jacobs 1974; Hollander 1976). Satisfaction, productivity, interpersonal ties, and the likelihood of leaving are all dependent on the terms of the contract and its fate at any given moment in time. What is demonstrated in the grook is perhaps the most basic form in which a contract exists. Individual members consent to be governed; in return, some smaller body agrees to govern in a beneficient manner. Phrased in terms of the grook, the majority consents to become the minority in the belief that their interests are more likely to be promoted.

One way to contrast small groups and large organizations is to view the latter as a group of groups (e.g., Simon 1957). This feature is illustrated in the grook and affords the wedge by which additional psychological concepts become relevant for organization theory. Two such relevant notions are link pins, people with membership in two or more overlapping groups who promote cooperation between the separate groups (Wager 1972), and ethnocentrism, ingroup loyalty coupled with outgroup deprecation. If one views an organization as a group of groups, this implies that there may be some competition among the several groups for scarce resources (Sapolsky 1972). This competition often leads members to overrate the virtues of their own group and to downgrade those of other groups (Le Vine and Campbell 1972). These divisive forces are often reduced when one or more members hold joint membership in or are acceptable to both groups (Likert 1961; Heiskanen 1967). Presumably, the "excluded groups" on the right side of Fig. 1.2 would exhibit some hostility toward the groups on the left side. The groups on the left side control the scarce resource of power, which has been removed from the control of the members on the right side. The left-side members themselves would probably have their own hostilities—toward the people in "higher" ingroups. Working against this tendency of excluded members to deprecate "included members" are the facts that there are link pins and that all groups may share the goal of leading a good life. To the extent that all groups share this goal despite their differences, and to the extent that they believe the leader is capable of improving their state, then intergroup hostility should decrease.

Anyone who samples the literature on organizations will soon notice a term that occurs over and over again, *rationality* (Diesing 1962). This concept does not necessarily mean that organizational actions are logical or sensible, but rather that they are intended, thought about, planned, calculated, or designed for a purpose. The emphasis is on the idea that what happens in an organization was at one point in time expected or planned to happen (Mintzberg 1978). The fact that organizations typically exhibit a great deal of turbulence, disorder, and unpredictability does not necessarily disprove the theory that their *origins* were rational or that they are trying to be rational.

Rather than demonstrate rationality as such, the grook shows the trouble one has in trying to apply this concept. If there is "calculation" or "intent" present in the grook, the only person to whom this might safely be attributed is the person on top. If "rationality" is used this way, it means an expedient set of alliances composed for the ultimate purpose of gaining control. Rationality lies in the several means that were used to gain control. We could say that the other members tacitly "consented" to this rational plan; but if we do this, we lose the force of the concept.

To keep the concept from becoming meaningless, one alternative is to adopt a convention suggested by Simon (1957, pp. 33-41)—the concept of *bounded rationality*. The essence of this notion is that individuals have perceptual as well as information-processing limits, and even though they may intend to act rationally, they can do so only in a limited fashion. This limited fashion consists of acting on the basis of sufficient knowledge rather than complete knowledge (the concept of satisficing); of using simple, unlaborious rules to search for a solution when a problem arises (e.g., searching in the immediate vicinity of the problem); and of using shortcuts whenever possible.

In terms of bounded rationality, we could say that the persons in the grook facilitated the form of control that finally emerged; when faced with decisions, they used simple decision rules (e.g., the majority wins) and applied a criterion of sufficiency (e.g., "If this agreement will enable us to get on with our work, let's accept it"). There was little review of all possible consequences. The members dealt with "here and now," and did so in the way that involved the least possible effort.

While some of us may balk at this unflattering portrait of mankind, to do so is to miss the point being made. The point is that *if* one assumes that the actors have limited rationality, then it follows that decisions will be made in terms of localized disturbances to which abbreviated analyses will be applied, with short-term recommendations as the result. A search for more stable solutions (i.e., those that will solve the problem once and for all) is unlikely; consequences are not given much attention, and apparently logical solutions may prove faulty as their consequences ramify. Furthermore, since the consequences of a decision often occur much later than the decision itself, it is difficult for the members to trace backward from these disruptive consequences to determine precisely what caused them. The members cannot make such an analysis, simply because there are too many competing explanations. Thus, the only thing members can do when a new problem arises is to engage in more localized problem-solving.

What all this suggests is that rationality is best understood as in the eye of the beholder. It is *his* aims and how he consciously sets out to accomplish them that constitute the clearest, most easily specified component of rationality. To say that "systems" or organizations engage in rational decision-making makes sense only if we can specify some set of persons who agree on some desired outcome, on a specified set of means to attain this outcome, on ways in which the specific means will be activated, and on how it will be known whether the desired outcome was attained or not. Since this fourfold agreement is more difficult when large numbers of persons are involved, it is likely that rationality will characterize mostly small groups of actors and that, at any moment in time, organizations will have several different and contradictory rationalities.

There are some newer models that take considerable liberty with the notion of rationality. Many of these seem more appropriate for examining the Brotherhood of Brothers. In particular, models which suggest that organizations are collectivities that "make do" suggest the value of relaxing the constraints of rational models.

A good example of this newer class of models is the attempt by Cohen, March, and Olsen to characterize organizations as garbage cans into which are dumped problems, people, choice situations, and solutions. The resulting definition of an organization is interesting:

> An organization is a collection of choices looking for problems, issues and feelings looking for decision situations in which they might be aired, solutions looking for issues to which they might be the answer, and decision makers looking for work (1972, p. 2).

A crucial variable that is emphasized in this model is timing. It is assumed that there is a continual stream of people, solutions, choices, and problems that flow in an organization. Every now and then some clusters of these elements coincide, and a decision is produced. In other words, problems may attach themselves first to one choice situation and then to another, and the same holds true for people and solutions.

These investigators have created a computer simulation to see how an organization behaves when it operates like a garbage can; they find an interesting property of decisions. Two major decision strategies in a garbage can organization are the strategies of *oversight* and *flight*. The strategy of *oversight* involves making quick choices. You make a choice whenever the important problems are attached to some other choice and before they can drift to the choice you're making. Having made the choice you solve nothing, since the problems are still attached to other choices. Likewise, the decision style of *flight* involves delaying a choice until the problems wander away and attach themselves to other choices. Once the problems have left, then you make the choice. Again the choice solves no problems, since none are attached to it.

This is not meant as a cynical commentary on organizations. Instead, it is simply what actually happens in a computer simulation when you set up organizations as if they were streams of people, choices, problems, and solutions. It's striking that most decisions involve flight and oversight because this fact suggests why organizations can keep making decisions yet never solve any of their problems.

© 1978 by the New York Times Company. Reprinted by permission.

While numerous other relationship linkages between the grook and organizational theory could be highlighted, a final set of subtleties should be noted; these suggest the unusual appropriateness of this display as an exhibit of organizing. There is motion and a glimpse of process and emergence in this example. It is also clear that much of whatever stability or organization exists in the Brotherhood exists in the minds of the actors. The actors, with one exception, conclude from their particularistic experiences that they are all members of a minority, that their groups are all members of a minority, and when this view of the world is superimposed on their collective activities, it becomes a self-fulfilling prophecy. They indeed act like and become the minority, even though a casual head count buttressed by a reflective moment would reveal that this is incorrect.

Conspicuously missing from the grook are two prominent elements in organizational theory: technology and the environment. Given the position we will develop, these omissions are not serious. Environments will be treated as the outcomes of organizing and as the creations of actors within the organization. Technology will be viewed as relevant solely for the information that it provides the organizational members and for the effects it has on equivocality.

The whole set of groups, factions, and fractions in the grook also has a decidedly arbitrary quality. It's apparent that the entire collection of people plus votes plus power attributions could be carved up differently. Different subsets of the 100 could easily be composed (e.g., losers and winners, supporters and supported). The point is that most collectivities and most objects on which collectivities work can be made sensible in a wide variety of ways. Furthermore, the various versions are relatively equivalent in their reasonableness. Organizations continuously make different kinds of sense of their inputs and of themselves. These continuous operations manage some equivocalities, ignore others, and create still others. Repeatedly organizations find themselves trying to stabilize the stream of experiences that flow through them and the streams of actions being directed at the flows. Positing "minorities" and "majorities" is just as good a device to make the world sensible as any other one.

Here is what we're up against when we try to think about organizing. First, about the thinking:

tactics for thinking about organizing

The problem of definition of terms and of statements of theory is like the problem of writing a menu. It is rather easy to say what it is one thinks he has eaten, rather more difficult to decide what to order, and most difficult to write the menu before the groceries have been delivered from the market, especially if one orders from a whimsical grocer who seldom delivers what you order. In many cases in science, one cannot know beforehand what will be found out, or even what will be interesting at a better-informed tomorrow (Crovitz 1970).

Second, here's what we're up against with the objects of that thinking: People often treat organizations as if they were clocks that can be read, counted, measured. If organizations are clocks, they are certainly unusual ones. Not only can they be misread, but it is also possible

(1) that the *frequency* with which the clock is *consulted* may modify the time it reports; (2) that the time the clock is expected to show may modify the time it actually reports; (3) if the observer dislikes the clock (let us say from an aesthetic viewpoint), it will report time differently than if he is fond of it; (4) if the observer sends someone else to consult the clock, it will report differently; (5) that the time indicated by other clocks adjacent to the one being consulted or the position of this clock relative to other clocks might influence the time the clock in question reports (Wallerstein and Sampson 1971, p. 45).

Our sympathies in inquiry lie with people who can think deeper than a fact. Facts do not speak for themselves (Gould 1977), and they are no more a science than a heap of stones or a pile of blueprints are a house. Organizations are

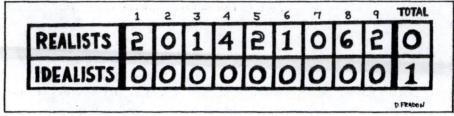

	1	2	3	4	5	6	7	8	9	TOTAL
REALISTS	2	0	1	4	2	1	0	6	2	0
IDEALISTS	0	0	0	0	0	0	0	0	0	1

D FRADON

Drawing by D. Fradon; © 1976 The New Yorker Magazine, Inc.

tough enough for us to comprehend without handicapping ourselves by ruling out certain ideas and methods (McCall 1977). There are lots of "shoulds" in organizational inquiry: laboratories live, structure is salvation, there are great men, there are great events, satisfaction suffices, power and money are all, machinery manages people, history has the upper hand, size dominates, it's all in your mind—or head or tools or coworkers, networks are ties that bind (and blind), statistical regression is regressive, paths are pathetic, grounded theory is groundless, participation is pat, etc. All of those slants on organizations are partly true, partly false, partly incomplete, and partly irrelevant.

To make sense of such diverse phenomena as heavy farm machinery, the Brotherhood of Brothers, and umpiring, we need a set of ideas that have generality, that deal with relations, that are stated at a fairly high level of abstraction, and that contain evocative images. As should now be apparent, the intent of this book is to develop ways to talk about organizations. This book is about organizational theorizing, not organizational theory. The concern is with ways to talk about organizations and with what these ways of talking single out for closer attention. In the context of the Brotherhood grook, some ways of talking about organizations were suggested; more will be introduced.

In the organizational theorizing that follows, we will not be timid about speculating (Bakan 1975; Moscovici 1972, p. 37; Lave and March 1974, pp. 9-84), striving for interest (Davis 1971), utilizing incongruity as a perspective, anthropomorphizing, reifying, inserting hyperbole, waxing discursive, glossing, improvising, examining alternatives to positivism, reframing, intuiting, and any other tricks that help counteract sluggish imaginations. In the course of directing these various bits and pieces of bias and action at organizations, certain ideas will emerge. The ideas are important, but so is the process by which they were achieved. Our joint interest in the activity of theorizing as well as the product of theorizing, coupled with our belief that the products of theorizing age quickly and have a short half-life (Koestler 1970), should be sufficient to explain why this is a book about organizational theorizing rather than about theory.

As a final exhibit of what it takes to think deeply and provocatively about organizations, consider madness (Lichtenstein 1971). Madness is to think of too many things in succession too fast or of one thing too exclusively (Auden and Kronenberger 1966, p. 351). Generating ideas about organizations sometimes borders on madness. People free-associate, introspect, rifle through piles of images, and play percentages that they'll find something that captures a portion of organizational reality everyone else has missed. They think of too many things, often too fast. At other times the passionate investigator becomes obsessed with a single image and can see or talk about nothing else. All the world becomes filled with least preferred coworkers, cognitive dissonance, prisoners' dilemmas, resource dependence, or garbage cans. That's functional, if unnerving, because it aids the development and exemplification of the obsession and it keeps something tangible in front of other investigators, something on which they can sharpen their contrasting arguments. In all of this, madness lies not far below the surface (Mol 1971; Chafetz 1970; Ziman 1970; Graves 1970; Merton 1969; Mitroff 1974; Weisskopf-Joelson 1971).

In the remainder of this chapter, six thinking tactics will be examined, each stated in the form of advice:

1 Know what you're doing.
2 Acknowledge tradeoffs.
3 Think "ing."
4 Mutate metaphors.
5 Incorporate interest.
6 Evoke minitheories.

Know What You're Doing

In 1941 John Steinbeck anticipated the foul-up in the Floon Beetle Expedition when he was on an expedition of his own in the Gulf of California (the Sea of Cortez) collecting biological specimens with Ed Ricketts (Hedgpeth 1971). Steinbeck became fascinated with a species of fish called the Mexican Sierra.

The Mexican Sierra is shaped like a trout, has brilliant blue spots, ranges from 15 inches to 2 feet, is slender, is a very rapid swimmer, is classified with mackerel-like forms although its meat is white and delicate and sweet, weighs up to 14 pounds, and occurs in the northern half of the Sea of Cortez (composite descriptions from Steinbeck 1941, p. 155, and Cannon 1973, p. 263, "Sierra Grande").

Permission MAD Magazine © 1975 by E. C. Publications, Inc.

Here is what the Sierra has to do with thinking:

The Mexican Sierra has 17 plus 15 plus 9 spines in the dorsal fin. These can easily be counted. But if the sierra strikes hard on the line so that our hands are burned, if the fish sounds and nearly escapes and finally comes in over the rail, his colors pulsing and his tail beating the air, a whole new relational externality has come into being—an entity which is more than the sum of the fish plus the fisherman. The only way to count the spines of the sierra unaffected by this second relational reality is to sit in a laboratory, open an evil-smelling jar, remove a stiff colorless fish from the formalin solution, count the spines, and write the truth. . . . There you have recorded a reality which cannot be assailed—probably the least important reality concerning either the fish or yourself.

It is good to know what you are doing. The man with his pickled fish has set down one truth and recorded in his experience many lies. The fish is not that color, that texture, that dead, nor does he smell that way (Steinbeck 1941, pp. 2-3).

Spine-counters are like clock-readers and people who count organizational trappings and report some of the least important realities. To get the organization into countable, measurable form is to strip it of what made it worth counting in the first place (Leach 1967). Spine-counting does record "a reality that cannot be assailed." And in the hands of wise observers (e.g., Johnson 1978; Bernard and Killworth 1973; Lave and March 1975; Miller 1977; Tukey 1977; Kimble 1978), that counted reality can be constructed with forethought and can stimulate those who can't stand the smell of formalin.

But what will more likely happen is that quantitative investigators forget that counting is only a means to understanding. They become means-centered and stop inquiring once the spines are counted, or they refine the count and do it again. In either case, the investigator does not move on to other realities or embed the count more richly. Whether one chooses to count spines, chide spine-counters, or fish, it's still good to know what you're doing. And this holds true for inquiry in general as well as for specific inquiries concerning organizational behavior.

Inquiry in general is based on the assumption that the paths to understanding in nature may be infinite and characterized by unique problems, but that all of these paths lead to *a* goal, *an* understanding of *one* nature.

These two connected themata of unlimited outer accessibility and delimited inner meaning can be vaguely depicted by the device of a maze having in its outer walls innumerable entrances, through each of which one can hopefully reach, sooner or later, the one mystery which lies at the center (Holton 1965, p. xxiii).

Now comes a disturbing possibility that makes it harder for us to know what we're doing. Returning to the maze analogy, Holton remarks,

> But another possibility has suggested itself more and more insistently; that at the inner-most chamber of the maze one would find *nothing*. . . . From a suitable distance, we cannot soundly claim that the historic development of science has proved nature to be understandable in a unique way, as distinct from documentable, manipulable, predictable within limits, or technically exploitable. What has happened is that the ground of the unknown has continually been shifted, the allegory has continually changed (1965, p. xxiii).

If areas of ignorance remain constant in size and continually shift, then it seems clear that ambivalent conceptual orientations toward the world will be more adaptive and accurate than unambivalent ones. Problem-solving seems to be favored by opposed sets of propositions, *both* of which are correct on some occasions (e.g., Bruyn 1966, pp. 23-83). The investigator who retains opposed conceptual orientations will be open to comprehending a larger portion of the referent event. It is not that scientists must become more tolerant of ambiguity: information that is received may lend clear support to a specific position and may therefore reduce uncertainty. But this less ambiguous view of a world should not be mistaken for a "correct" view; instead, the scientist needs to search for information that supports opposing explanations of an observed event. The event itself probably contains properties such that *both* explanations may appear to be valid at one time or another, even though they are opposed. And the scientist who has nurtured more than one point of view will be better able to adapt to this "multiple contingency environment."

To know what we're doing when we inquire into anything is to know the limits of that inquiry:

> We seem to know more and more about how to live without finding out any more about why it is worthwhile to live. . . . The main point to bear in mind, however, is that the primary purpose of both revealed knowledge and of artistic knowledge is to make the individual feel better about the world as it is. The emphasis (in art) is on altering or enlarging the individual's experience of the world, not on changing the world itself to serve man's desires. . . . [T]here should be nothing disjunctive about a culture which sets out on the one hand to control the external world for man's welfare and at the same time attempts to adjust man to what is unadjustable in his condition. Experience has shown that he is not likely to do either one well enough to render the other superfluous (Morison 1965, pp. 256, 257, 261).

To know what we're doing when we inquire into the specific topic of organizational behavior is to know, first of all, what intellectual territory that phrase designates.

In the first edition of this book I argued that the phrase *organizational behavior* should not be used because it seemed to confuse rather than clarify the questions organization watchers asked. I'm still not crazy about the phrase, but I've become a bit more mellow about it.

After reviewing some problems created by the term *organizational behavior*, I will discuss the sense in which the term does seem to be a useful designation to retain. The phrase *organizational behavior* is troublesome because one is never certain whether it means behavior that occurs in a specific place, behavior with reference to some certain place, behavior controlled by an organization, behavior that creates an organization, or just what. The trouble deepens if we inquire further. Behavior is behavior, isn't it? What is gained by introducing the qualifier *organizational?* If we search for instances of organizational behavior, we may be tempted to look for unique behaviors that occur when people act within organizational roles.

The problem with this type of search should be obvious. Events inside organizations resemble events outside organizations; sensitivities of the worker inside are continuous with sensitivities of the worker outside. Since people have as much desire to integrate the various portions of their lives as to compartmentalize them, what happens inside affects what happens outside, and vice versa (e.g., Salaman 1971). Staffan Linder (1970), for example, argues that people try to bring the yield on their working time into line with the yield on their other activities, such as leisure activities. When a person's productivity rises, the yield of his working time increases; this generates pressure to increase the yield from other activities.

Suppose that in my work one hour of writing produces one-third of an article. Now suppose that by using a dictating machine I increase my production to one-half of an article per hour. It used to take me three hours to produce an article; now it takes me two hours. Each of those hours has increased in value. Linder argues that two hours of recreation now have to count for more. To accomplish this I add expensive consumer goods to amplify the yield from my consumption time. I trade in my Instamatic for a Hasselblad so that I'll get more return from my two hours of photography. But I have to pay a great deal for the Hasselblad, which tightens the screws on me to become even more productive and to earn even more, which in turn makes me try to squeeze even more out of my photography. I then become one more member of the "harried leisure class."

This is a roundabout way of saying that continuity from setting to setting is more likely than discontinuity. In that sense, behavior is behavior, and though its form may be shaped by the particular setting in which it unfolds, it still unfolds with a certain degree of orderliness, regularity, and predictability. Rather than searching for unique behaviors that occur within an organization and then building a theory about this uniqueness, it seems more useful to build theories about the particular ways that enduring individual dispositions are *expressed* in an organizational setting, and to build theories about the effects of this expression. Organizations may pose unique problems for their members and they may furnish unique mechanisms by which these problems are handled, but it is still people who implement these mechanisms, and the behaviors are the same behaviors that implement family, recreational, or community mechanisms (e.g., Bradney 1957).

The argument that organizational behavior is continuous with behavior in other settings can be made from a different perspective. There are several investigators who argue that action involves sequences of acts that unfold intact once they are triggered (e.g., Mandler 1964; Roby 1966). This assumption can be coupled with the further one that people notice those stimuli that enable response sequences to be unfolded:

An act is an impulse that maintains the life process by the selection of certain sorts of stimuli it needs. Thus, the organism creates its environment. The stimulus is the occasion for the expression of the impulse. Stimuli are means, tendency is the real thing. Intelligence is the selection of stimuli that will set free and maintain life and aid in rebuilding it (Mead 1956, p. 120).

To rephrase Mead's point, people notice stimuli that permit them to do what they want and/or need to do. Thus behavior can be viewed as responses in search of pretexts for expression. Though an organization may contain stimuli unlike those encountered in nonorganizational settings, these stimuli remain only potential stimuli until they are noticed. And Mead's point is that response repertoires control noticing. The person carries this repertoire and its implications for noticing everywhere. If an observer gains an understanding of response repertoires, and the conditions under which attention is controlled by the content of these repertoires, then a more substantial theory about organizations and behaviors can be built. The theory would concentrate on attention as well as on action. It would essentially ask the question, "How are the processes and contents of attention influenced by the conditions of task-based interdependency found in those settings we conventionally designate as organizations?" Rendered in this form the question is complex, but it is also much more specific than the question, "What is organizational behavior and what affects it?" Defining organizational behavior in terms of processes of attention directs the investigator toward specific processes and properties within an organization that might ordinarily be overlooked. The investigator is sensitized to a specific set of events and behaviors in a way that is impossible given a more general definition of organizational behavior.

Walter Nord (1976) has recently taken issue with some of my gripes about the term *organizational behavior*, and he makes some good points. Nord notes, first, that the term serves as a useful reminder that problems within organizations must be approached at both the psychological and sociological level. Attention to both individual behavior and formal organizational properties are essential in this field, and the attractiveness of the phrase *organizational behavior* is that it is composed of a word from each of the two foundation disciplines. Thus the term is a useful reminder that interdisciplinary approaches should be directed at any inquiry into organizations, and a further reminder that organizations need to be examined as sites for both collective and individual behavior.

Nord's second point is that behavior may have continuity, but some determinants are more important in organizational settings than in other ones. He notes that formal authority has more important consequences for behavior inside organizations than outside. Other possibilities that Nord might have cited in this line of argument are that power is more important in organizational settings, and physical attraction is less so. The term *organizational behavior* also directs attention to a place, a hierarchy, circumscribed hours, input, output, transformation processes, accountability, effort expenditure, controls, finance, and competition.

Nord's final point is that the phrase implies an interest in knowledge that can be used. He goes on to note that the emphasis in the phrase *organizational behavior* is more clinical and practical than theoretical. There is room for debate on this point. As Derek Pugh (1966) has said, "applied psychology is a contradiction in terms because there is yet no coherent body of acceptable theory and data which can be drawn upon and applied once we get beyond the level of learning of perceptual and motor skills."

Similar arguments can be found in Merton (1963), Krech (1968), Heiskanen (1967), and Minogue (1973). Organizational theory needs to ask better questions to improve what it has to apply. Questions may well improve as we get closer to the data, as we do better thick descriptions of organizations, and as we try our hand at thinking prescriptively (Nystrom and Starbuck 1977).

In summary, several things can be said about the term *organizational behavior*. The term suggests that both psychology and sociology are combined in this topic, but then conventional disciplines such as psychology and sociology are quite arbitrary collections of activities (Campbell 1969). It is not necessarily in the best interests of vigorous development of organizational theorizing to incorporate intact disciplines. The qualifier "organizational" also has a kind of stiffness and frozenness that the word "organizing" does not. "Organizational" as a qualifier also suggests that the topic of interest is substance rather than pattern and form. We believe instead that the crucial issues in organizational inquiry turn on issues of pattern and form, not on issues of substance.

To illustrate this important point we can look at the complicated issue of reification (Haworth 1959). Reification means to treat an abstract concept as if it referred to a thing. In the case of organization, if we read that "an organization acts" we could assume that because there is the single noun-word "organization," something in nature must correspond to it—something that is independent, unique, unchanging, and capable of entering subject-predicate relations with other things. What we want to avoid is treating organization as a separate force or agent. What we want to do instead is look at behaviors that are eventful, process-like, and that possess some kind of distinctive quality that make it reasonable to call them *organizational*.

Throughout this book we will refer to organizations acting. When we say that "an organization acts," we mean this as a shorthand statement which, when translated, results in a conjunction of statements, each one of which describes a double interact (see Chapter 4) between two or more human beings, one of whom can even be imagined.

Whenever organizations act—the university gave tenure, the government negotiated, the bakery searched its memory, the orchestra enacted chaos—people act. And any assertion that organizations act can be decomposed into some set of interacts among individuals such that if these people had not generated and meshed a specific set of their actions, and if these actions had not been generated by and meshed among any other people, then the organization would not have performed the act attributed to it.

The important points made by the attribution of actions to organizations are that organizational activities are social rather than solitary, and that these activities are specified sufficiently that a variety of people can contribute the necessary components that allow the pattern to persist. The pattern can withstand a turnover of personnel as well as some variation in the actual behaviors people contribute. It is the persistence of the pattern through contributions made by interchangeable people that distinguishes organizations from other collectivities such as mobs, families, or patient-therapist dyads where changes in "personnel" produce fundamental changes in the process and the outcome.

Organization forms outlast their originators (Weick and Gilfillan 1971) and are relatively impervious to personal redefinition (Berkowitz 1956). People move into and out of these forms; surprising constancy is maintained in the outcomes (Warwick 1975). The fact that forms transcend specific individuals means that it is reasonable to say that an organization acts, because it is the persisting form that coordinates actions of transient personnel and that produces the outcomes.

When we say that an organization acts we mean to emphasize that double interacts, not solitary acts, are the raw materials that are assembled into processes. We also mean to emphasize that it is the assemblage, the *pattern* of interacts, that determines the outcomes—not the personal qualities of single individuals.

When we assert that an organization acts, it will also be true that that shorthand phrase can be decomposed into a set of interlocked behaviors between two or more persons and a set of assembly rules by which those behaviors were assembled and sequenced to produce an outcome.

The phrase *organizational behavior* does have the valuable effect of reminding researchers that in the final analysis, organizational theorizing comes down to predictions of behavior. While this particular book may not result in many of those predictions, it remains true that eventually all such formulations have to deal in one way or another with behavioral-dependent variables. Organizational behavior is a symbol around which diverse researchers can rally, and since those researchers are good company, I see no reason to destroy their pretext for gathering together.

Acknowledge Tradeoffs

A person who can identify the inevitable tradeoffs in inquiry and relax gracefully having done so is a seasoned inquirer. One version of these tradeoffs is found in Thorngate's (1976) postulate of commensurate complexity. This postulate states that it is impossible for a theory of social behavior to be simultaneously general, accurate, and simple. The more general a simple theory is, for example, the less accurate it will be in predicting specifics.

To grasp the implications of this postulate imagine the face of a clock (see Fig. 2.1). At twelve o'clock is inscribed the word *general*, at four o'clock is inscribed the word *accurate*, and at eight o'clock is inscribed the word *simple*. The mnemonic device to store away these observations is simply the word GAS (or SAG). If we array this postulate across the clock face, we can see the dilemma inherent in any research. If you try to secure any two of the virtues of generality, accuracy, and simplicity, you automatically sacrifice the third one.

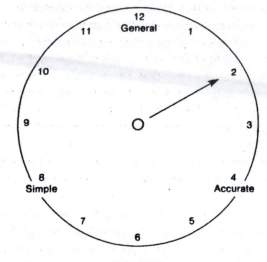

Figure 2.1

Consider some examples. Two o'clock research is general and accurate but is also difficult. Psychoanalytic theory (Fenichel 1945), Levinson's book on organizational diagnosis (Levinson 1972), and Bateson's (1972) work are good examples. Six o'clock research is accurate and simple, but its generality is suspect. Coalition theory (Komorita and Chertkoff 1973), much of which is tied to highly contrived situations, is a good example of this position. It's interesting that lab studies as well as case studies share positions at six o'clock. Both preserve accuracy and simplicity and sacrifice general relevance. The final position, ten o'clock research, combines generality and simplicity at the expense of accuracy. Concepts such as the organized anarchy, loose coupling, deviation amplification, and the Peter Principle illustrate this position.

Failure to accept the inevitable tradeoffs implied in the GAS formulation seems to be at the heart of many current research problems. Investigators act as if they can simultaneously accomplish all three aims in their explanations, and that delusion is at the heart of much trivial, inconclusive research. The solution would seem to be either robust compromises or alternation rather than attempts to accomplish all three. If one accepts the reality that at most only two of those three virtues can be realized, then many rules and constraints in inquiry take on a new interpretation. This can be illustrated if we look at three mixed positions: two o'clock research, six o'clock research, and ten o'clock research.

If one intentionally sets out to do *two o'clock research*, then Occam's Razor (Luchins and Luchins 1965) is sacrificed in favor of intentional overdetermination. The concept of *overdetermination* states that there are usually more factors that act to produce a single behavior than are really necessary to have it occur. The concept was first described by Freud in 1896 when he tried to account for symptoms of hysteria. Used in that context the idea meant essentially that a single bit of behavior served simultaneously to reduce tensions generated by several motives. Occam's Razor, a venerated concept in natural sciences, contains a tacit plea for economy in psychological explanations. Fewer and simpler concepts are to be preferred to more and more complicated concepts.

The concept of overdetermination says that a given bit of behavior should be regarded and analyzed as expressing a maximum number of psychological factors. If a maximum number of psychological determinants are expressed in a minimum amount of behavior, then invoking a minimal explanation will exclude the majority of determinants that in fact are influencing the behavior. Thus an explanation that satisfies Occam's Razor should be disturbing, not satisfying. That feeling of disturbance coupled with a search for overdetermined explanations is more likely to occur if people self-consciously try to do two o'clock inquiry.

People who try to generate explanations that have generality and accuracy will probably enlarge questions rather than try to shrink them. Several of Steinbeck's (1941) attempts at speculative metaphysics illustrate this strategy. For example, the observation that prehistoric animals had the greatest amount of armor just before they became extinct becomes enlarged into a set of speculations about the equivalent armor in human societies and the question of whether that human armor has developed to a point where it too is at its maximum, hinting at extinction. This line of questioning exemplifies two o'clock research because it is grounded in concrete observations (the presence of armor prior to extinction), but the accurate observation is enlarged and generalized to other species.

Six o'clock inquiry is illustrated by recent arguments of noted investigators such as Cronbach (1975) and Campbell (1975) that case studies are better tools of inquiry than they first imagined. Cronbach describes "interpretation in context" and suggests that journalists (Behrens 1977) and playwrights may serve as more accurate models of what psychologists can realistically do than can physical scientists. Because many psychological findings are unstable over time, Cronbach concludes that we should try harder to make our interpretations specific to situations. This suggestion renders generality of secondary importance.

Campbell's (1975) recent second thoughts about case studies stem from his insight that investigators who use case studies can obtain the equivalent of degrees of freedom in statistical tests by using multiple theoretical implications. The argument is this:

> In a case study done by an alert social scientist who has thorough local acquaintance, the theory he uses to explain the focal difference also generates predictions or expectations on dozens of other aspects of the culture, and he does not retain the theory unless most of these are also confirmed. In some sense, he has tested the theory with degrees of freedom coming from multiple implications of any one theory (1975, pp. 181-82).

Thus the intensive case study may have a capacity to reject theories. If people become compulsive about recording the thought experiments that emerge in a given setting from a given theory, and if they record both the implication and the test, then it is likely that they will not be so culpable when confronted by people who use more quantitative strategies.

Qualitative researchers need not blindly spot more quantitative opponents the advantage, even on the issue of confirmation. Lancelot White, a well-known physicist and historian of ideas, has argued that the truth value of any statement in science in the last analysis is evaluated by one criterion only: "how deeply acquainted with the phenomena, how non-defensive, how truly open to all facets of his experiencing, is the scientist who perceived the pattern and put it to test" (Rowan 1974, p. 95).

Lest all of this be interpreted as license for endless, groundless, needless case studies of organizations, it's important to realize that investigators must simultaneously proliferate their theoretical degrees of freedom as well as their observations. Many pseudo-observers, trying to imitate Woodward and Bernstein's Watergate coup, seem bent on describing everything and, as a result, describe nothing. It can be argued that the current upswing in social science enthusiasm for ethnography, thick description, grounded theory, and case studies is partly a symptom of the Watergate *Zeitgeist*. What's worrisome is that relatively little discernment seems to be applied to the zeal for description (Leonard 1977). Seemingly, the more that is contained in the description, the better the description is felt to be.

Two things are necessary to offset those trends. First, more than ever we need to invest in theory to keep some intellectual control over the burgeoning set of case descriptions (e.g., Smith and Pohland 1976). Second, those people who insist on doing case descriptions should be encouraged to adopt the model of theoretical degrees of freedom and to supply a contextual embedding along with at least partial theoretical interpretation of those descriptions they feel other people should take the time to read.

Many of my favorite concepts, ideas, and studies in organizational theory are a mixture of simplicity and generality and fall at the *ten o'clock position*.

That these concepts also have modest accuracy (and sometimes irk people because of this) came as no particular surprise when I discovered it, although it was pleasant to see how neatly my experiences in the classroom could fit into the compact world of the GAS argument. The attractiveness of explanations such as the garbage can, organized anarchy, or the distinction between exit, voice, and loyalty (Hirschman 1970) is the fact that they are simple, easy to remember, portable, and seem to apply in a wide variety of situations. But when you really press these explanations in any specific situation, you find it hard to spot something that is nothing but a garbage can or loose coupling or specific exit versus voice alternatives. Qualifications and amendments become so detailed in the face of this imprecision that the original general and simple explanation soon disappears.

Once again, intentional effort devoted to ten o'clock inquiry need not be an embarrassment. It remains true that any explanation dreamed up by anyone will be true for some other person at some time at some place. All explanations, no matter how bizarre, are likely to be valid part of the time. It's simply up to the originator of the idea to be smart enough or lucky enough to find those sites where the theory is accurately supported.

The concept of ten o'clock research also provides a good excuse to examine other tabooed issues in science. For example, Ravetz, a historian of science, argues that the social sciences may be misplacing their energies by trying to ape the natural sciences. This theme, which is common enough, becomes more interesting when Ravetz then asserts that the so-called facts of social science may be of a different form than those facts associated with mature mathematical and experimental sciences. Rather than being simple, impersonal, elementary, and indubitable assertions, Ravetz feels that the typical product of a social scientist will more likely be aphorisms: "an expression of a deep personal understanding of its objects in a condensed and communicable form" (1971, p. 375) (e.g., "Everybody wants to be somebody; nobody wants to grow," or "What we do not understand we do not possess").

The idea that aphorisms could be bearers of knowledge has distinguished roots, including some of Francis Bacon's early writings:

> But the writing in Aphorisms hath many excellent virtues, whereto the writing in method [science] doth not approach. For first, it trieth the writer, whether he be superficial or solid; for Aphorisms, except they should be ridiculous, cannot be made but of the pith and heart of sciences; for discourse of illustration is cut off; recitals of examples are cut off; discourse of connection and order is cut off; descriptions of practice are cut off; so there remaineth nothing to fill the Aphorisms but some good quantity of observation; and therefore no man can suffice, nor in reason will attempt, to write Aphorisms, but he that is sound and grounded (cited in Stern 1963, p. 105).

The interesting characteristic of aphorisms is that knowledge is distilled rather than deduced, and that it has a developing character much like interpretations in context. Thus, it's conceivable that people doing ten o'clock research can argue that they're in the business of producing aphorisms rather than deduced knowledge; they might tailor their activities of inquiring accordingly, and might count it as a plus when people routinely think of their world as populated with such things as organized anarchies, seesaws, and octopuses.

In suggesting that aphorisms rather than deductions may be the form that social facts take, Ravetz is not blind to drawbacks associated with aphoristic knowledge. Aphorisms are not the conclusions of a tightly structured argument, which means that they are difficult to modify through criticisms of particular details, they do not go through the same rigorous processes of development and standardization as do other scientific results, which means they have been developed in a much less rigorous fashion. Aphorisms express private understandings, which means that their terms often have important nuances of meaning that are lost when the aphorisms are removed from their original context.

Aphorisms, pure and simple, don't have the permanence and objectivity of laws. But this doesn't mean that they are necessarily inferior. Aphorisms can move inquiry along; they can help people see facets of problems they hadn't seen before; they can force people to keep asking questions, possibly improving the quality of questions that get asked; and they have the obvious advantage of honesty. If a discipline proceeds as if it is mature when in fact it isn't, and if it proceeds as if it can generate facts when it can't, then remodeling itself to produce the best aphorisms possible is a potentially healthy way to redefine its identity.

Aphorisms are relevant to another taboo topic: speculation. Speculation involves consecutive logical thought that starts with premises or data and proceeds, through inferences, to arrive at conclusions or judgments. What sets speculation apart from reasoning is the fact that there is some uncertainty in the premises or some incompleteness in the data and, therefore, there is more tentativeness to the conclusions reached. But the important points to remember about speculation are that it is constrained activity, it unfolds in an orderly manner, and when the raw materials on which it operates are insufficient, premises or data are invented so that the process can continue and possibly arrive at a provocative conclusion.

Speculation brings feelings and intuitions into conscious awareness, a process that leads the speculator more deeply into the phenomenon about which he is speculating. Speculation exemplifies ten o'clock research. Accuracy is not a major constraint because the process of reasoning doesn't grind to a halt in the absence of information. It continues. This means that speculation is quite as credible a way to conduct inquiry as are many of the other strategies which have received a better press.

It's interesting that many writers have suggested that speculation actually predominates in social science. Consider the following comment by C. H. Cooley:

> It is perhaps not sufficiently understood that 19/20's of what men of science write, and what the public takes for science, is not such but an overflow of speculative discussion not necessarily less biased or more grounded than any other matter of the kind. No doubt this has a scientific value in that from the flood of conjecture fruitful hypotheses may emerge, but in the meantime all men should know that it *is* conjecture (1931, pp. 148-49).

In discussing tradeoffs I have argued that there is virtue in such things as speculation, armchair theorizing, aphorisms, overdetermined explanations, enlarged questions, complicated explanations, and journalism. Each of those recommendations was made without apology on the assumption that it's impossible for any explanation to be simultaneously general, accurate, and simple. To know what we are doing is to be realistic rather than arrogant about what can be accomplished at any one time in an inquiry.

This line of analysis has several implications. A sound research program would consist of a portfolio that contained explanations and investigations at all twelve positions on the clockface. If I'm right that much organizational theory converges on the ten o'clock position, then we have eleven other locations that need attention.

The argument implies that each individual should locate a position on the clockface, banish any unnecessary guilt that is tied to ideals that can't possibly be realized from that position, and somehow keep in touch with work at all of the other eleven positions, especially the one directly opposite the located position. If, for example, my style of scholarship falls at ten o'clock, then I should try especially hard to locate people at the four o'clock position, and I should be certain that I understand their work and maintain some contact with that work. Better still might be the solution in which I alternate my research style and systematically try to move among the various positions over the duration of a year or a career.

I think much organizational research is uninformative and pedestrian partly because people have tried to make it general *and* accurate *and* simple. In trying to accommodate all three of these aims, none have been realized vigorously; the result has been bland assertions.

Furthermore, much of the low morale among social scientists may be traced to the fact that lay people don't seem to implement their findings or give social scientists sufficient credit and support for their work. If you look at the tradeoffs in the GAS model, you can see why these reactions by lay people are inevitable. Scientists want to do relevant research that also has generality. But a completely general explanation (twelve o'clock research) is hard to generate and may, in fact, be nonexistent. This means that the person who wants to be relevant has the following choice: the person can either be *wrong* as he moves from twelve o'clock toward the ten o'clock position, or he can be *obscure* as he moves from twelve o'clock to two o'clock. It's very unlikely that scientists who move in either direction will be regarded as saviors. It's good to know what you're doing.

Think "ing"

Organizations deal with streams of materials, people, money, time, solutions, problems, and choices. Streams can be a useful metaphor to portray the continuous flux associated with organizations, but there are some subtleties in this image. A stream might be visualized as a single homogenous viscous flow that moves at a constant rate. Such a visualization is unduly limiting as a portrait of organizational processes, and a more appropriate image would be that of multiple, heterogenous flows of diverse viscosity moving at variable rates. If you can visualize something moving between two points, and then visualize the points also moving, that's what flows in organizations are like.

> The proverb has it that we never step twice into the same river. It is equally true that we never go to work twice in the same undertaking. It is also equally false; for these words "river" and "undertaking" do not denote unchanging substances, but continuing forms. The language of business and administration is full of such words. Capital, revenue, profit and loss; stock, throughput, turnover, plant; staff, wastage, workload, capacity; all these and a hundred others refer to relations and aspects of relations between inflows and outflows, distinguished by administrators in the complex process which it is their job to regulate. Some of these words define the state of a balance at a point in time, like the balance in a bank account or the water level in a reservoir. Others define a rate of flow, such as the output from a production line or the volume of water over a dam, in some unit of time. Yet others define the relation between two rates of flow, as do profit and loss. All are descriptive of relationships. There is nothing unusual in this. The familiar forms of language conceal from us the extent to which the objects of our attention are not "things" but relations extended in time. I stress this, because the most essential common characteristic of the administrator's job in any organization is that he has to regulate a process extended in time (Vickers 1967. p. 68).

As Vickers points out, processes are elusive, and difficult to describe. That doesn't make them any less important since, as Vickers also notes, streams, flows, and changes are the essence of what managers manage. It is the very difficulty of comprehending processes that leads managers, in frustration, into spine-counting and other static pasttimes. When they mistake these snapshots for the important realities in organizations, the probabilities increase that they will tinker with the wrong things, destroy natural controls that are in place, and basically meddle the organization into a mess. In the language of the following chapter, insensitivity to process promotes the destruction of devia-tion-counteracting causal relationships.

It is the very fact that processes elude both researchers and managers, which makes it more important for us to suggest ways in which people can gain at least intellectual control over this property of organizations.

Figure 2.2, "read" from left to right, shows a process. That figure portrays a "schematic representation of a unicellular animal moving from one spot to another by extending a tubular pseudopod and pulling itself up through this extended capillary (Von Foerster 1967, p. 869).

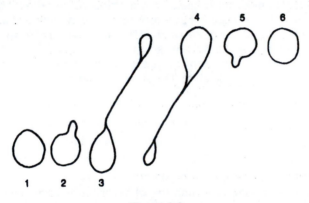

Figure 2.2

The pseudopod exhibit provides a good example of the intricacies in a process. Notice, first, that there are both spatial and temporal aspects of this illustration. The spatial aspects are preserved by nouns ("animal," "spot," "pseudopod," "capillary") and the temporal aspects by verbs and verb forms ("moving," "extending," "pulling"). The verbs and verb forms in the descriptive statement capture the process features of this exhibit. Motion, change, and the flow of time would not be apparent without the verb and verb forms. However, verbs aren't enough to portray processes; you also need memory. It is only through memory that temporal abstracts of events can be computed and stored and that the appropriateness of a specific verb can be demonstrated. From spatial information about location of the object, plus memory of that location, plus the addition of a suitable word that abstracts temporal features of a situation such as "moving," the observer is able to build up from successive views of changed spatial location the idea that a single organism is moving, rather than the alternative possibility that six different organisms are being viewed. Verbs anticipate sequences of events and bind together the various changed appearances that occur when the object becomes transformed. The process of moving requires time, it extends through time, and it involves change. Without verbs, people would not see motion, change, and flow; people would see only static displays and spines.

The point that verbs and verb forms are crucial in process descriptions can be broadened to include the argument that process descriptions rely heavily on relational words of all kinds. Connections among nouns are the stuff of process. This is why we have repeatedly mentioned the importance of relationships for organizing and why the next chapter will dwell on interdependence.

> There is not a conjunction or a preposition, and hardly an adverbial phrase, syntactic form, or inflection of voice, in human speech, that does not express some shading or other of relation which we at some moment actually feel to exist between the larger objects of our thought. If we speak objectively, . . . we ought to say a feeling of *and*, a feeling of *if*, a feeling of *but*, and feeling of *by*, quite as readily as we say a feeling of *blue* or a feeling of *cold*. Yet we do not: so inveterate has our habit become of recognizing the existence of the substantive parts alone, that language almost refuses to lend itself to any other use (James 1950, vol. 1, pp. 245-46).

Whenever people talk about organizations they are tempted to use lots of nouns, but these seem to impose a spurious stability on the settings being described. In the interest of better organizational understanding we should urge people to stamp out nouns. If students of organization become stingy in their use of nouns, generous in their use of verbs, and extravagant in their use of gerunds, then more attention would be paid to process and we'd learn about how to see it and manage it.

The idea of process implies impermanence. The image of organizations that we prefer is one which argues that organizations keep falling apart and that they require chronic rebuilding. Processes continually need to be reaccomplished. Most administrators know this; most students of organizations need to be reminded of it. The imagery of processes "unfolding" can be misleading, because it suggests a kind of inevitability to the unfolding. The fact that this unfolding is problematic, must be engineered, and can be bungled needs to be kept uppermost in organizational theorizing.

Process imagery also means concern with flows, with flux, and with momentary appearances. The raw materials from which processes are formed usually consist of the interests and activities of individuals that become meshed. The fact that these activities and interests undergo continuous change is the reason why process views typically comment on short-lived appearances that soon resolve into other appearances.

Consistent with the process image, organizing can be thought of as a set of recipes for connecting episodes of social interaction in an orderly manner. These episodes, later to be called *interlocked cycles*, constitute the ingredients that are made orderly by organizing recipes.

As an illustration of the recipes associated with organizing, three can be mentioned. Three processes will be described later as comprising the bulk of organizing activity. These are *enactment* (bracketing some portion of the stream of experience for further attention), *selection* (imposing some finite set of interpretations on the bracketed portion), and *retention* (storage of inter- preted segments for future application). When these three processes are viewed as recipes for building an organization, they look like this:

1 Sort the social cycles available to you into three categories: selection, enactment, retention.

2 Arrange these three categories in the following sequence: enactment, selection, retention.

3 Connect these three processes with four causal linkages:

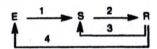

What this brief recipe has done is enable a person to take a pile of senseless social cycles and form them into a sensible arrangement. Notice that we describe this as *an* arrangement. Those same cycles could have been sorted into any number of different categories and could have been linked by any number of different linkages. The question of *who* designs and applies such recipes will vary among organizations. We are trying to develop an all-purpose format for thinking about organizations of all kinds. For that reason, observers will have to specify the contents in which they are interested.

When an orchestra leader rehearses his orchestra on a piece of new music, he has available to him quite a different set of cycles for assemblage than does a manager who has to prepare for an audit or a surgeon who has to assemble a bypass operation. For the moment, what all those activities share is the fact that they are not solitary performances. Sets of people will be involved in their execution, those social activities are basically directed at puzzling displays (strange music, assorted financial records, clogged arteries), and the intent of the activities is to modify the puzzles in the direction of greater clarity.

Crucial questions implied by a process analysis include (1) who applies recipes and builds processes, (2) what knowledge the builder has concerning resources available for assemblage, (3) what criteria the builder uses to determine how puzzling the inputs are and what is needed to manage those inputs, (4) the extent to which the builder uses past modes of assemblage to constrain present activities of process building, (5) the amount of variance in the quality of the cycles being assembled (that is, do some take a great deal of time to unfold? Are some unpracticed? Are some jaded?), and so on.

The view that recipes are the core of organizing is fairly common. Alfred Schutz invokes the image of a person who tries to figure out how to master a situation. A person in this position will:

> appeal to his stock of recipes, to the rules and skills arising out of his vocational life or his practical experiences. He will certainly find many systematized solutions in his standardized knowledge. He may perhaps consult an expert, but again he will get nothing else than recipes and systematized solutions. His choice will be a deliberated one, and having rehearsed all the possibilities of action open to him in the future perfect tense, he will put into action that solution which seems to have the greatest chance of success (1964, p. 78).

Schutz later describes recipes as being both a scheme for expression and a scheme for interpretation. A recipe is a scheme for expression in the sense that it contains directives for action. It tells how to handle people and situations so that satisfactory results are obtained and so that undesirable consequences are minimized. Recipes, viewed as schemes of interpretation, are more subtle. The recipe serves as a scheme of interpretation in that it provides an "automatic" explanation of what people who act in certain ways are up to. Since recipes usually produce certain results, a person viewed as abiding by a recipe is presumed to be intending the outcome typically associated with that result.

Most recipes associated with organizing are expressive rather than interpretive: "If you want to adapt, build an enactment process that maximizes the variety of inputs you pay attention to." If we looked closely at what happens inside an organization we would expect to find that members make sense out of the actions of other members by also using recipes as schemes for interpretation. Thus, when someone is observed to do oddball things and to encourage others to do the same, that person may be seen as trying to promote adaptation through using a recipe that encourages those activities. Sensible foolishness, however, runs the danger that it may be embedded in other recipes that suggest less serious intent.

Simon's (1962) treatment of recipes is most directly related to organizing. He equates recipes with process descriptions, and he contrasts these with state descriptions or blueprints. A state description reads, "A circle is the locus of all points equidistant from a given point." A recipe for that circle would read, "Rotate a compass with one arm fixed until the other arm has returned to its starting point." Recipes provide the means to generate structures that have the characteristics you want. The trick in organizations is to coordinate blueprints and recipes. The prototypic question in organizations becomes: given that blueprint, what recipe will produce it? Adapted to organizing, the question becomes: given our need for a sensible enacted environment, how do we produce it?

Thus, organizing resembles a grammar, code, or set of recipes. The physical world that people confront contains the raw materials that processes of mind will elaborate or simplify into diverse patterns for the sake of action. These activities of elaborating, simplifying, and patterning are collective activities in the case of organizing. Organizing involves shared recipes for building, and it involves arranging processes to cope with the equivocal nature of streams of experience. The processes themselves are also streams. They are social, and they involve multiple actors. The outcomes of organizing are reasonable interpretations of a slice of experience; these slices are treated as being amendable as well as prescriptive for future activities. Thus processes are assembled from flows, directed at flows, and summarize flows.

Mutate Metaphors

Metaphors are abundant in organizational theory; organizations have variously been portrayed as anarchies (Cohen and March 1974), seesaws (Hedberg, Nystrom, and Starbuck 1976), space stations (Weick 1977), garbage cans (Cohen, March, and Olsen 1972), savage tribes (Turner 1977), octopoid (Geertz 1973), marketplaces (Georgiou 1973), and data processing schedules (Borovits and Segev 1977). Diverse as they are, each metaphor has articulated some property of organizations that might otherwise have gone unnoticed (Fernandez 1972). And we judge this articulation to be crucial.

Metaphor is defined as a "figure of speech in which a term is transferred from the object it ordinarily designates to an object it may designate only by implicit comparison or analogy, as in the phrase, evening of life" (*American Heritage Dictionary*, 1976, p. 825). Metaphor supplies language with flexibility, expressibility, and a way to expand the language (Billow 1977). Many theorists agree with Ortony (1975) that metaphors are necessary, and not just nice.

Ortony's enthusiasm for metaphors is grounded in three considerations. First, metaphors provide a compact version of an event without the need for the message to spell out all the details. The details are implicit in the metaphor and can be reconstructed later. "He dived into the water like a fearless warrior" is a quick, concise description that invites embellishment and that directs the embellishment of details by some reader. It is *not* necessary to say that he dived into the water bravely, strongly, fearlessly, aggressively, in a determined manner, and so forth. Metaphor, in this compactness, "enables the predication of a chunk of characteristics in a word or two that would otherwise require a long list of characteristics individually predicated" (Ortony 1975, p. 49).

Second, metaphors enable people to predicate characteristics that are unnamable. It's frequently impossible for people to find the appropriate words; when faced with this impasse, people use metaphors to portray what they cannot portray literally. Percy (1975) argues this point with force and emphasizes that a metaphor is rarely a mistake. The apparently mistaken image more often captures some significant quality that belongs uniquely to an object or event. Metaphors often portray the quiddity of an object, "the essential nature or ultimate form of something; what makes something to be the type of thing that it is" (*Webster's Third New International Dictionary*, 1966, p. 1865).

Ortony presents a marvelous example of the horrors when one uses a metaphor to portray that which is *already* expressible:

> Suppose someone said, "Oranges are the baseballs of the fruit-lover!" On being asked what was meant by this extraordinarily obscure remark, imagine the proud speaker to reply, "Oh—that's a metaphor; don't you see, oranges are round and so are baseballs—it's clever isn't it?" Now according to our view the function of metaphor is to express succinctly what can only be said very circuitously if, indeed, it can be said at all. Our literary giant, however, anticipates an appropriate distinctive set comprising one easily nameable characteristic (if he anticipates anything). His metaphor fails because what he wanted to say was that oranges are round, and there was nothing preventing him saying just that! . . . People simply do not use metaphors to transfer *one* characteristic, even if it is a distinctive one, when there is a ready literal way of making the point (Ortony 1975, p. 50).

Just to see what inexpressibility can do, ponder this comment made by a child after she tasted her first glass of soda water: "It tasted like my foot's asleep."

Ortony's third point is that metaphors are closer to perceived experience and therefore are more vivid emotionally, sensorially, and cognitively. Not only does the "sleeping foot" in the previous paragraph convey the inexpressible, it evokes a vivid multisense image.

One of the most original suggestions about metaphors is Mary Catherine Bateson's (1972, p. 285) suggestion that "each person is his own central metaphor." One meaning of this is to say of any puzzling object such as a tree or an organization, "That's a me." I am the metaphor by which I can initially comprehend the organizational things around me. I look out and what I see are things that are like myself.

> To see the tree as a god or as a woman, as a dryad, is a more accurate way of looking at a tree than our usual casual attitude that treats it as a separate and static object. Like a woman, a tree grows, interacts with its environ-

ment, and dies. To anthropomorphize the tree gives us access to a certain truth about it, and the same is true when we anthropomorphize the orderly and unfolding process of the universe (M. C. Bateson 1972, p. 290).

With this as background we can look more closely at metaphors associated with business. To introduce this topic and to illustrate the idea of metaphor as mistake, a childhood experience described by Walker Percy is relevant.

I remember hunting as a boy in south Alabama with my father and brother and a Negro guide. At the edge of some woods we saw a wonderful bird. He flew as swift and straight as an arrow, then all of a sudden folded his wings and dropped like a stone into the woods. I asked what the bird was. The guide said it was a blue-dollar hawk. Later my father told me that the Negro had got it wrong: it was really a blue darter hawk. I can still remember my disappointment at the correction. What was so impressive about the bird was its dazzling speed and the effect of alternation of its wings, as if it were flying by a kind of oaring motion (1975, p. 64).

Think back about Percy's question. He asked, "What is it?" He didn't ask what it did. Yet his father described what the bird did and what color it was! It was a blue darter hawk. For Percy that wasn't enough. There was something unique about the bird, something more than darting and diving. Percy was looking for some poetry to validate his vivid impression. He found it when he heard blue-dollar hawk; he lost it when the mistake was corrected.

But did the guide make a mistake? Metaphors treat things that are different as if they are alike, and technically that's a mistake. Managers talk about the climate of their organization and themselves as quarterbacks and conductors. Those are metaphors and mistakes. But the mistakes are only partial, because people see more things than they can describe in words. A metaphor can often capture some of these distinctive, powerful, private realities that are tough to describe to someone else. That's why it's sad that managers usually make such poor choices in the metaphors they use.

There is one metaphor that dominates the business world. That metaphor is the military. It suggests the way people in business think about themselves and what they do (e.g., Cooney 1978; I. Miller 1969).

Consider these samples of organizational talk. Organizations have a staff, line, and chain of command. They develop strategy and tactics. Organizations give people marching orders, pass muster, attack competitors, recruit MBAs, conduct basic training, confer with the brass at headquarters, wage campaigns, assess the rank and file, field well-drilled salesmen, deplore a garrison mentality, retreat, gather intelligence, do battle, fire traitors, recruit spies, consider mutiny, employ diversionary tactics, launch frontal assaults, discipline their troops, and lament that the code of conduct doesn't work.

Why does the military metaphor have such a grip on managers? For one thing, a military metaphor is an ideal self-fulfilling prophecy. Suppose I go into a situation assuming that the person I'm about to meet wants to fight. That person sees my hostile, menacing appearance and responds in kind with a hostile display. So I conclude that my original prediction was correct: the other person did want to fight. It never dawns on me that *I'm* the one who created the fight. It's the same with business. If I assume that doing business is like waging war, then this presumption creates the very wars that I predicted. Since I never realize the true origins of those wars in my own presumptions, the wars and the combat go on and on.

But military metaphors might persist for other reasons. People don't like to deal with uncertainty and disorder, so they impose military trappings like hierarchies and they impose spans of control to conceal the disorder. Military imagery probably also persists because it is tough, macho, exciting.

One might even suppose that military metaphors persist because business attracts authoritarian people to powerful positions where those people then impose their view of the world on others. Remember, authoritarian people are not just autocrats. They adhere to conventional values and condemn those who don't; they are opposed to anything that is subjective and tender-minded; they are preoccupied with dominance-submission, strong-weak, and leader-follower in any relationship; they have an uncritical attitude toward their own group, and they are concerned with knowing the right people rather than with any exchange of affection. Those characteristics sound just like what you would expect to find in a military organization. If that same pattern is also found among the top people in nonmilitary organizations, then it is not too surprising that as their vision diffuses down through the organization, people will describe the place with military language.

Whatever its origins, the military metaphor is a bad choice when used alone because it forces people to entertain a very limited set of solutions to solve any problem and a very limited set of ways to organize themselves. They solve problems by discharging people (honorably or otherwise), tightening controls, introducing discipline, sending for reinforcements, or clarifying responsibilities—since that's what you do when an army sags. And the only way they know to organize themselves is into some kind of hierarchy.

Chronic usage of the military metaphor will lead people repeatedly to overlook a different kind of organization, one that values improvisation rather than forecasting, dwells on opportunities rather than constraints, invents solutions rather than borrows them, devises new actions rather than defends past actions, values argument more highly than serenity, and encourages doubt and contradiction rather than belief. That kind of organization has advantages that a military organization doesn't, but to see those advantages, different metaphors are needed.

George Orwell once said, "there is a huge dump of wornout metaphors which have lost all evocative power and are merely used because they save people the trouble of inventing phrases for themselves."

Military images save managers the trouble of inventing richer ways to understand and conduct business. And that's sad, because military images restrict flexibility, encourage narrow solutions, assert nothing very interesting about organizations, and are self-perpetuating. Other metaphors are needed to capture different private realities that exist right alongside those military realities.

Cultivate Interest

Intentionally striving to develop interesting ideas is an important thinking tactic. We have just begun to understand how to develop those ideas. This section relies wholly on Murray Davis's (1971) analysis of interesting theories in social science and what contributes to their appeal. The relevant arguments from Davis's analysis are the following:

1 All interesting theories share the quality that they constitute an attack on assumptions taken for granted by an audience.

2 People find noninteresting those propositions that affirm their assumption ground (that's obvious), that do not speak to their assumption ground (that's irrelevant), or that deny their assumption ground (that's absurd).

3 Laymen and experts have a dilemma that Davis labels *the double dialectic.* Anyone who wishes to assert something that both laymen and experts will find interesting is up against the following situation: "On the one hand, his proposition will interest experts only if it denies the ground assumption of their discipline. On the other hand, his proposition will interest laymen only if it denies a ground assumption of their common sense world. But since the ground assumption of experts is already a denial of a ground assumption of laymen, he will find that any proposition which interests experts (because it denies their ground assumption) will not interest laymen (because it affirms their ground assumption), and vice versa. What will be interesting to one will be obvious to the other" (Davis 1971, p. 331).

Davis suggests 12 categories into which interesting propositions can be sorted; these categories are quite relevant for propositions about organizations. To reconstruct the 12 categories from memory, the reader can use a mnemonic device suggested by Ben Auger, "Go cover faces." Those 12 letters stand for assumptions about:

1 Generalization

2 Organization

3 Causation

4 Opposition

5 Co-variance

6 Co-existence

7 Co-relation

8 Function

9 Abstraction

10 Composition

11 Evaluation

12 Stabilization

When someone makes an assumption about, say, generalization and reads a theory, experiment, survey, case study, or even an opinion that denies that assumption, then the person is apt to respond, "That's interesting." This is most likely if the assumptions are weakly held (Davis 1971, p. 343). We will go through each assumption briefly so that you can see how to work consciously toward developing interesting statements about organizations.

GENERALIZATION
If a person assumes that a phenomenon is local and if it turns out to be general (e.g., Freud asserts that sexual behavior is not confined to adults, it's also found in children) or assumes it to be general and it turns out to be local (e.g., in no other country do people smile as much as people in America do), then that person should find these observations and ideas interesting. The same pattern should hold true concerning organizational theory. If it is assumed that organized anarchies are found only in public-sector organizations (e.g., Rainey, Backoff, and Levine 1976) and they are in reality found also in private organizations, then those latter observations should be interesting. If hierarchy, an organizational form assumed to be universal, is not found in organizations that are still successful, then this should be interesting (e.g., Maruyama 1974).

The same determinants of interest should also hold true for practicing managers. This is where the power of Davis's suggestions becomes even more apparent. All people in organizations have assumptions and things they take for granted, and all of those assumptions contain some hint of extent or pervasiveness in them. Any assumption, be it "organizations are incapable of admitting it when they make a mistake" or "organizations are obsessed with forming committees," is assumed to hold true for everyone or someone or some group in between. Whatever the assumed scope of generality, data that *deny* that scope should be interesting. Any assumptions that practicing managers make about something being either general or local create the background for interesting new assertions to be made.

ORGANIZATION

Interest will develop when people assume that a phenomenon is disorganized or unstructured and then discover that it is really organized, or when they discover that a phenomenon is disorganized when they in fact assumed it to be organized. The fact that people who seem to be autonomous and into their own thing in actuality are responsive to an organized underground with specific limits on acceptable behavior illustrates the first half of this assumption; the second half is illustrated by the observation that the presumed unity in women's movements in fact is not there (Curtis 1976).

Those who find order and organization amidst the apparent chaos of crowds and mobs (e.g., Milgram and Toch 1969; Swanson 1970; Berk 1974) are perhaps the best exemplars of this category, as are those who show a lack of structure in government decision-making where structure was presumed to exist (Allison 1971).

CAUSATION

What seems to be the independent variable in a causal relationship turns out to be the dependent variable (deviant actions don't cause deviant labels, deviant labeling causes deviant actions) or what seems to be the dependent phenomenon in a causal relationship is in reality the independent phenomenon (participative management styles don't increase productivity, the presence of productivity leads managers to adopt more participative management styles).

OPPOSITION

This assumption involves things that are similar and opposite. What seem to be similar phenomena are in fact opposite (radio and television were thought to be similar until McLuhan argued that they were opposite), or what seem to be opposite phenomena in reality are similar (people who join opposing social movements are in fact similar because both show the pattern of a true believer).

CO-VARIATION

What seems to be a positive co-variation between phenomena is in reality a negative co-variation, and vice versa. Davis cites two relevant examples of this assumption. The assumption that lower-income people are charged less for goods and services turns out to be wrong and lower-income people in fact pay more for these goods. To exemplify the other point, it was thought that a social group's desire for revolution decreased as the group's standard of living went up, but in fact it increases.

Davis describes another form of this assumption: that a presumed linear co-variation between phenomena is in reality a curvilinear co-variation. These disconfirmations come in many forms: the upper and lower class have more similar traits with each other than either does to the middle class, top management and workers are more alike than either is to the middle management. In all of these cases the extremes are more similar to each other than they are to the mean.

CO-EXISTENCE

Love and marriage, thought by many to be compatible, have been asserted to be in fact incompatible. Phenomena assumed to be incapable of existing together in reality can exist together (for instance, love and hate can co-exist in an ambivalent person or relationship). Davis makes the further interesting comment that propositions involving co-existence are relatively rare in the social sciences, where there seem to be very few things that are so incompatible with one another that they deny the existence of one another. This very assertion by Davis, however, may be culture-bound because the "social psychology of the nice person where everyone is presumed to get along with everyone else appears to be a peculiarly American product" (Moscovici 1972, p. 18).

CO-RELATION

The pattern of assumptions and denials for co-relation is this: what seemed to be independent phenomena are in reality interdependent; those phenomena assumed to be related and interdependent are in reality independent. As an example of the first difference, social class and mental illness were thought for some time to be unrelated, and were later found to be related. Climate was assumed to be related to suicide, and was later shown to be unrelated, which exemplifies the latter pattern of disconfirmation.

The category of co-relation probably accounts for much of the boredom associated with organization inquiry. People have heard repeatedly that everything is related to everything else. Having heard this often enough, people begin to assume it in most cases. As a result, when a social scientist reports the "news" that birth order is related to personality, the discovery is actually fascinating, but to many people it simply fits within the general expectation that things are related; the discovery, then, is branded as obvious. There are, however, some current examples that go against this tendency. Cancer and fast-food burgers were assumed to be unrelated until Barry Commoner suggested otherwise, a report that was branded absurd more than it was labeled interesting.

Among organizational theorists, especially those who prefer systems theory, the assertion that organizational parts are coupled less often and less tightly than they presume is the occasion for the experience of interest. This may be one reason why concepts such as loose coupling, organized anarchies, and garbage cans have received so much attention so quickly. It is not that these ideas are so much better than other ideas, but rather that they are so much different from prevailing assumptions of interdependence, systems, and tightly coupled events. If these newer images of independence and autonomy diffuse widely, then it shouldn't be long before people who emphasize the presence of rich linkages among phenomena will once more be making the interesting assertions that promise to revitalize organizational inquiry.

FUNCTION

The assumption here is that what seems to be a phenomenon that functions ineffectively as a means to attain an end is in fact a phenomenon that functions effectively. Again, the reverse of this assumption is also included in this category.

The assumption that long meetings accomplish nothing is a good illustration for this category. Evidence suggests that during long meetings where nothing much seems to get done on the manifest agenda, a great deal of information is in fact being exchanged, and members are learning more about each other and how to accommodate to each other's idiosyncratic styles; this learning improves meeting productivity over the long run. Something that was assumed to be dysfunctional turns out to be functional, and that's interesting.

Propositions that fall into this category seem to have political implications. Propositions of the form "what seems to function ineffectively in fact functions effectively" have conservative implications. People should not try to change an obviously defective social institution which in reality has useful consequences (Gans 1972). Radical implications are associated with assertions that seemingly successful social institutions in fact are dysfunctional and should be changed (e.g., schools make pupils stupid, jails create criminals, doctors produce disease, affirmative action hastens segregation).

Analyses of functions are unusually good starting points in organizational theory. Looking for unexpected functions and dysfunctions is a useful pretext to become absorbed into a phenomenon and to think about it carefully. I mention this because many people are highly critical of functional analyses, not so much because they are a fallible form of analysis, but because of the political implications mentioned earlier. Once these political overtones—which are not as black and white as they are said to be—are stripped away, there remains a useful way to begin examining any phenomenon.

ABSTRACTION

This pairing is built on the following disconfirmation: what seems to be an individual phenomenon is really holistic; what seems to be holistic is in reality individual. Suicide, thought to be an individual characteristic, is in reality a societal characteristic; territoriality, thought to be a societal characteristic, is in reality an individual characteristic.

Earlier we saw this category in Nord's argument that one advantage of the term *organizational behavior* is that it preserves a word from each of the two root disciplines. Some of the tension within organizational research stems from the fact that both psychologists and sociologists indirectly try to deny the assumption ground of the other. If I believe that the real locus of human phenomena is at the individual level, then every piece of well-crafted sociology should seem interesting to me, unless I hold my assumption strongly (sociology is absurd) or if the sociology seems so removed from individuals that it has no bearing on my assumptions (sociology is irrelevant). And the same thing holds true for people who assume that the social level explains most phenomena.

As a further complication, the field of social psychology—which is summarized within the Kiesler series, of which this volume is a part—seems to cover an intermediate position on the individual-social dimension. The field is about individuals in social settings, and this means that it's partly psychology and partly sociology. Viewed in terms of the present analysis, this intermediate position could be the death knell of the field. No matter what assumptions an individual has, whether they be social or individual, social psychology, because of its intermediate position, should affirm them. This means that *everyone* should regard the findings of social psychology as obvious, which should in turn mean that the field agonizes over its identity and value more than most. It does (e.g., I. Silverman 1977).

In a way, the agonizing of social psychologists is unnecessary. The very fact of intermediacy could mean, first, that social psychology is relevant to every person, whether that person assumes that individual characteristics or social characteristics predominate. More importantly, whatever a person assumes about crucial determinants, social psychology should contain findings that deny the sole importance of that which the person assumes to be crucial. Everyone should find social psychology interesting because of this dynamic. The fact that in the eyes of social psychologists no one seems to find them interesting suggests either that they are masochistic or that they have strayed from their original mixed character (they are now nothing but psychology or nothing but sociology) or that eclectic positions incorporate all possible assumptions anyone can make, and through their continuous affirmation of these assumptions they produce endless obvious findings.

COMPOSITION

What seems to be heterogeneous phenomena are actually composed of a single element; what seems to be a single phenomenon is in reality composed of assorted heterogeneous elements. As an example of the first part of this assumption, Simmel (Wolff 1950) argued that the three-person family and the three-class society are alike in sharing the triadic form (Bonoma 1976 disagrees).

As an example of a phenomenon assumed to be singular that in fact turns out to be heterogeneous, stratification appears to be composed of a variety of independent phenomena including economic class, status, prestige, and political power.

Inquirers who use the first pattern in this category use a reduction strategy in which they look for the simple in the apparently complex. Occam's Razor provides the cutting edge for people who favor this strategy, a strategy that is in the Platonic tradition. The opposite strategy, a strategy in the Aristotelian tradition, is one in which interesting propositions are generated by finding complexity in the simple.

EVALUATION

What seems to be bad is really good; what seems to be good is really bad. Cancer is good because it's evidence of growth. Families are bad because they stifle adult development. This form of generating interest involves selective highlighting of accepted values.

Davis outlines two strategies that involve interest and evaluation.

First, a person can generate interest in a phenomenon by first assessing his audience's appraisal of an object and then choosing as his indicator of the phenomenon those aspects that represent the opposite of their appraisal.

> Thus, if a social theorist wishes to counter his audience's appraisal of American Society as great or as awful, he need merely select, to serve as his indicators of the moral worth of American Society as a whole, those of its aspects which are generally considered bad (like pollution, pockets of poverty, materialism, etc.) or those of its aspects which are generally considered good (like technology, average income, abundant consumer goods, etc.) (Davis 1971, p. 321).

The second way to control interest using evaluation is to change the standard against which the phenomenon is being compared.

> Comparison baselines for a social phenomenon include (1) other social phenomena of the same logical type, (2) the same social phenomenon in the past (recent or distant), (3) future projections of the social phenomenon (short run or long run), and (4) some positive or negative ideal version of the social phenomenon. Thus if a social theorist wishes to counter his audience's appraisal of American Society as great or as awful, he need merely compare it to (1) other societies (Sweden, Nazi Germany, etc.), (2) its past history (the "gay" nineties, the depression, etc.), (3) its potential futures (2001, 1984, etc.) or (4) some utopian or distopian society (Marx's pure communism, Hobbes' state of nature, etc.) (Davis 1971, pp. 321-22).

Adjustments of indicators and baselines are common among theorists and practicing managers alike. When one experiences the sensation of hearing an interesting assertion, and when that interest seemingly is tied to an unexpected difference in evaluation, the listener would be well advised first to discount the sensation by so much as it has been inflated by selective use of indicators and baselines; then, having removed these confounds, the listener should see what remains as the core of the interesting suggestion. When someone starts out with the assertion that we've been doing everything wrong (i.e., what we thought was good is bad), be attentive to what the person does *not* say and what the person omits as plausible indicators and plausible comparisons.

And that certainly holds true for evaluating the assertions made in this book. I will repeatedly highlight instances where what seems good is bad (managers disrupt controls, they don't impose them) and where what seems bad is good (chaos preserves adaptabiity). These assertions can be interesting because they deny background assumptions, but they accomplish this denial by relying on indicators and comparisons that not everyone attends to regularly. The reader may agree or disagree with my choices of indicators and comparisons, but the reader should be aware that I have made choices and that it is those choices in part that make these assertions interesting. I'm not unique in doing this, however. Any piece of social science that has any bearing whatsoever on accepted values will invariably provoke judgments of interest, irrelevance, obviousness, or absurdity, depending on the values it connects with and the strength with which they are held. Evaluation, like other categories we've reviewed, is a pervasive ground for judgments of interest.

STABILIZATION

What seems to be unchanging does change; what seems to be changing is unchanging. Organizations, thought to be stable, in fact keep falling apart and need elaborate maintenance mechanisms to ward off threats to stability. Conflict-ridden organizations, thought to be unstable, can often continue indefinitely.

The assertion that what seems unstable is in fact stable is well exemplified by arguments that conflict is functional and persists. Models of apparent instability in organizations—models that describe anarchy, irrationality, aimlessness, and disjointed incrementalism—are not sufficiently developed that they can demonstrate clearly that the apparent chaos they depict is durable. But such development seems likely, and it should not be long before such temporary structures as organizational tents (Hedberg, Nystrom, and Starbuck 1976) are seen to be quite stable structures, their flimsy appearance notwithstanding.

Leaving aside now the 12 categories and looking at the phenomenon of interest itself, any person who inquires into organizations and tries to make assertions about them would be naive to neglect the assumption ground of the audience. Suggestions made concerning the nature of organizations need not intentionally strive to deny whatever assumptions are found or consolidated, but potential reactions of observers should be understandable in terms of arguments developed here.

Intentional cultivation of interest is not quite as ludicrous as it might appear. If any theory is true somewhere, sometime for someone, then you as an inquirer might as well work with theories that interest you as theories that don't, since whatever you find interesting should be found interesting by someone else and be relevant to still other people. Pursuit of an interesting inaccurate theory can also be justified because the offshoots of the thinking, the things observed in the process of speculating, may themselves be more accurate. Interest is a good point of departure and can lead to relevant material.

Figure-ground reversals, a metaphor that we use repeatedly throughout this text, are an ideal medium for generating interest. The ground is the background assumption that is taken for granted. If that ground suddenly becomes figure, then what was assumed to be holistic in fact becomes individual; that which is organized (the original figure-ground configuration) becomes disorganized. The reaction is, "That's interesting." Try the demonstration described on page 181 to see this for yourself.

People seem to find a proposition interesting not because it tells them some truth they did not already know, but because it tells them some truth they thought they already knew was wrong. That's why organizational theory can be so interesting, but also why it risks the indictment of being obvious. Everyone is in constant contact with organizations, and as a result, everyone develops a thick, overlearned set of assumptions about organizations. The more diverse those assumptions are, the greater the likelihood that any assertion which denies one assumption will also affirm another one and thereby be branded obvious—a candidate for the Golden Fleece award (Shaffer 1977).

But underneath all of these considerations lies the fascinating, seemingly inevitable crunch between academics and practitioners, a crunch that seems especially intense in the field of organizational theory where ivory-tower types continually brush up against have-you-ever-met-a-payroll types. There seems to be no way around the dilemma that what will be interesting to one will be obvious to the other.

The propositions of these specialized journals and technical texts that are found interesting by their professional readers are actually of the form: "What everybody, except experts on the subject, believes is true is in fact true." No one will recognize that the proposition is of this form until the proposition is brought to the attention of non-experts. However, the more a person's proposition is found to be interesting by the experts of his field, the more he will be tempted to bring it to the attention of these non-experts. Should he be foolish enough to reveal the proposition which interested his colleagues to his non-professional friends, he will usually find that they are not impressed. Should he be even more foolish enough to disseminate this proposition to a wider public through popularizing it in newspapers and magazines, he will succeed only in convincing more people of the poverty of his discipline (Davis 1971, p. 331).

Thus, it's understandable why managers and academics stick to themselves and dazzle the members of their own clan, and it's understandable why scientific popularizers are loved by the public and loathed by the academics. A popularizer such as Carl Sagan (Goodell 1977) bypasses the assumption ground of his colleagues and makes assertions that deny assumptions of the intelligent man on the street. Colleagues get miffed that Sagan gets credit for stuff that everyone else in the field knows. They fail to realize that had they been less parochial and had they understood that laymen assume differently, they too might have relieved the man on the street of his oppressive feeling that the world is no good and could have, at least for the moment, given him the experience of interesting times.

Evoke Minitheories

Many people have good implicit theories about organizing, but they find it difficult to get access to them. Several of the ideas presented in this book are baldly evocative. They are included partly to trigger associations so that the reader can discover chains of ideas whose relevance for understanding organizations had not been previously noticed. The process of evocation can be illustrated in terms of college campuses.

Most people reading this book have access to college campuses. This access is all that is needed to uncover what may be some of the most valuable ideas that can be found about organizations. The technique to be used is a combination of interpolation and unobtrusive measures.

This technique will be illustrated in terms of colleges, but it can be adapted to any place that one finds interesting. A stroll around a campus will reveal that there are statues of famous people. Some of these people are national heroes; others are generous donors to the college. Suppose a count is made of how many busts there are of each kind, and suppose that there are more busts of donors than of national heroes. On the basis of this observation *alone*, predict the answer to each of the following questions:

1 Will the college have open or closed library stacks for undergraduates?

2 Will the faculty be listed by rank or alphabetically in the college catalog?

3 Will more space in the alumni magazine be devoted to necrology or to current activities of living alumni?

4 What percentage of the periodicals housed in the library will have broken runs?

5 How many windows in the dorms are broken each year?

6 What percentage of the student body stays on campus during weekends?

7 What percentage of the total operating budget is spent on beautification of the grounds?

8 In what location will the portraits of past college presidents be hung?

9 Will faculty offices have wood or steel furniture?

10 What is the average distance from a faculty office to the nearest restroom?

Your first inclination may be to say that you cannot get from busts to books. On that we disagree. If one persists, the prediction begins to tip one way or the other. For example, in thinking about open versus closed stacks, many people find that one or the other possibility begins to sound more plausible given the predominance of donor busts. When this happens, they must be absolutely ruthless in trying to capture the reasons *why* they think that prediction seems more plausible. That "why" is a budding contribution to organizational theory.

What the preceding ten "unrelated" items do is help uncover implicit theories that are held and that may be quite valuable if followed up more systematically. The further advantage of those items is that they are visible, countable, and one does not have to bother anyone to collect the data nor can anyone deflect the data for reasons of stubbornness or ingratiation. In this kind of testing, feedback is swift. For example, an excess of donor busts may suggest that alumni (do donors equal alumni?) feel strong affection for the college (but donations are tax-deductible), affection that lingers because the college treated them (colleges don't treat, people do) like human beings. And part of being treated like a human being is having people trust you. Presto! There should be open stacks. One can then go to the library and find out whether this assumption is right or wrong. If the assumption is right, then hold on to the explanation temporarily and see if it can predict the next item on the list. In this case, the incipient theory that humane treatment begets affection runs directly into the problem of trying to predict whether the faculty are listed alphabetically or by rank in the catalog. Now one may ask such things as: Does humane treatment of students imply humane treatment of faculty? Which is more humane, recognition by achievement (listed by rank) or equal recognition (listed alphabetically)? Who decides how college catalogs are composed, and what is that person's relationship to donors, to faculty, and so forth?

It should be emphasized that in examining everyday places like campuses, what is found is secondary to the incipient reasons for expecting to find it. It is the *reasons* that are important to uncover, because these may supply the grit for a better set of ideas about organizations. The word *interpolation* may be used to describe this strategy because the objective is to figure out, given two items (an observation and a prediction about an independent event), what links them. Once a prediction is tested, there are still two observations (busts, closed stacks), and the objective is to figure out what relates them.

Because of the very independence among the ten items listed, if a prediction survives the first item, then it faces a new challenge at the next item. The diversity of the items forces a move to a higher level of abstraction if the predictions are to continue to be supported. It is just this raising of the level of abstraction of ideas that improves the probability that whatever ideas finally emerge will generalize to settings other than college campuses. If a person starts at the top of the list and can successfully predict through to the bottom of the list, *whatever* theory brought this about is worthy of close attention by anyone interested in organizations.

Conclusion

Drawing by Koren; © *1976 The New Yorker Magazine, Inc.*

Koren's crowd could just as easily be a gathering of organizational theorists as a gathering of practicing managers. In either case the people sound much like a swimmer immortalized by Somerset Maugham: "She plunged into a sea of platitudes, and with the powerful breast stroke of a channel swimmer made her confident way toward the white cliffs of the obvious" (1967, p. 174).

To escape platitudes isn't easy, but it can be done. We've tried in this chapter to outline some suggestions that will give the reader access to images of organization that are neither commonplace nor trivially cute.

The main suggestion was that the diversity in the phenomenon be matched by diversity in the inquirer so that more of the phenomenon can be comprehended and made sensible. (This is the idea of requisite variety spelled out in Chapter 7). The reader should have sufficient grasp of this suggestion to see why there is a tinge of madness as well as a tinge of theatrics involved in being diverse enough to grasp the diversity that exists elsewhere. Above all, the excursions into madness and theatrics have to be done self-consciously with the person knowing full well what is being done and knowing full well its limitations.

Diversity is enhanced by the adoption of ambivalent conceptual orientations, ambivalent inquiring practices, and varying positions on the issues of generality, accuracy, and simplicity. Those who successfully sustain this ambivalence are more likely to remain relevant to practitioners than those who stick with one set of assumptions and techniques that dazzle colleagues but put practicing managers to sleep.

Diversity is also enhanced when inquirers take phenomena like organizational behavior with a grain of salt and when they write aphorisms, speculate, do journalism, sit in the armchair, develop cases, and enlarge their questions without effusive apologies.

Diversity also means trying to grasp the flows, rhythms, and streams of organizations, a tough undertaking that seems to work best when launched as an inquiry into recipes, codes, or grammars. To grasp flows is often to dig deeply into metaphors since they are compact, articulate, eloquent, vivid, and even accessible if one uses oneself as a metaphor.

Diversity means understanding that assumption grounds color a person's receptiveness, attention, and effort expenditure on strange displays, and this mediation of reactions occurs whether the theorist likes it or not. *GO COVER FACES* portrays a dozen categories of interest, but surely there are more; the diverse inquirer should try to find/create those additions by contemplating private "mistaken" metaphors about organizations.

Gaining access to buried themes, chains of associations, and ideas is tough, but part of the difficulty is that people feel reluctant to expose some of their private understandings lest they be thought foolish. That might happen, but since there's already a little madness in the theorizing, mere foolishness is nothing.

All you need to remember while thinking about organizing is that there's a bit of absurdity in all of us, theorists and managers alike. That absurdity can be turned to one's advantage, and I've tried to show how. But whether exploited, tolerated, or suppressed, that touch of absurdity lies just below the surface and breaks through in strange forms: "The folly of mistaking a paradox for a discovery, a metaphor for a proof, a torrent of verbiage for a spring of capital truths, and oneself for an oracle is inborn in us" (Valery 1895, quoted in Siu 1968, p. 75).

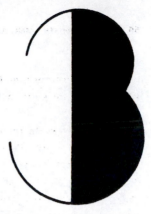

In the last chapter William James urged that we talk about feelings of "and," "if," "but," and "by," and this chapter takes that injunction seriously.

interdependence and organizing

Words such as *connection, relation, link, network, interdependence,* and *reciprocal* are plentiful in literature on organizations. It is important to gain some experience with this way of viewing the world. The purpose of this chapter is to introduce some tools and ideas that can be used to think through some of the issues of connection as they involve organization. In the next chapter we will look at quite molecular forms of connection, interpersonal contingencies between pairs of actors. In this chapter we are talking about connections in general. The ideas to be developed here are equally relevant for connections between a therapist and client, parasite and host, nation and nation, subscribers and advertisers, an individual's failure and depression, or team expansion and fog.

To familiarize the reader with the general notion of interdependence, we will first examine two examples. Then the question of what the examples have in common will be answered by having the reader generate a personal display of interdependence using personal experience. In exploring this display, we will examine several characteristics of it that are also found in the examples and that are basic characteristics of any setting characterized by interdependence.

People and Spirit Levels

A graphic way to demonstrate interdependence is by means of a piece of laboratory apparatus suggested by Alex Bavelas (the same one) and used by Raven and Eachus (1963) (see Fig. 3.1).

In Fig. 3.1 three people are seated at the corners of an equilateral triangle; there are knobs in front of them, and in front of each knob is a carpenter's

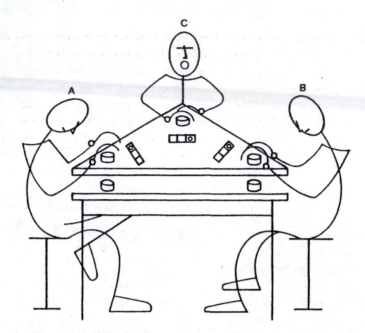

Fig. 3.1 The spirit level task. (From Raven and Eachus 1963, p. 309.)

spirit level—a piece of wood with a bubble in the center of it. If the level is put on a surface that is tilted, the bubble will not remain in the center, but when the surface is perfectly flat the bubble will be in the center. Simple as this tool is, it can portray most of the dramas of interdependence that occur in everyday life.

To see this point, look at person A in Fig. 3.1. If person A turns the knob in front of him, this raises or lowers his corner, depending on which way he turns the knob. Notice the precise direction the spirit level is facing. Suppose that the table is tilted and that the bubble is not in the center. Suppose further that A wants to get the bubble into the center. How can this be done? *A can't do it alone.* Persons B and C have total control over the plane of the table that person A must tilt to get the bubble centered. To see this property, notice where the circle is located in A's spirit level. If A turns his knob he will lower or raise his corner, but that simply moves the level up and down. This vertical movement is irrelevant to A's problem; A needs control over horizontal movement. And it is this kind of control that is in the hands of both B and C. As diagrammed in Fig. 3.1, the bubble is located in the left hand end. This means that the triangle is higher at person C's point than it is at person B's point. If C were to lower the point and B were to raise the point, then the bubble in A's level would come back to the center.

Thus, given the way the spirit levels are pointed, person A is dependent on both person B and person C if the goal is to center the bubble. A is dependent in the sense that he has no direct control over this outcome. A does have some indirect control over this outcome, and it is this feature that makes the exact display of spirit levels in Fig. 3.1 an example of interdependence rather than an example of dependence. We said that A has indirect control over whether his own level can be made horizontal. To see why this is so, simply put yourself in B's chair. B has the same problem that A has. He also can't control directly the table movements that will center his bubble; his fate is in the hands of A and C. As diagrammed, if C lowers his corner and A raises his, then B's bubble will be centered. Thus A is dependent on B and C to center his level, but B is also dependent on A and C to center his. And the same holds true for C. Any one person's fate depends upon what the other two people do, but the person who is dependent on the others can also partially control their fate.

The fascinating part of this simple exercise is that it can be used to create an incredible variety of interdependent situations simply by changing the placement of the levels. In Fig. 3.1 everyone's fate is in the hands of everyone else. If we move the levels so they are directed as shown in Fig. 3.2, then each individual gains more control over his own fate. The form of interdependence depicted here is weaker than was true in Fig. 3.1 in the sense that each individual has partial control over his own fate and is thereby less dependent on the other members; it is also weaker in the sense that each is dependent on and also can affect the fate of only one other individual. In Fig. 3.2 the only crucial person in person A's universe is person C. If C remains passive and doesn't turn his knob at all, then all A has to do is raise his corner, and eventually the bubble will go back to the center. The drama in this setup lies in the fact that even though in A's view C is crucial and B is irrelevant, if we shift around to C's position, C could care less what happens to A: the crucial person is B. However, even though B is crucial to C, if we shift to B's position we find that B could care less what happens to C because A is vital.

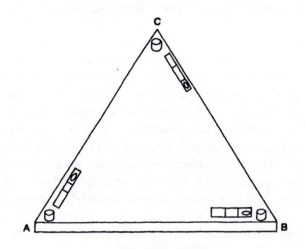

Figure 3.2

Figure 3.1 illustrated a situation of mutual interdependence, and Fig. 3.2 illustrates sequential interdependence. Sequential interdependence is the simplest type of interdependent situation that involves the use of some kind of intermediary in social interaction, and mediated interaction is the essence of organization (Guetzkow 1961). In Fig. 3.2, person A is interested in the outcomes that another person, person C, can offer. But A can offer C nothing. Instead, A has to rely on the actions of somebody else, B, who can offer something of value to C. Situations similar to this in everyday life include the plant manager who relies on supervisors to control the work quality of workers, the child who works through the softer parent to get desired outcomes from the other parent, and the nation that asks another nation to sound out a third regarding some possible agreement.

"Nobody Ever Dies of Overpopulation"

The phrase "nobody ever dies of overpopulation" comes from an editorial written by Garrett Hardin (1971) concerning the population explosion. His point of departure was the catastrophe that occurred in East Bengal in November 1970 when 500,000 people were killed by a cyclone. Hardin asks the question, "What killed these unfortunate people?" The obvious answer is the cyclone. Hardin argues that it's just as plausible to argue that overpopulation killed these 500,000 people. The area where they lived is barely above sea level, making anyone who lives there vulnerable to being killed by even quite ordinary storms. Hardin feels that if it were not for the fact that Pakistan is so overcrowded, "no sane man would bring his family to such a place. Ecologically speaking, a delta belongs to the river and the sea; man intrudes there at his peril."

Hardin feels that we tend to exaggerate the effect of something like a cyclone and to underplay the effect of something like overpopulation simply because if we identified overpopulation as a strong determinant, then we would have to deal with the unpleasant question, "How can we control population without recourse to repugnant measures?" (Hardin and Baden 1977). By saying that the cyclone caused the deaths, then we can comfortably say that fate, not human responsibility, was at the root of the problem. As another example, Hardin mentions the fact that every year diseases like tuberculosis, leprosy, or animal parasites "cause" the deaths of millions of people. His argument is that malnutrition is intimately connected with overpopulation.

Another population example of interdependence is found in the work of Ehrlich, Ehrlich, and Holdren (1973). They note that as the population increases cities expand and push out into farm land. This has the consequence that air pollution becomes a mixture of agricultural chemicals and the conventional urban pollutants such as power plant emissions and automobile exhaust fumes. The basic component of the urban pollution is sulfur dioxide, which drastically slows and eventually paralyzes the cleansing mechanisms of the lungs. When cities expand and encroach on agricultural lands, this has the serious consequence that a slowing of the cleansing mechanism in the lungs means that the carcinogens in agricultural chemicals reside in the lungs for a longer time before they are cleansed out. And the longer a human being is exposed to these carcinogens, the higher the probability of death from a terminal disease. Notice that if we apply Hardin's phrase, we would be tempted to say that people die from lung cancer rather than overpopulation, which was the original reason that the cities were expanding and that the urban pollutants became fatally mixed with agricultural pollutants.

Causal Structures in Group Discussions

General properties of these two examples can be uncovered with an exhibit you can generate. Please read and follow these instructions *before* you read the portion of this chapter which follows the exercise.

In Fig. 3.3 you will see 12 different boxes that each contain a brief phrase. Each of these 12 phrases describes some typical event that occurs during a classroom lecture, group discussion, seminar, or planning meeting. Think back to the most recent classroom or workgroup discussion you've been in. It's important that you have a specific session in mind and that it be vivid in your memory. Once you've chosen the particular session that you want to analyze, enter the identifying information about this session at the top of Fig. 3.3. This will help you later if you forget what this diagram represents but wish to refer back to some of the ideas in this diagram.

Fill out this diagram: draw on this figure both arrows and plus and minus signs that describe accurately your meeting experience. Basically you're asking yourself which labeled events in that meeting affected which other events. When you feel that some event affects some other event, represent this by an arrow. For example, suppose that when your feelings of boredom (10) changed—that is, they either went up or down—this change affected the number of ideas you thought of (5). If you think that was the case, then draw an arrow from box 10 to box 5, with the point of the arrow at 5 and the blunt end of the arrow at 10. This arrow simply says that when feelings of boredom change, this change causes a change in the number of ideas you think of.

Work your way systematically around the diagram. First look at box 1, "Number of people making comments," and ask yourself, as the number changes (more people make comments or fewer people make comments), does

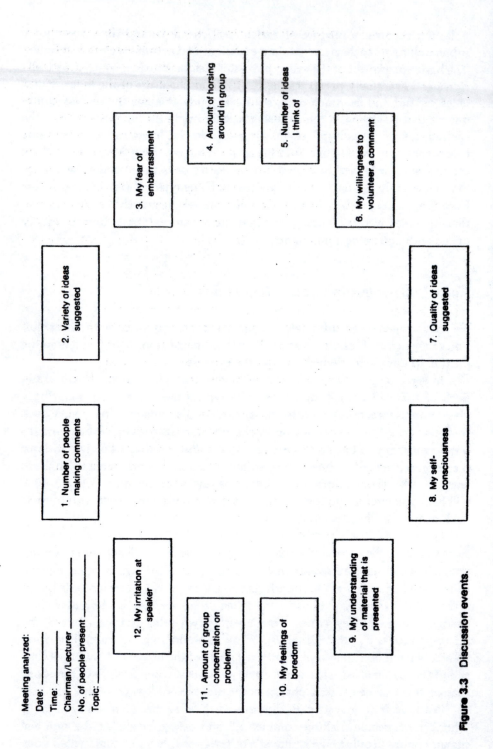

Meeting analyzed:
Date: _____
Time: _____
Chairman/Lecturer _____
No. of people present _____
Topic: _____

1. Number of people making comments

2. Variety of ideas suggested

3. My fear of embarrassment

4. Amount of horsing around in group

5. Number of ideas I think of

6. My willingness to volunteer a comment

7. Quality of ideas suggested

8. My self-consciousness

9. My understanding of material that is presented

10. My feelings of boredom

11. Amount of group concentration on problem

12. My irritation at speaker

Figure 3.3 Discussion events.

this affect box 2, box 3, and so on? (These boxes represent *variables* in the discussion.) Once you have examined all 11 events other than box 1 and have asked yourself whether a change in variable 1 produces a change in these other events, then switch to variable 2 and ask, "As the 'variety of ideas suggested' changes, does this affect box 3, box 4, and so on?" Whenever something does have an effect on something else, connect those two events by an arrow.

In addition to drawing arrows among the events you should also place either a plus or a minus sign next to *each* arrow that you draw. When you draw an arrow, that simply says that the event at the blunt end of the arrow has an effect on the event at the sharp end of the arrow. The plus and minus designation permits you to identify what kind of effect occurs. A plus sign means that the two connected events change in the *same* direction. For example, suppose you had an arrow going from box 10 to box 5 showing that when your feelings of boredom change this affects the number of ideas you have. Suppose further that as your boredom increases, the number of ideas you have also increases (when you get bored your mind wanders and you dream up ideas to entertain yourself). And suppose that as your boredom decreases the number of ideas you have also decreases. In both of these cases the connected variables change in the *same* direction. When one goes up the other one goes up; when one goes down the other one goes down. In your diagram, put a plus sign next to every arrow connecting variables that move in the *same* direction.

Some events that you connect, however, will move in opposite directions. For example, it is conceivable that when your feeling of boredom increases your idea production decreases. Or similarly, as your feelings of boredom decrease, the number of ideas you have goes up. In both of these cases when one event changes in one direction, the event to which it is related by a causal arrow changes in the *opposite* direction. Wherever you have two events linked by an arrow and the two events move in *opposite* directions, then put a minus sign next to that arrow.

In summary, take some actual discussion experience that you've recently had and, using the 12 events in Fig. 3.3, portray what happened. Indicate which events affected which other events and the direction of these effects. Take your time completing this exercise. The more carefully you work on it, the more you will understand subsequent ideas presented in this book.

DO NOT READ ANY FURTHER IN THIS TEXT UNTIL YOU HAVE COMPLETED FIG. 3.3 ACCORDING TO THE INSTRUCTIONS GIVEN IMMEDIATELY ABOVE.

Analysis of Interdependence

OVERVIEW OF FIGURE 3.3

Each numbered event in your cause map is a variable: each event can assume a variety of values. Each of the 12 variables you've connected is either interdependent, dependent, independent, or irrelevant. Any variable that has arrows coming into it and arrows going out from it is interdependent: it is affected by and affects other variables. Any variable that only has arrows coming to it but has no arrows going away from it is a dependent variable. And any variable that has arrows going away from it but has no arrows coming into it is an independent variable.

Just on the basis of this crude tally, it is probably the case that more of your variables are interdependent than either independent or dependent. Whether that's true or not, the point is that the discussion configuration resembles the situations of the spirit level and overpopulation.

In Chapter 1 we talked about causal loops and causal circuits; these should be visible in your diagram. Take one of the *inter*dependent variables as a starting point. Starting with that variable, see if you can trace a pathway by following the arrows that will eventually lead you back to the variable that you started with. You are trying to start with an interdependent variable and locate some path of arrows that will lead you back to that starting point. Every complete path that you find is a causal loop. If you can find no loops, then draw in a hypothetical one—using a different-colored pencil—to aid your understanding of the following points.

CAUSAL LOOPS AND CONTROL

Pick out one of your loops and count the number of negative signs contained in that loop. If there is an even number of negative signs (e.g., 0, 2, 4, etc.), then that loop is a deviation-amplifying loop (Maruyama 1963), a vicious circle (Wender 1968), or a regenerative loop (Bateson 1972, p. 109). The potential significance of such a loop can be seen if you trace what happens when one variable in that loop increases. You will find that the variable you started with increases even further once you have completed the circuit and it continues to increase every time you complete the cycle. In a causal loop with an even number of negative signs there is no regulation or control. Once a variable begins to move in a particular direction, either up or down, the variable will continue to move in that same direction until the system is destroyed or until some dramatic change occurs (Goldsmith 1971).

To see how control operates look at portions *A* and *B* of Fig. 3.4. In portion *A* there is an even number of negative signs: zero. In that kind of situation any change in one of the variables will be amplified, and a vicious

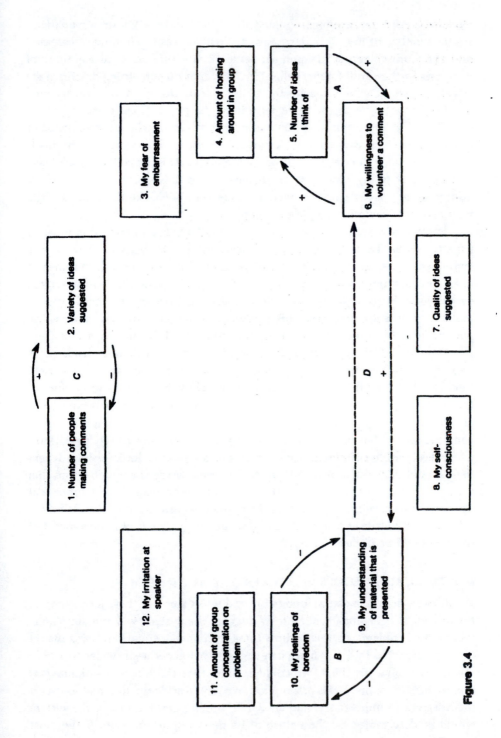

Figure 3.4

circle will result. For example, suppose that I have difficulty thinking up ideas. As the number of my ideas decreases, my willingness to comment decreases; and as my unwillingness to comment decreases, the number of ideas I think of decreases further until I either fall asleep, leave, or do something drastic to get attention—all of which change the system. In a closed loop with an even number of negative signs, there is nothing to prevent the spiraling I just described. The same spiraling holds true for portion *B*, which is composed of two negative signs, again an even number. If my boredom increases, this leads to a decrease in my understanding of the material that is presented, which leads to an increase in my boredom, which should lead to a further decrease in my understanding, etc. Again this vicious circle goes unchecked, a characteristic feature of any deviation-amplifying loop.

In some of your loops, however, you may have found an odd number of negative signs. These loops are particularly interesting because they impose stabilities on organizing processes. In portion *C* there is an odd number of negative signs (one). If you trace through several circuits in that pair of related events you will see how self-regulation occurs. Suppose the number of people making comments increases. This produces an increase in variety of ideas, which then produces a decrease in the number of commenters (they get overloaded), which leads to a decrease in variety, which then leads more people to make comments. Both people making comments and idea variety fluctuate, but they fluctuate around some middle value. This is so because of the relationship between these two events, a relationship that leads them to be controlled and self-regulating rather than uncontrolled and amplified. Any causal loop that has an odd number of negative signs counteracts deviations.

When people examine relations in organizations they look for interdependent variables, causal loops, and the presence or absence of control. Loops that are deviation-counteracting mean that the system is basically stable; loops that are deviation-amplifying mean that the system is basically unstable. Whether this instability leads to constructive or destructive growth is of importance, but this point will be discussed later.

MULTIPLE CAUSAL LOOPS AND THE FATE OF THE SYSTEM

When more than one causal loop exists and when some of these loops suggest the system will explode while others suggest the system will remain stable, there is the problem of knowing how to analyze such a situation. Using the set of loops depicted in Fig. 3.5 we can suggest two general strategies to use in making this analysis. First, we could assume that the loops are of *unequal* importance. If we make this assumption, we would scale the different loops on their degrees of importance, and we would predict that the fate of the system would be determined by the nature of its most important loop. If the most

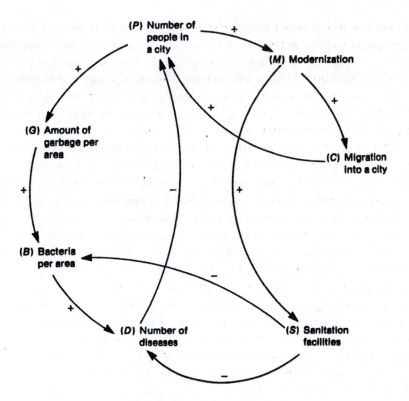

Fig. 3.5 (From Maruyama 1963.)

important loop is deviation-counteracting, then the *system* in which the loop is embedded will be deviation-counteracting. If the most important loop is deviation-amplifying, then the system will be deviation-amplifying. The difficulty with this method of predicting is that the judgment of a loop's importance may often be purely arbitrary.

However, there are some ways in which this problem of arbitrariness can be solved. It is possible, for example, to define importance in terms of the number of inputs to and outputs from the different elements in the system. The general rule would be: the greater the number of inputs to and/or outputs from an element, the more important that element is. Having assessed the individual elements, we would then search for that loop which contained the greatest number of important elements, and we would predict that the nature of that loop would determine the fate of the system. For example, if we examine the elements in Fig. 3.5, we find that some of them have more than one output (this is true of elements *P*, *M*, and *S*) and some of them have more than one input (this is true of elements *P*, *D*, and *B*). Now if we assume that the five elements with more than one output or more than one input are the most important elements in the system, then we look within this system for that closed loop that contains the greatest number of these important elements (the loop goes from P to M to S to B to D to P). Since this loop has an even number of negative signs (two), it is deviation-amplifying. Thus we say that the most important loop within this system is deviation-amplifying, and therefore the entire system is deviation-amplifying; we predict that it will eventually destroy itself unless one of the relationships changes in sign, another relationship is added, or some relationship is deleted.

All this pertains to the situation in which the investigator assumes that the loops are of unequal importance. If we make the assumption that the loops are of *equal* importance, then we can solve the problem of predicting the fate of the system in a different way. It seems plausible that we could talk about the fate of the system *as a system* by counting the number of negative loops, just as we previously counted the number of negative relationships. By a *negative loop* we mean a closed loop that contains an odd number of negative causal relationships. We would predict that any system will survive as a system only if it contains an odd number of these negative loops. If the system contains an even number of negative loops, then their effects will cancel one another, and the remaining positive cycles will amplify whatever deviations may occur. Another way of reaching the same prediction would be to count the total number of negative relationships in the whole system, counting each negative more than once if it appeared in more than one loop. If the total number was odd, the system would be deviation-counteracting; if it was even, the system would be deviation-amplifying.

Now we can refer back to Fig. 3.5. In this figure *one* of the four loops is negative ($PGBDP$), and there is a total of five negative causal relationships (counting the one between D and P three times, since it takes part in three loops).

Since both these numbers are odd, whatever happens within this system, regardless of where it happens, will eventually be reversed. The system, according to this prediction, is a deviation-counteracting system. This prediction differs from the earlier prediction based on the assumption that the loops were of unequal strength, thereby illustrating the point that assumptions make a difference. It is conceivable that both conclusions about this system are correct. The system will continue for some period of time, but due to such things as the differential speed with which the cycles are completed, the magnitude of the changes at each variable, the tightness of the couplings among variables, the number of times each loop is activated, and the effects of exogenous variables, increasing amounts of instability could be introduced.

The tactic of using arrows and plus and minus signs is simply a means to portray situations of complex interdependence in such a way that one can then ask better questions about these situations. These cause maps do impose some order on the domain being analyzed, and it will be our argument that this ordering can be informative to both participants and observers.

ARBITRARY CAUSE AND EFFECT

When any two events are related interdependently, designating one of those two *cause* and the other *effect* is an arbitrary designation. If you examine any causal loop you will see why. In any causal loop no variable is any more or less important than any other variable. No variable in a loop controls other variables without itself being controlled by them. You can start the sequence anywhere you want by changing any variable. That change initially looks like a cause that triggers subsequent events in the loop. But the changes within the loop keep happening and eventually come back and modify the initial change which you had intentionally made. And that cycling back means that what was originally a cause is now suddenly an effect. This is a prominent feature of any structure of causal circuits. It should be kept in mind when you are tempted to argue that some changes are more important than other ones. If you have a genuine causal circuit, then any change made anywhere will eventually itself be changed by the consequences it triggers.

Drawing by Levin; © *1976 The New Yorker Magazine, Inc.*

UPTIGHT VARIABLES

Earlier we substituted the word *variable* for the word *event* to signify that an event can take on a variety of values. The number of ideas I think of, for example, can vary between 0 and 37, my fear of embarrassment can vary from slight to monumental, and so forth. Although it is sometimes hard to specify the limits within which a variable can change, the reader probably does have some feel for what it means to say that variables can take on different values. Normally when a variable moves between its upper and lower limits, these changes promote adaptation and stability.

But in any causal loop the limits between which a variable varies can produce rather dramatic consequences. One of these consequences is "uptight variables":

> When, under stress, a variable must take the value close to its upper or lower limit of tolerance, we shall say, borrowing a phrase from the youth culture, that the system is "uptight" in respect to this variable, or lacks "flexibility" in this respect. But, because the variables are interlinked, to be uptight in respect to one variable commonly means that other variables cannot be changed without pushing the uptight variable. The loss of flexibility thus spreads through the system. In extreme cases, the system will only accept those changes which *change the tolerance limits* for the uptight variable. For example, an overpopulated society looks for those changes (increased food, new roads, more houses, etc.) which will make the pathological and pathogenic conditions of overpopulation more comfortable. But these ad hoc changes are precisely those which in longer time can lead to more fundamental ecological pathology. The pathologies of our time may broadly be said to be the accumulated results of this process—the eating up of flexibility in response to stresses of one sort or another (especially the stress of population pressure) and the refusal to bear with those byproducts of stress (e.g., epidemic and famine) which are the age-old correctives for population excess (G. W. Bateson, 1972, pp. 496-97).

Suppose that one of the variables in the discussion group diagram (Fig. 3.3) is pushed to its limits: irritation (box 12) is at an all-time high or quality of ideas (box 7) is as low as it can go. If this happens, then all *other* variables related to that single uptight variable will now also become frozen, and that's true even if they are *not* near the extremes of their limits. Remember that the variables are interdependent, and this means that they are responsive to the changes made in those variables to which they are connected. If one of those variables to which they are connected is frozen and does not change, then the related variables won't fluctuate, either.

When variables freeze up danger results because they are then unavailable to absorb changes occasioned by normal fluctuations. Think back to portion C in Fig. 3.4. On any one day, the variety of ideas being suggested may be quite high, quite low, or right in the middle. And some of the things that happen in that discussion will have an effect on variety. People are able to adapt to these fluctuations and to stabilize them because of the deviation-counteracting loop that relates people and variety. Suppose the discussion starts off with very little variety in what is produced. That discouraging start really doesn't matter.

In a deviation-counteracting loop, the relationships are present that allow the group to adapt to lowered variety, whatever caused it. In the presence of low variety, more people speak up, which raises variety. The presence of the deviation-counteracting relationship, plus the fact that these two variables are free to vary and absorb some of these external buffetings, helps stabilize the discussions.

Bateson is worried about what happens when variables lose their variability. Suppose people get stuck on the same idea or everyone wants to talk at once or everyone is preoccupied and wants everyone else to talk. In any of those cases the variable is not free to move except in one direction. Consequently, its capacity to absorb some of the buffeting from the environment is drastically reduced.

In a discussion situation there are several variables that could become uptight. If by chance you diagramed a meeting with which you were very dissatisfied, one of the first things you should look for is the likelihood that deviation-amplifying loops are present. Secondly, you should look to see if some variables are uptight and have thereby frozen the variation in related variables. If you discover that variables are uptight or locked into deviation-amplifying circuits, what should you do?

PATTERNS ARE MORE CRUCIAL THAN SUBSTANCES

What do you do with a system that is stuck? One thing you don't do is tamper with a single variable. The basic property of interdependence is that patterns and *relations* among variables are the realities that you have to deal with; substances are trivial. If a loop is uptight it won't do any good to work on single variables. The only place that you can make a significant change is *between* variables. Those relationships are what give order to the events you have depicted.

To see this point examine portions B and D of Fig. 3.4. In portion B a vicious circle is operating. Bordeom cuts down on understanding, which increases boredom, which cuts down on understanding even more. Suppose I want to change that. I can't operate on my boredom and somehow develop more tolerance, nor can I somehow operate independently on my understanding so as to deepen it. The reason those changes won't make any difference is that they take no account of the causal ties between these two events. Even if I develop more tolerance, all that happens is I expand slightly the limits within which the variable varies. What remains unchanged is the fact that boredom is linked to understanding by an amplifying relationship.

I could change that vicious circle by adding a new variable into the loop, a solution depicted in portion D. If I could generate a world in which my understanding of the material that is presented would not affect my boredom directly but rather would affect my willingness to make comments, and if my willingness to make comments (variable 6) were tied to my understanding of material in the ways that are designated by the signs in portion *D*, then a stable relationship is created.

The sequence will be traced through to show how control has been achieved. Suppose my boredom increases. This leads to a decrease in my understanding of the material. But now, with the addition of the new linkage to variable 6, my decrease in understanding triggers an increase in my willingness to comment; this in turn increases my understanding of the material, which then finally decreases my boredom. By adding a third variable in the ways depicted in portion *D*, I have regained some control over a potentially vicious circle and now have a more stable set of events.

By relating variable 6 a situation of an even number of negative signs was transformed into a situation of an odd number of negatives. To reiterate an important point, it was *not* the fact that I became willing to volunteer comments that stabilized this system and gave it additional flexibility. Merely volunteering comments had nothing to do with this outcome. What *did* produce the outcome was the way in which this activity of commenting became related to the other events of boredom and understanding. If I had incorporated "willingness to comment" into my cause map, but had related it to understanding with a plus rather than a minus sign (when my understanding goes down I say nothing), then the causal loop would have been even less stable. It all depends on the relationships involved.

DISSOLVING RANDOMNESS

It is also a property of causal circuits that they generate a nonrandom response to a random event at that position in the circuit at which the random event occurred. This is a subtle but crucial point for organizational analyses. If there is an accidental change in value of one of the variables in a circuit, the characteristics of the *circuit* will even out that fluctuation as it moves around the circuit so that when it finally arrives back at the point of the original accident, the accident has been made orderly. By characteristics of the *circuit* we mean such things as its threshold of activity, its patterns of plus and minus relationships, how long it takes a circular sequence to complete itself, and so on. These characteristics of the circuit act as constraints on any random fluctuation and tend to even out what occurs.

For example, take the extended causal loop that combines portions *B* and *D* of Fig. 3.4. Suppose a random impulse leads me to start making comments about everything to everyone (variable 6 goes up for no particular reason). More comments leads to more understanding, less boredom, greater understanding, and finally *fewer* comments. Thus, the original random increase in comments, through the events triggered in this causal circuit, eventually makes of this random commenting a nonrandom, orderly response. This outcome occurred because of the patterns of plus and minus relationships in that causal loop, the amount of time it took for the events to cycle through (time is left unspecified in this particular example), and the amount by which a prior variable had to change before it triggered a subsequent variable (as discussed in this example I have assumed that the thresholds are very low—that is, a minor fluctuation is sufficient to trigger the next variable along the circuit).

SMALL BEGINNINGS

Deviation-amplifying loops can be either vicious or virtuous circles, and it is important that this broader implication be understood. Any chance event such as a small crack in a rock that gathers water or a farmer who builds his home on a homogeneous agricultural plain can become amplified into a tree that grows out of a rock or people congregating around the original farmer to form a city. The process, not the initial crack or location, generated the complex outcome (Maruyama 1963).

What is striking are the disproportions involved. A small initial deviation that is highly probable—such as a wagon breaking down—may develop into a deviation that is very improbable—a city. This final outcome is improbable if one believes in unidirectional causality rather than causal loops. With sufficient cycling, small deviations can be amplified into complex homogeneous events, a sequence that can be quite misleading to analysts (see Waddington 1977, pp. 145-60).

Let's return to the city in an agricultural plain. Once the farmer opens a farm at a chance spot on it, other farmers follow his example; soon one of the farmers opens a tool shop where the farmers congregate. Later a food stand opens next to the tool shop, and a village grows. The village makes it easier to market crops, which attracts still more farmers; eventually a city develops. Now, if an analyst looks for a geographical cause as to why this particular spot and not some other became a city, he won't find it. He won't find it because "it" is not there. The amplifying processes generated the complexity. And because the final outcome is so complex, there are that many more false leads concerning "things" or single variables that could have "caused" this city to form in this place. All of these clues are misleading because none of them "caused" the city to be located in just that spot. The truth will be lost to analysts, especially to the person who views reality as consisting solely of things and structures rather than relations and processes.

The analytic problem can be illustrated by a different example, one discussed by Wender (1968). Suppose we observe that an adult experiences social rejection in response to social ineptitude, and that this sequence also is associated with lowered self esteem and withdrawal. The process looks like that portrayed in Fig. 3.6. As shown in Fig. 3.6, the person now faces rejection, and that's what sustains the misery. But that isn't how it started.

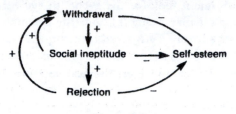

Figure 3.6

As an adolescent the person was fat and pimply, withdrew in embarrassment, and failed to acquire social skills. Thus Fig. 3.6 should be extended to reveal the factors shown in Fig. 3.7. The acne and obesity disappeared, but the withdrawal and social ineptitude persisted because of their amplifying linkage. This means that what started the problem no longer exists to sustain it. "Insight" into the *origins* probably won't help either, because they're no longer responsible for what holds the misery (rejection) in place. If the original event has disappeared and left no trace, then it may even be undiscoverable.

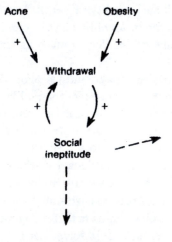

Figure 3.7

Deviation-amplifying circuits mock a search for original single causes that are proportional in size to the effect that is now observed (e.g., a tiny little stream could never have carved out that huge Grand Canyon). An outcome produced for one reason may continue for other reasons due to amplification. The same may hold true for your maps of discussions. If you diagramed an unsatisfactory session, it is probably fruitless to look for the first minor deviation that produced the present unhappiness. Loops operating here and now are what the organizational analyst needs to study. After studying the pattern, the analyst may conclude that what needs to be done is that the direction of some variable should be reversed. That's the topic we turn to.

REVERSING A VARIABLE

Deviation-amplifying loops often cause trouble because their variables are moving in the "wrong" direction. If in portion B of Fig. 3.4 boredom goes up, I'm in trouble because it can only get worse, something that also happens in portion A when I block and can't think of any ideas. In both those cases, if the direction in which the variables are moving could be reversed, I'd be in much better shape (Ashton 1976). This is where activities such as reflection and contemplation come in and make great sense (LeShan 1976; Low 1976; TenHouten and Kaplan 1973; Pearce 1973, 1975; Siu 1974). These activities frequently result in reversing of variables and a reversal of one's fate.

A set of connected variables thought to be associated with depression (Wender 1968) illustrate this point eloquently in Fig. 3.8; these loops and connections are self-explanatory and almost painful to work through. Given the bare structure shown in Fig. 3.8 it is easy to see why depression can persist and get worse.

But the causal network of depression portrayed in Fig. 3.8 is vulnerable, and one point of vulnerability is "aid from others." As a person's self-evaluation drops, depression increases, coping ability decreases, one has to depend on others for aid, which lowers even further one's self-evaluation, and so on. This vicious circle is fueled by the interpretation that getting aid from others is a sign of weakness and dependence. Upon reflection, however, the meaning of aid can shift from one of weakness to the more positive interpretation that it's okay to ask for help and it's great to have others who care enough to come to

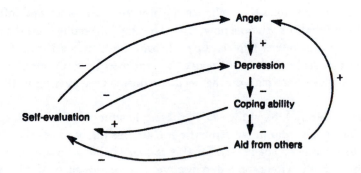

Figure 3.8

one's aid (Lyon 1977). If, after reflection, that interpretation becomes salient, then the negative sign between aid and self-evaluation in Fig. 3.8 becomes a positive sign, which turns amplification into stability.

Reversal need not take the form of a reversal of sign. It can take the form of a reversing of direction, the dynamic we mentioned in the first paragraph of this section. If coping ability can be increased by training and/or a success experience, then the downward spiral of depression can be halted and self-evaluation can increase. Because of the consensual element in organizing, reversal of direction may require social action and redefinition. And because of the density of linkage, reversing a direction may be difficult because inertia and prior understandings work against the redirection.

NONLOOPS

It is fairly common for people to draw a map of their experience and find no loops. The meaning of this outcome is not completely clear, and the reader is urged to add to our modest thoughts on this topic.

An absence of loops seems to mean most economically that an insufficient number or the wrong variables were included in the experience map. If everything is related, then a failure to find relations simply means one is looking at the wrong things. If "my fear of embarrassment" reduces "my willingness to volunteer comments," but nothing on the map affects my fear, this simply means the list of variables is incomplete. We assume that something affects my fear.

This is not, however, the sole possibility concerning loops. Events may not be interrelated richly and unidirectional causality may be a correct rather than an incorrect perception. It may be correct because that's the way things are or because that's the way they appear to fallible perceivers who invariably influence the data they are gathering (see Salancik and Pfeffer 1977, pp. 449-52, on priming).

The perception of nonloops may operate in the service of hubris, pride, or other egocentric pastimes that enhance the stature of the actor and inflate the apparent magnitude of personal power. This has the interesting twist that people who are not on a "power trip" and people who have high self-esteem should report more causal circuits and report the world to be more interdependent than do those who are high on the need for power or wavering in their self-esteem.

If one wishes to look at the same problem in situational terms, it could be argued that people who move around a lot are less likely to see the world as full of causal circuits. The reason for this is that people who are mobile may not stay in a situation long enough to discover the consequences of their actions. The consequences do not come back and affect transients, because transients have moved to a new setting. Transients are left with the impression that what they did had an effect. What they fail to see is that if they had stayed, the effect in turn would have influenced them.

The presence of nonloops may mask the fact that variables are related by step-functions (and the threshold for triggering the next variable is seldom exceeded) or by nonmonotonic relationships (the same variable causes both a decrease and an increase in a related variable, and the effects are thought to cancel and therefore are not related). Time lags in responsiveness may mask loops.

Loops may not occur because the variable that originated the relationship (e.g., acne) may not be present in the same form when the effect finally circles back to the origin. If variables are consensual labels and if variables change, then it shouldn't be surprising that loops can't occur if the origins of the causal sequence are no longer present.

An absence of loops may simply be testimonial to human frailties such as people being unable to describe their inner cognitive processes (Nisbett and Wilson 1977; Smith and Miller 1978), people being severely limited in the capacity to process information or people being immersed in routines that *do* simply run off without feedback to their origins.

DISCREDITING A CAUSE MAP

The possibilities for changing a cause map are quite straightforward, so we will simply list them. Assume that in a cause map a simple linear relationship is stored: the greater the number of criticisms, the higher the quality of performance. Changing that linear sequence could take any one of the following forms:

1 The causal direction could be reversed: the quality of performance causes the number of criticisms received.

2 The sign of the linkage could be changed: as criticisms increase the quality of performance decreases.

3 Two variables could be decoupled: criticism has no effect on quality.

4 The direction of the relationship could be removed: criticisms affect quality, but there is no regularity to the direction in which this relationship moves.

5 Dissolve the variables: there is no such thing as criticism or quality of performance.

6 The coupling could be tightened: criticisms always, immediately, and in direct proportion affect the quality of performance, an assertion that is stronger than the one originally formed. This introduces change in the speed with which the cycle is completed and in the amount of influence exerted on other variables that are related to these two.

7   The coupling can be loosened: criticisms have a very modest regular effect on the quality of performance.

8   The effects of the originating variable are canceled by another pathway: even though criticisms affect quality directly, they also affect the patience of one's peers, and as this patience wears thin the quality of performance goes down. Therefore, criticisms may improve quality, but they have even more effect on peers and peer pressure decreases quality, which undercuts any direct effect from criticisms.

9   The variables are related in a curvilinear manner: criticisms affect quality of performance directly up to a point, but beyond that criticisms have just the opposite effect—they degrade quality.

The reader can add other changes to this list, but the point should be clear that anything that is done to form a cause map can be undone to change it. Obviously some of the nine changes we've mentioned are more severe forms of change, are more difficult to accomplish, and are more likely to be acceptable in certain kinds of organizations. Those potential differences may provide a wedge to categorize people within organizations in terms of the kinds of cognitive changes they are willing and able to make in their cause maps.

Conclusion

Most managers get into trouble because they forget to think in circles. I mean this literally. Managerial problems persist because managers continue to believe that there are such things as unilateral causation, independent and dependent variables, origins, and terminations. Examples are everywhere: leadership style affects productivity, parents socialize children, stimuli affect responses, ends affect means, desires affect actions. Those assertions are wrong because each of them demonstrably also operates in the opposite direction: productivity affects leadership style (Lowin and Craig 1968), children socialize parents (Osofsky 1971), responses affect stimuli (Gombrich 1960), means affect ends (Hirschman and Lindblom 1962), actions affect desires (Bem 1967). In every one of these examples causation is circular, not linear. And the same thing holds true for most organizational events.

Suppose you thumb through books to find the answer to some question you have. Your first temptation might be to say that the question caused focused searching. But that's not the way it works. Searching is circular. You start with a question, you stumble onto some apparently relevant item, which in turn affects subsequent searching, which in turn redirects your question, etc.

If you become obsessed with interdependence and causal loops, then lots of issues take on a new look.

If you take loops seriously, for example, then you realize that some very sacred ideas such as self-power and self-determination are fictions. If most of our behavior is embedded in causal circuits, then whatever we do will come back to haunt and control us. The revenge of the environment is perhaps the most obvious example. Those things we unilaterally did to the environment now are coming back to undo us.

John Steinbeck, writing in the late 1930s, described a set of deviation-amplifying causal loops that anticipated ecological concerns by several years:

> At one time an important game bird in Norway, the willow grouse, was so clearly threatened with extinction that it was thought wise to establish protective regulations and to place a bounty on its chief enemy, a hawk which was known to feed heavily on it. Quantities of the hawks were exterminated, but despite such drastic measures the grouse disappeared actually more rapidly than before. The naively applied customary remedies had obviously failed. But instead of becoming discouraged and quietistically letting this bird go the way of the great auk and the passenger pigeon, the authorities enlarged the scope of their investigations until the anomaly was explained. An ecological analysis into the *relational* [italics added] aspects of the situation disclosed that a parasitic disease, coccidiosis, was epizootic among the grouse. In its incipient stages, this disease so reduced the flying speed of the grouse that the mildly ill individuals became easy prey for the hawks. In living largely off the slightly ill birds, the hawks prevented them from developing the disease in its full intensity and so spreading it more widely and quickly to otherwise healthy fowl. Thus the presumed enemies of the grouse, by controlling the epizootic aspects of the disease, proved to be friends in disguise (1941, pp. 144-45).

Through the mechanism of a deviation-amplifying circuit, minor deviations (a few less hawks) created the conditions under which the survival of the grouse became precarious. Hubris was revenged by causal loops.

As a different variation of the interdependence theme, G. W. Bateson (1971) has argued that one of the major insane premises in Western thought is the belief that we have self-control. He illustrates this by discussing alcoholics. Alcoholism is inevitable as long as the drinker maintains the illusion, "I am captain of my soul and I can stay sober." That claim is an illusion, because drinking is circular. The only way you can prove that you are the captain of your soul is to test the proposition by exposing yourself to the challenge of a drinking situation. For alcoholics, these tests typically fail. Actually, when the test fails the alcoholic is demonstrating that the idea of self-control is fallacious, that he doesn't have control, that the problem is bigger than he is. He is only part of a larger circuit (Finlay 1978). But as long as he continues to believe or has foisted on him the belief that he has self-power, he'll blame his failures on external circumstances, preserve the illusion that he can control his fate, and continue to go on binges until he hits bottom.

What gives plausibility to this analysis is the fact that the most successful cure for alcoholism, the program of Alcoholics Anonymous, involves a credo that directly reverses the premises that may produce alcoholism and other problems. A major tenet of the AA credo is that "there is a power greater than you; once an alcoholic, always an alcoholic." Notice that such a premise falsifies the idea that one is captain of his soul. It says instead that the alcoholic and his drinking are part of a larger system that neither rewards nor punishes, that his relation to this greater power is both complementary and submissive, and all of these lessons are eloquently summarized in AA's insistence that members be anonymous (Bill 1957, pp. 286-94). The practice of anonymity merely restates the idea that all of us are in part-whole relationships.

Still another implication of thinking in circles is that it explains why self-fulfilling prophecies are inevitable. They are inevitable because whatever a person does comes back and does him in. William James asked the question, "Is life worth living?" He replied that you can make the answer come out either way. "Faith beforehand in an uncertified result is the only thing that makes the result come true" (1956, p. 59). If you despair and refuse to believe that life is worth living, then indeed it won't be, and your own self-destruction will prove it. However, believe that it is worth living and that belief will help to create the fact. That's more than homely advice. Like the AA credo, it confirms the reality of loops and disavows the reality of linear causation.

Most "things" in organizations are actually relationships, variables tied together in systematic fashion. Events, therefore, depend on the strength of these ties, the direction of influence, the time it takes for information in the form of differences to move around circuits. The word *organization* is a noun, and it is also a myth. If you look for an organization you won't find it. What you will find is that there are events, linked together, that transpire within concrete walls and these sequences, their pathways, and their timing are the forms we erroneously make into substances when we talk about an organization. Just as the skin is a misleading boundary for marking off where a person ends and the environment starts, so are the walls of an organization. Events inside organizations and organisms are locked into causal circuits that extend beyond these artificial boundaries.

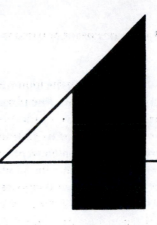

Organizing is accomplished by processes. But before we can talk about these processes, we need to describe their elements.

Processes contain individual behaviors that are interlocked

interlocked behaviors and organizing

among two or more people. The behaviors of one person are contingent on the behaviors of another person(s), and these contingencies are called *interacts*. The unit of analysis in organizing is contingent response patterns, patterns in which an action by actor *A* evokes a specific response in actor *B* (so far this is an interact), which is then responded to by actor *A* (this complete sequence is a *double interact*).

Hollander and Willis (1967) argue that double interacts are the basic unit for describing interpersonal influence. Since organizing involves control, influence, and authority, a description of organizing benefits from using the double interact as the unit of analysis. To see why this is so, suppose that a supervisor wants to get a worker to stop doing task *A* and start doing task *B*. The worker's action is the doing of task *A*; the supervisor tries to influence the worker to do task *B*. Obviously, we must know how the worker responds to this directive before we can make any statement about the complete influence attempt. But to determine the worker's response, we need a specific description of the original activity as a basis for comparison. The worker's typical response pattern will probably be altered in some way by the supervisor's directive, and before we can understand the meaning of this alteration, we need to know the action that was already underway. This is the point in Atkinson and Cartwright's (1964) important argument that many existing theories of motivation are inadequate because they fail to take account of ongoing activity and the forces sustaining it when a substitute activity is proposed.

The purpose of this chapter is to describe a variety of ways to conceptualize interlocked behaviors, including F. H. Allport's (1962) concept of collective structure, Wallace's (1961) concept of mutual equivalence structure, and Kelley's

(1968) work with the minimal social situation. The chapter also illustrates how sets of interacts are assembled into processes, and how processes constitute the organization.

It is important to understand that we are equating the term *organizational structure* with the concept of interlocked behaviors (e.g., Krippendorf 1971). The structure that determines how an organization acts and how it appears is the same structure that is established by regular patterns of interlocked behaviors.

The Concept of Collective Structure

Allport's concept of collective structure can be introduced by the following question: When someone says that "the group imposes norms on its members," precisely what does the word *group* refer to? If it is not people who impose norms, then we are at a loss to know who does impose them, and why these particular norms were chosen. The developmental sequence implied is that first a group forms and *then* there is a convergence on rules for maintaining the group.

Allport suggests that it makes more sense to reverse this sequence. He argues that convergence *precedes*, and is a necessary condition for, the emergence of groups. Thus an initial overlap among people in their beliefs—an overlap that *looks like* behavior controlled by norms—makes it possible for more enduring social relationships to emerge. When two people encounter one another, there is some possibility that each can benefit the other. For each, the contact with another person affords the possibility of increased need-satisfaction and self-expression (Brockett 1975). But these opportunities can be preserved only if each can count on the continued presence of the other person.

Note that a preliminary convergence of interest occurs because each anticipates that the other can provide a benefit and each has a similar notion of how this can be accomplished. Having *first* converged on shared ideas of how a structure can form (i.e., on means), the persons *then* activate a repetitive series of interlocked behaviors—that is, they form a collective structure. The range of their behaviors narrows *before* a group forms, not after; the group is made possible by this narrowing and convergence. In Allport's words, whenever

> there is a pluralistic situation in which in order for an individual (or class of individuals) to perform some act (or have some experience) that he "desires" to perform (or for which he is "set") it is necessary that *another* person (or persons) perform certain acts (either similar or different and complementary to his own), we have what can be called a fact of collective structure. It is either collectively actualized or potential (1962, p. 17).

The crucial point in Allport's collective structure is that people converge first on issues of means rather than on issues of ends. Individuals come together because each wants to perform *some* act and needs the other person to do certain things in order to make performance possible. People don't have to agree on goals to act collectively. They can pursue quite different ends for quite different reasons. All they ask of one another at these initial stages is the contribution of their action. Why that person consents to make the contribution or why that contribution is needed is secondary to the fact that the contribution is made. Partners in a collective structure share space, time, and energy, but they need not share visions, aspirations, or intentions. That sharing comes much later, if it ever comes at all.

THE DEVELOPMENT OF MEANS-CONVERGENCE

The priority of means convergence in the formation of collective structure can be described more formally by a four-stage model of group development in which people agree to exchange means and to facilitate the accomplishment of one another's designs—whatever they may be—before they try to exchange ends and work toward some common goal.

The four stages of the model are summarized in Fig. 4.1. Notice in Fig. 4.1 that the traditional assertion that groups form around common goals has been replaced by the assertion that groups form around common means. All groups presumably form among people who are pursuing *diverse ends*. It is common to assert that individual differences exist, but the full implication of this assertion often gets lost in discussions of collective behavior. In any potential collectivity, members have different interests, capabilities, preferences, and so forth. They want to accomplish different things. However, to achieve some of these diverse ends concerted, interlocked, actions are required.

As a structure begins to form, members converge first on common means, *not* on common goals. In the early stages of formation, it is not essential to agree on ends in order to implement interdependence. Instead the more basic agreement involves interdependence as a means to pursue ends that need not

Fig. 4.1 A model of group development.

be similar. It should be recalled that a basic property of reciprocal actions is that a member emits some behavior, *any behavior*, which is valuable to the other person; in return the member receives a behavior that is valuable. There is no immediate requirement for a shared goal. Rather, there is a commitment to pursue diverse ends through the common means of collectively structured behavior.

Perhaps the most important consequence of treating the developmental sequence as starting with *diverse-ends* → *common means* is that it preserves the crucial point that people *create* social structure. Considerable group theorizing assumes that social structure influences people, their actions, and their decisions. The problem is that we do not know where the structure came from, what it looks like, or precisely who does the influencing. A reversal of sequence and the postulation that diverse ends are *followed by* common means avoids this problem. An example of the argument that persons constrain social structure is found in March and Simon. They argue that

> the basic features of organization structure and function derive from the characteristics of human problem-solving process and rational human choice. Because of the limits of human intellective capacities in comparison with the complexities of the problems that individuals and organizations face, rational behavior calls for simplified models that capture the main features of a problem without capturing all of its complexities (1958, p. 169).

Once the members converge on interlocked behaviors as the means to pursue diverse ends, there occurs a subtle shift away from diverse to *common ends*. The diverse ends remain, but they become subordinated to an emerging set of shared ends. This shift is one of the most striking that occurs in group life and it is exceedingly complex.

One of the initial ends shared in common is that of preserving and perpetuating the collective structure which has been instrumental in aiding individuals to get what they want. Evidence of this convergence is found in the articulation and enforcement of norms, categorization of members and actions (Steiner 1955), increased regularity in frequency and form of interpersonal communication, and explication of boundaries.

But there is a more subtle sense in which common ends follow rather than precede common means. An important insight that occurs in a variety of sources (e.g., Skinner 1966; Garfinkel 1962; Bem 1967; Chapter 7 in this volume) is that meaning is often retrospective, not prospective. Actions occur for any of several reasons, and only when the actions are completed is it possible for a person to review them and know what decision was made or what intention was present. By positing that common means precede common ends, and by restricting the concept of common ends mostly to events that preserve a collective structure in which diverse ends can be pursued, then it is possible to look more closely at group behaviors and make sense of them in their own right.

We are also in a better position to understand capricious, self-oriented acts that are common in the early stages of a group. Given the present model, it is clear that some behaviors may be oriented to an incipient common goal, but most are not. And yet, when a person retrospectively sorts out the meaning of a group and becomes more or less involved in it, *all* of the events that occurred earlier may affect the reconstruction. It will *not* be just the "goal-oriented" behaviors that are noticed; all behaviors will be noticed. Thus, it is not surprising that diversity is prominent in any aggregate of persons and that people may leave before the common goal is attained. Diverse ends remain salient because persons have coalesced around means and not ends, and because the ends that they eventually do share in common (1) are tied to the actual behaviors which have taken place in this group (i.e., the perceived ends make sensible those immediately prior behaviors that were generated within the group) and (2) the ends that are shared concern mostly the preservation of a collective structure.

Perhaps the most fascinating phase of the developmental sequence occurs when common ends are followed by *diverse means*. There are several reasons why this shift may occur. First, when some convergence on common ends has occurred, it is typical to find that groups implement a division of labor to aid task performance. They exploit with greater intensity the unique resources that are available. Thus, members are valued more for what they do not share with others than for what they do share. And, as Merton (1940) has shown, when tasks are specialized, persons tend to become more attentive to their component task and less concerned with the larger assignment of which it is a part. They become less concerned with how their contribution will fit with the contributions of others.

But there are two additional reasons why means should diversify. One concerns stabilization of attribution (Kelley 1967; Kelley and Thibaut 1969) and the other concerns increased pressures toward individuated action. First, means may diversify because a durable collective structure does impose stability and order. But if some portion of the continually changing world becomes orderly, other portions could in comparison seem even more disorderly, unpredictable, and ambiguous than they actually are. Precisely because some portion of the world makes sense, other portions make even less sense. The basic dynamic operating here is a "contrast effect." These increasingly sharp contrasts should be unsettling, individuals should have a sense of increased ambiguity, and this means there should be a higher incidence of idiosyncratic behavior. Persons should act in more dissimilar ways. It has been demonstrated in several studies (e.g., Sherif and Harvey 1952) that as the environment becomes more ambiguous, persons act in more individual ways. This proposition has figured prominently in the work of Sherif and Sherif (1969) and in Lazarus's research on psychological stress (1966). Stated formally, the contention is that "ambiguity permits maximum latitude for idiosyncratic interpretations of situations, based on the individual's psychological structure" (Lazarus 1966, p. 118). In the absence of an external anchor for actions, the person uses the only remaining anchor, namely himself. Thus, it is suggested that when a collective structure forms and serves to stabilize some portion of the world, other portions that are less orderly become noticed, and because of the operation of a contrast effect, the less orderly portions appear even more ambiguous than they may be. This ambiguity fosters diversity of action (diverse means).

But there is a second reason why diverse means may follow common ends. The complete model proposed here argues that there are diverse ends, followed by common means, followed by common ends. Notice that there are two adjacent steps that involve commonality and sharing. There are two stages where accommodation, convergence, concessions, and compromise have been required for the group to remain intact. Thus, it seems reasonable to argue that a second dynamic that pushes toward diverse means is that of increased pressure to reestablish and assert uniquenesss (Simmel 1971; Fromkin 1973), to demonstrate dissimilarity from the associates with whom one has become interdependent. Interdependence does entail costs, and these costs become more apparent at later stages in a group.

The model completes itself because as means diversify, as persons act in more idiosyncratic ways, they begin to pursue different ends. Having acted in an increasingly dissimilar manner from their associates, dissimilar ends become defined, preferences and desires diverge, and the group once again consists of members with *diverse ends*.

The model covers both the history of a group from its formation to dissolution, and repeated events within the same group among the same members. In short, it traces the fate of a set of reciprocal behaviors over time. If a group consists of only a single set of reciprocal behaviors that become disengaged when the task is completed, then the model traces the entire history of the group. If the group stays together, and reciprocities change over time, then *each* set of interlocked behaviors should follow the proposed sequence.

With this material as background, we can see the durability, both of Barnard's definition of a formal organization as a "system of consciously coordinated activities or forces of two or more persons" (1938, p. 73) and of his insistence that "it is not persons, but the services or acts or action or influences of persons, which should be treated as constituting organizations" (p. 83). People coordinate means, and that coordination is the forerunner of complex organizations.

The importance of means convergence was also implicit earlier in the spirit level exercise with which Chapter 3 was introduced. If you reexamine that structure and the specific problems it poses, you will see that the conflicts arise because means (raising and lowering the relevant plane of the table), not ends (getting the bubble centered), are where interdependence is focused. In the spirit level task each person needs the other person's behavior of knob-turning and each can contribute turns that make it worthwhile for others to supply their turning. But the task can be performed without people having to agree also on why they need those turns, why turns are important, and so on. They coordinate activities, not desires.

PARTIAL INCLUSION

Other implications should be noted. Allport shares Barnard's view that organizations are grounded in interlocked behaviors rather than interlocked people, and he crystallizes this view in the concept of *partial inclusion* (see also M. C. Bateson 1972, p. 160). A person does not invest all behavior in a single group; commitments and interlockings are dispersed among several groups. Once this point is recognized, then it is more apparent why some predictions about groups are not confirmed. The simple reason is that a member has interlocked fewer behaviors with other members than the investigator assumed.

This is a persistent problem in the attraction and cohesion literature, for example. Several of these studies make the implicit assumption that if someone interacts with you, or helps or agrees with you, then you will like *all* of that person and will become wholly interdependent with that person when performing joint tasks (Shibutani 1971). But there is no reason to think that involvement is this complete. Reciprocities involve specific actions, and once a given reciprocity is established, other ones may or may not be established. It is possible that some person other than one's present partner might be more suitable for producing closure in other behaviors. The consequence is that some behaviors are interlocked with one person and some with another.

It is in this sense that Thibaut and Kelley's (1959) concept of the Comparison Level for Alternatives (*CLalt*) is partly correct and partly incomplete. The concept states that a group member has some standard of acceptable outcomes, and if the outcomes attained are above this point, the person will be dependent on the group and will remain a member. If outcomes fall below this point, however, the person will search for other groups where higher outcomes can be achieved.

The value of this notion is that it helps to explain why groups form and disband, and why persons enter and leave. But the concept is incomplete because it is tied to people rather than behaviors. With respect to some behaviors, interlocking could yield outcomes above the *CLalt*, but with regard to other behaviors, the same group might be inadequate to produce closure. Thus it is probable that, for any group member, some behaviors are above the *CLalt* and some below.

A literal application of Thibaut and Kelley's concept would suggest that the person would sum up all current outcomes, good and bad, and, on the basis of this sum, would either stay or leave. Our point is that the person may do *both*. The person stays in the group in the sense that some behaviors remain interlocked with its members, and at the same time leaves the group in the sense of looking outside for significant persons who can provide reciprocation for other behaviors. Thus any person is typically a member of several groups; to predict that person's behavior in any one group, we must know the investment that person has in the behaviors interlocked in the group *plus* the extent to which significant behaviors are tied elsewhere. Only if this information is available will it be possible to predict how much effort a person will expend to preserve ties with the group and how much energy will be put into the execution of group tasks.

Theorists differ in their opinions regarding how much of a person is engaged in performing organizational activities. Several (e.g., F. H. Allport 1955, 1962; Katz and Kahn 1966; Steiner 1955; Tannenbaum 1968) argue that only selected behaviors of individuals are necessary for organizational functioning, and that it is these specific behaviors that are interlocked with those of other members. While it is true that whole persons rather than parts are hired, it is not true that all member behaviors are of equal importance. Other investigators, while acknowledging the fact of partial inclusion, discuss its implications for morale, satisfaction, productivity, and growth of the person involved (e.g., McGregor 1960). Essentially, they argue that if more of the person were engaged by the organization, then satisfaction and productivity would increase.

In their eagerness to "moralize" about the dysfunctions of partial inclusion, investigators have overlooked some of its dynamics. People are interested in being both alone and together and in having both social ties and independence (Simmel 1971). Given these dual interests, it follows that partial inclusion provides conditions under which both interests can be realized. Some of the person's behaviors are interlocked with those of other people; others are not. The organizational member is simultaneously individual and socialized. Furthermore, interlocked behaviors and the collective structure that they produce are commonly protected by the individual, so that the rewards that result from this interlocking are assured and are produced with regularity.

Once a collective structure forms, people take steps to insure that it is preserved. This means that when there is partial inclusion or interlocking of some behaviors, additional behaviors of the individual may come under the control of this collective structure, because of the person's desire to stabilize it. It is the production of these structural assurances (Allport 1962) which suggests that the actor may take responsibility for integrating more of herself into the organization. She does so by binding additional behaviors to the organization so that collective structure may be maintained.

If one takes seriously the possibility that meaning is retrospective then part of the debate regarding partial inclusion dissolves. If a person interlocks some behaviors, and if the interlocked behaviors are protected by structural assurances, then it is possible that this subset of behaviors will become meaningful and attain closure when viewed retrospectively. An actor's *organizational life* consists of the things that are done at the organization and that are reconstructed into a meaningful life. While it may appear to an outside observer that the actor's capacities are not being used to the fullest, this may not be the actor's circumstance at all. The meaning of the organization and of the actor's participation in it are defined solely in terms of what is done there. It is actions that control the definition of what organizational behavior is.

There is the further point that behaviors not interlocked in the direct pursuit of organizational requirements might be interlocked informally with those of other workers. Most theorists acknowledge this possibility. This point can be summarized in terms of the argument that only parts of members are wanted and that members must "realize" this and act accordingly (e.g., Katz and Kahn 1966). Our point is that the actor, unaided, tends to put closure around the actions he performs no matter how extensive or limited the involvement. It is unnecessary that people "realize" the fact of partial inclusion. They really can't do otherwise. It is true that people may retain desires or ambitions which are thwarted in a present job, but these exist apart from partial inclusion. A person does not have the desires and ambitions *because* only part of his talents are being used. The person simply has partial inclusion and desires.

CONCLUSION

The concept of collective structure by no means includes everything that is in a group. As should be apparent, there is virtually no end to the list of symptoms one could use to characterize a group. The relevant point about collective structure is that it is assumed to be a basic building block for the creation of larger collectivities. The concept retains the fact that groups are composed of individuals and that groups are defined in terms of observable behaviors, but it does not overlook the fact that groups are unique. The concept anchors this uniqueness in a property not found in isolated individuals: repetitive interstructured behaviors.

Mutual Equivalence Structures

The discussion of collective structure implied that even though ties among people are minimal, coordination can occur; that instrumental acts (means) are crucial; and that sharing of beliefs is not essential to the perpetuation of interlocked behaviors. These tacit suggestions are made explicit in Wallace's (1961) concept of mutual equivalence structures, and that is why the concept has been added to this discussion (see also McCarl 1976).

Wallace starts with the assumption that individual actions are either consummatory or instrumental. Consummatory actions are concluding actions that typically involve consuming a reward. Instrumental actions are initial activities or means that allow the consummatory activities to occur. The instrumental activities provide the conditions under which the pleasurable consummatory activities can then occur.

A mutual equivalence structure comes into existence when my ability to perform my consummatory act depends on *someone else* performing an instrumental act. Furthermore, my performance of my instrumental act has the function of eliciting the other's instrumental act. If this pattern holds, and if I keep repeating my instrumental act, then the two of us have organized our strivings into a mutual equivalence structure. For example, Dorothy Parker supposedly said, "I hate writing, I love having written." Parker's loathed instrumental act of writing releases the publisher's instrumental act of turning on printing presses, which then allows Parker to bask in the consummatory act of having written a book and the publisher to enjoy the consummatory act of selling a best seller.

The basic mutual equivalence structure is diagramed in Fig. 4.2. Person A and person B are two different people. Fig. 4.2 shows that each person's consummatory act (a_2, b_2) is released by the instrumental act (a_1, b_1) of the other. The arrows in Fig. 4.2 are read as "is followed by." Thus the arrow from

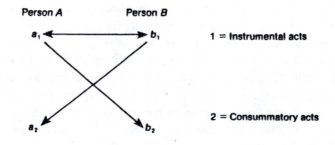

Figure 4.2

a_1 to b_2 is read as, "The instrumental act made by person A is followed by the consummatory act of person B." Another way to read Fig. 4.2 would be to say that person A does a_1 in order to be able to do a_2. The world of person B is read similarly.

As an example of a mutual equivalence structure in operation, consider the tooth fairy. A child loses a tooth, places it under a pillow, the tooth fairy exchanges money for the tooth, and both the tooth fairy and child enjoy consummatory activities, either spending money or observing pleasure and amazement. If we depict the child as A and the tooth fairy as B, the ritual looks like that pictured in Fig. 4.3.

Notice that even though Fig. 4.3 seems to differ from Fig. 4.2, in fact it is equivalent. The arrow from a_1 to b_2 shown in Fig. 4.2 is implied in Fig. 4.3 by the fact that when the child puts the tooth under the pillow, this eventually makes it possible for the tooth fairy to engage in pleasurable observations. The arrow from b_1 to a_2 in Fig. 4.3 portrays that when the tooth fairy exchanges the tooth for money this allows the child to have the pleasurable consummatory act of buying candy and enjoying it. The arrow from a_1 to b_1 in Fig. 4.3 signifies that when the child performs the instrumental act of placing a tooth under the pillow, this elicits the tooth fairy's instrumental act of exchanging coins for the tooth. And the dotted arrow from b_1 to a_1 in Fig. 4.3 similarly signifies that the tooth fairy's acts of exchanging coins for a tooth will, in the future, lead the child to repeat the process so that both the tooth fairy and the child can once again complete their consummatory acts. Notice that in this example, neither person can perform the consummatory act directly. The child doesn't just find coins under the pillow whenever they are desired, nor does the tooth fairy experience a spontaneous outpouring of mystification and delight whenever desired. These outcomes occur only when the *other* person performs an instrumental act.

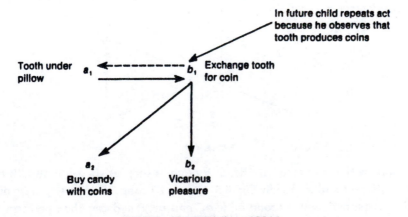

Fig. 4.3   (From Wallace 1961.)

MUTUAL EQUIVALENCE AND MINIMAL KNOWLEDGE

With these tools in hand it is now possible to examine the beauty of Wallace's proposal: a mutual equivalence structure can be built and sustained *without* people knowing the motives of another person, without people having to share goals, and it is not even necessary that people see the entire structure or know who their partners are. What is crucial in a mutual equivalence structure is mutual prediction, not mutual sharing. To build and sustain such a structure, all you need to know is (1) that a person's behavior in some circumstances is predictable, and (2) that other behaviors can be predictably related to one's own activities.

A mutual equivalence structure is very much like an *implicit* contract. Parties to an implicit contract (Wolff 1950, pp. 317-19) don't have to know each other well, they don't have to share goals, and they don't have to visualize the exact nature of their interdependence for an orderly transaction to unfold. The crucial fact is that each person's ability to engage in consummatory behavior (get income, secure a house) depends on the instrumental behavior of the other (put the house up for sale, get the money to buy the house). Real estate transactions make only minimal demands for sharing. What they require for successful execution is mutual prediction, not mutual sharing. That's the point of Wallace's structure.

The fact that people don't have to be aware of the complete structure for it to function smoothly can be illustrated by Fig. 4.4. Suppose that person A and person B have interlocked their behaviors into a mutual equivalence structure, *but* each has a different view of what is happening. There is little overlap in their cause maps.

Suppose that in person A's head the map looks like Fig. 4.4. Person A knows that whenever he does a_1, person B will respond with b_2 and then b_1, after which person A can do a_2.

Figure 4.4

Suppose that in person B's head, though, a map of the *same* situation is totally different and looks like Fig. 4.5. Person B's map tells him that if he does b_1, then person A will respond with a_1, and person B can then perform b_2.

Each person has an incomplete view of the situation, and neither understands it fully, yet flawless coordination results. Why? If we merge the two

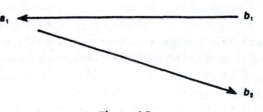

Figure 4.5

maps, place one on top of the other, we get a structure like that pictured in Fig. 4.6. If we summarize the circuit in person A's map (Fig. 4.4) going from a_1 through b_2 up to b_1 with a simpler arrow going from a_1 to b_1, it will be seen that these two persons, with their imperfect maps, still have a mutual equivalence structure. Their two incomplete versions are equivalent because they permit each person to sustain the same social interaction even though each sees it differently.

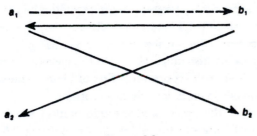

Figure 4.6

The very slight demands on sharing that are required to sustain a mutual equivalence structure provide some of the background for our repeated assertion in this book that shared goals aren't necessary for organizations to sustain themselves or for them to hold together. Shared goals may make the interaction more rewarding or more enjoyable, but shared goals aren't the glue that holds the organization together. People can get along reasonably well without shared goals, and Wallace's analysis shows why this is possible.

MUTUAL EQUIVALENCE AND MINIMAL SHARING

To see some of nuances of the mutual equivalence structure, consider the plight of a stranger who is trying to get oriented in a new organization or a new country. The stranger doesn't know what is going on; he can't interpret what the natives are doing, nor can he express himself in a way that is understandable and acceptable to them. He can't fit in. What could his problems be if we examine them in the context of a mutual equivalence structure? Conceivably he can't separate instrumental from consummatory activities (e.g., do they eat to live, or do they live to eat?), or he can't discover the contingencies (the arrows).

More likely is the possibility that he can't meet one of the three conditions for forming a mutual equivalence structure that Wallace specifies. The first of these three conditions is that a person must perceive that within the limits of the system in which he finds himself, his ability to perform his own consummatory act depends on his partner performing his instrumental act. The stranger may be in the predicament of wondering if he can perform a consummatory act, wondering how consummatory and instrumental acts differ, or he may simply be unable to find a partner.

The second condition necessary for the formation of a mutual equivalence structure is that the person must perceive that performance of his instrumental act serves to elicit the instrumental act of his partner. Notice that this has nothing to do with sharing: it is concerned with prediction. When I perform my instrumental act, I am able to *predict* that my partner will perform his instrumental act. The stranger may have trouble building such structures because he doesn't realize that his act elicits someone else's act. If any of the contingencies in the previous paragraph are not met, this will also cause problems for the linking of instrumental behaviors between two people.

Finally, a mutual equivalence structure forms only when the person repeatedly performs his instrumental act. In the case of the stranger this may be impossible because of the continuous flux of people and situations and the inability to impose labels on any of these situations.

A quick review of the conditions for the formation of a mutual equivalence structure will show how basically solitary this activity is. The person first has to perceive that some of his consummatory activities require that someone (anyone) else perform an instrumental act. Others become salient only as performers of instrumental acts that provide the occasion for consummatory activities. The person also has to perceive that others will produce their instrumental acts in response to his own instrumental acts. And that's where mutual prediction becomes important. But even then the necessity for mutual prediction is cushioned by the third condition: that the person repeatedly performs his instrumental act. If the child puts a tooth under the pillow night after night, then this should stabilize the occurrence of the tooth fairy's instrumental acts and make their acts more predictable. By repeated activation of instrumental acts, the mutual equivalence structure is continually activated and the ties among the contingencies are made stronger. This process resembles what Allport calls the provision of "structural assurances."

MUTUAL EQUIVALENCE AND MAXIMAL COMPLEXITY

Another nuance in Wallace's analysis is that "individuals can produce a sociocultural system which is beyond their own comprehension" (1961, p. 38). This is possible if person A's map is as complex a map as she can maintain, person

B's map is as complex as he can maintain, and the maps are not identical. When these conditions hold and when the maps are summed, the totality of the maps will contain a mutual equivalence structure, *but* the total structure of the maps (that is, *all* their lines and contingencies) will be more complex than one or both of them can grasp.

This nuance sets the stage for a fascinating peek at why organizations may flounder. Lindblom's (1959) analyses of muddling through suggest that organizations exhibit an incremental disjointed pattern of decision-making because they are simply too complex for people to comprehend. Small incremental changes are a means to cope with this complexity and retain stability. Wallace arrives at this issue of complexity in a rather similar manner, arguing that equivalence structures can be quite complex yet stable if an individual relies on a few simple rules to sustain a part in them. There is the additional assumption that because sharing is unnecessary, people can build more complex structures than any of them can comprehend and these structures can survive.

If administrators are overconscientious about trying to plan rationally for the future, they may produce a plan that artificially *simplifies* the complexity involved and unnecessarily admonishes people to work toward goal consensus and consensus on values. These managerial acts could handicap rather than help a group because members could evolve a more complex structure capable of coping with more complex inputs if they did not have to be explicit about how they plan to cope with information and if they did not have to agree on means and ends. Attempts to make a structure "understandable" to everyone could lead managers to introduce excessive simplification and limited linkages among people.

Minimal Social Situation: Pure Organizing

A further idea of how collective structures develop and function can be gained from a laboratory technology developed by Sidowski (1957), which preserves most features found in collective structures and mutual equivalence structures. This technology is labeled the *minimal social situation,* and the extensions of it by Kelley and his associates are of particular relevance for us (see discussions by Gergen 1974, pp. 415-31; Burnstein 1969).

The situation is best characterized as austere. Two persons are put in separate rooms, without knowledge of each other's presence. Each can press one of two buttons that control the outcomes of the *other* person. One button delivers a punishment, the other a reward. Neither person controls her own outcomes directly, but she does affect what happens to the other person. The question is this: is it possible, and if so under what conditions, for two persons to arrive at a "mutually advantageous" solution, in which each receives rewards and avoids punishments?

Studies (Kelley, Thibaut, Radloff, and Mundy 1962; Rabinowitz, Kelley, and Rosenblatt 1966) show that persons *are* able to produce mutually advantageous interactions, a fact that in itself is surprising since the relationship develops *"unconsciously* (without realization of the relationship), *unintentionally* (without deliberately planning to do so), and *tacitly* (without words or speech)" (Rabinowitz, Kelley, and Rosenblatt 1966, p. 194). Notice how this reinforces the point that mutual sharing isn't crucial and that minimal knowledge is sufficient for interlocking to occur.

An important set of studies in the mid 1960s involving the minimal social situation made considerable progress in specifying the conditions under which this mutually profitable interchange can be established. Rabinowitz, Kelley, and Rosenblatt (1966) found that discovery of solutions is a function of the pattern of interdependence and the conditions of response timing that prevail between the two persons. When the two persons are in the pattern of interdependence labeled mutual fate control (each person has complete control over the other's outcomes), mutually advantageous solutions are more likely if the responses of the two persons are synchronized rather than randomly timed.

However, when the two persons are in a relationship where one has fate control and the other has behavioral control (the person with behavioral control is in a position to control the actions but not outcomes of the other person), then there is a greater likelihood that they will arrive at a mutually advantageous solution if their responses are unsynchronized.

The distinction between fate control and behavioral control can be illustrated in terms of the two components of the minimal social situation: the behavior of button-pressing and the outcomes of reward or punishment. Fate control occurs when person *A* controls the outcomes for person *B*. Regardless of which button *B* presses, he will receive either a reward or punishment, depending on which button *A* pushes. *B*'s fate is totally in the hands of *A*, and he can do nothing to change this fate. Mutual fate control means that *A* has this kind of control over *B*, and *B* has this kind of control over *A*. Transformed back into the minimal social situation, the contingencies look like Fig. 4.7.

In a situation of behavioral control, the outcomes are controlled indirectly. If person *A* has behavioral control over person *B*, whenever *A* pushes a button *B* will receive *either* a reward or a punishment, depending on which button *B* presses. *A* does not control *B*'s final outcome directly, but *A*'s action does determine which of *B*'s button will deliver a reward and which will deliver a punishment. *A* can determine which of *B*'s buttons is the "good" one to push, but *A* can't make *B* push it. Thus *A* does exert some control over *B*, because over time *B* will repeatedly press the button that brings good outcomes and will avoid pressing the button that brings bad outcomes.

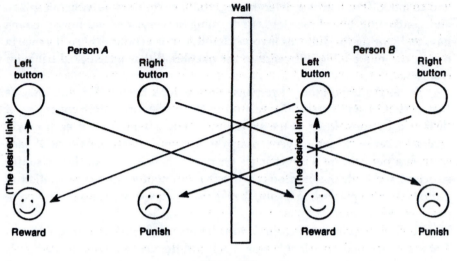

Figure 4.7

Transformed back into the minimal social situation, the contingencies look like Fig. 4.8.

If person *A* pushes the top button, this pairs person *B*'s top button with a punishing outcome and *B*'s bottom button with a rewarding outcome. If *A* keeps pushing the top button, presumably *B* will prefer to push the bottom button to insure good outcomes. *A* has controlled *B*'s behavior. If, however, *A* pushes the bottom button, then *B* will need to push the top button to experience good outcomes.

The issue of response timing assumes importance because in any attempt at interlocking, the behaviors of all parties occur either simultaneously or in sequence. Conversation is sequential behavior, as is card playing, making offers

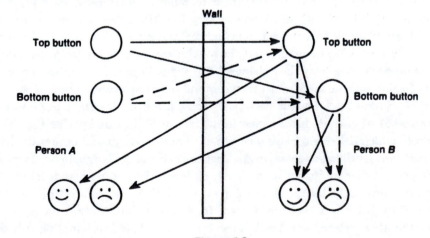

Figure 4.8

and counteroffers, teaching, interviewing, trading securities, driving rail spikes, and conducting board meetings. Performing surgery, making music, baling hay, and scoring touchdowns involve simultaneous actions. This difference in timing can make a big difference in the likelihood that interlocked behavior will form.

To see the importance of response timing, look back at Fig. 4.7. Imagine that person *A* and person *B* synchronize their responses. Both push one of their two buttons down at the same time. Now assume that if each player *receives* a reward, each player repeats the behavior on the next turn; if each receives a punishment, each changes the previous behavior. With this simple structure and with simultaneous responding, no matter what combination of buttons the two players start with, they'll always develop a mutually advantageous solution.

To illustrate, suppose person *A* starts by pushing his left button and person *B* starts by pushing her right button. Person *A* delivers a reward to Person *B*, which means *B* will push her right button again on the next turn ("win stay"). *B* delivers a punishment to *A*, which means *A* will change his response on the next turn and will now push his right button ("lose change"). Both people take their next turn. On this next turn person *B* has once again delivered a punishment to person *A*, but this time *A* has also delivered a punishment to *B*. Both players have lost, so both players should change. *B* should now start pushing her left button, and *A* should return again to his left button. Now, on only the third turn, when *B* pushes the left button she will deliver a reward to *A*, when *A* pushes his left button he will deliver a reward to *B*, both win, both stay with their rewarding responses, and a stable structure has been built without either intending it or understanding it.

The simple change of making the two players take turns, in this very same game, can make it *impossible* for them to build a structure. If both players accidentally reward each other on the very first trial, then a stable structure might arise. But if this doesn't happen, the players will never get a stable, mutually rewarding structure. To show why this is true we keep the same assumption of "win stay, lose change," and the only modification we make is that the players take turns rather than respond simultaneously. Person *A* pushes the left button and rewards person *B*. Then *B* pushes the right button and punishes *A*. *A* changes his response in the face of his loss and pushes the right button, which delivers a punishment to *B*. *B* now changes and pushes the left button, which delivers a reward to *A*. *A* persists in pressing his right button, which delivers another punishment to *B*, which leads *B* to change and deliver a punishment to *A*, which leads *A* to change and deliver a reward to *B*, which leads *B* to deliver another punishment to *A*, and so on. Only if the players scramble their actions and break loose from the simple but tempting rule of win stay/lose change is there even a chance that something rewarding will be built.

Oddly enough, the same simultaneous responding that was such a blessing in a situation of mutual fate control turns out to be a curse in a mixed situation of fate control-behavioral control. To see this, suppose both parties in Fig. 4.8 push their top button. Person A delivers a punishment to person B, and B delivers a reward to A. A hits the top button again and B hits the bottom button. As a result, B gets a reward and A gets a punishment. A now switches to his bottom button, and B sticks with her bottom button. The result of this is that B is now punished, and so is A. At this juncture, in the situation of mutual fate control, the stage is set for both to change and then both to win. Watch what happens. A switches from his bottom button to his top button; so does B. Because of the pattern of this interdependence, A now delivers a punishment to B and B rewards A for doing so. There's no way out. Unless these two players can break the synchrony of their responses, they have a knot (Laing 1970).

These intricate interpersonal puzzles are not just some idle pasttime invented to amuse experimenters. These microcosms of the difficulties involved in meshing behaviors of individuals do not change materially when more consequential behaviors are involved.

Suppose, for example, that we examine an attempt by a salesman of frozen pizza pie shells to get a bowling alley proprietor to be a steady customer. And let's use a different format to represent the contingencies. The pattern of interdependence is identical with those depicted earlier; now we are simply shifting to a matrix format often used to display such patterns.

The bowling alley proprietor would find it more rewarding if she could get a discount on her orders for shells, and unrewarding if she didn't. The salesman would find it rewarding if he could be the exclusive supplier of shells to the bowling alley, and unrewarding if he couldn't. Each person has control of the other's fate. The salesman controls whether the proprietor will get a rewarding discount, and the proprietor controls whether the salesman will get a rewarding exclusive supplier arrangement. In each cell pictured in Fig. 4.9, the sign above the diagonal depicts whether that combination is rewarding (+) or unrewarding (−) for the person listed at the top of the table, and the sign below the diagonal conveys the same information for the person listed at the side of the table.

Notice that this situation of mutual fate control unfolds with the same pattern as was true in the minimal social situation. If the two parties synchronize their responses, they're likely to agree and build a stable alliance. If they alternate their offers, they'll have more trouble building a stable structure.

We can easily represent the salesman-proprietor interdependence in terms of fate control-behavioral control by replacing the issue of discounts with the issue of whether the salesman will visit the proprietor once a week or once a

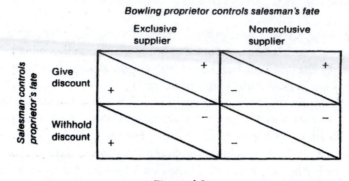

Figure 4.9

year. The proprietor still exercises fate control over the salesman, because she can decide whether to make the salesman the exclusive or nonexclusive supplier. In this modified version, the salesman exercises behavior control over the proprietor, because he controls how often he visits the proprietor. By varying his suggestions about how frequently he will visit, the salesman can make some of the proprietor's behaviors more rewarding than other ones. If the salesman says he'll make weekly visits, it is more rewarding for the proprietor to choose the salesman as an exclusive supplier to avoid the nuisance of a person dropping in every week to pick up a tiny order. If the salesman, on the other hand, suggests yearly visits, then it becomes more attractive for the proprietor to use him as a nonexclusive supplier. Given this pattern of interdependence, and its representation in Fig. 4.10, if these two people synchronize their responding, they're unlikely to establish a durable set of interlocked behaviors.

The example of the pizza salesman gives us a good opportunity to look more closely at similarities and dissimilarities between button-pressing and selling pizza. In the real world, the buttons are usually labeled, you generate the matrix rather than have it presented to you intact, you know your own payoffs, and you often know the other person's payoffs as well as the labels on that person's buttons.

And yet, it is easy to think of conditions in everyday life where you're not sure what the matrix is or what the labels are. The whole reason you try to build a collective structure may be to get some clarity on issues such as these. And in real life, matrices are sometimes handed to you intact. In the real world people do try to close deals by mail. Assume a salesman and a purchasing agent both try to reach agreements on a contract; both communicate by mail, both mail their offers on the same day, both receive the offers on the same day, and both make their replies on the same day. If their form of interdependence is mutual fate control, they'll make a deal; if it isn't, they may not. Notice, on

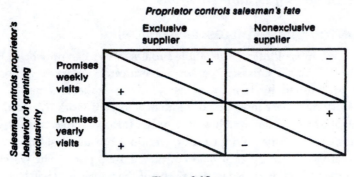

Figure 4.10

the other hand, that phone conversations are often occasions of ad lib, unsynchronized, nonsimultaneous responding. People talk rapidly, and proposals are presented in an alternating rather than a simultaneous sequence. Under these conditions, stable interactions should be harder to form in a mutual fate control situation than in a mixed situation.

While the minimal social situation, collective structures, and mutual equivalence structures may all seem bare, they are not barren. They are building blocks that can be aggregated into enormously complicated structures without the necessity of any single person knowing, understanding, or even visualizing that entire structure. If participants try to figure out these situations, they might have the very same trouble that readers do in trying to follow step by step the tortuous contingencies that occur when different combinations of buttons are punched in different sequences. Participants are spared from the laborious calculations that the reader just had to wade through. Win stay, lose change is enough.

And that's the point of using simple social structures as building blocks. They function with only incomplete knowledge among their inhabitants. The attractive feature of this is that we know most organizations function quite well even though no one knows quite what's going on. As we've seen, no one needs to know. The coordination is built into simple structures, the assemblage of which creates units more complex than anyone can comprehend. This greater complexity allows these structures to be used to cope with, manage, and resolve issues that are more complex than any participant can visualize or articulate. In this sense the outcomes are truly collective and truly are not represented in the perceptions of any one actor. Quite dissimilar and quite cryptic cause maps can be sufficient to sustain complicated social entities. That is the lesson implicit in interacts and that is why they are given such centrality in the present view of organizing.

The Assembling of Double Interacts

DOUBLE INTERACTS AS STABLE SUBASSEMBLIES

Our prior mentions of interacts as stable subassemblies can now be elaborated. The concept of stable subassembly was introduced by Herbert Simon (1962) and was personified by two hypothetical watchmakers named Hora and Tempus. Both men were interrupted frequently in their work by people calling on the telephone to order watches. But only Hora was able to survive these interruptions and prosper. Tempus soon went out of business. Why?

The watches made by each man contained 1000 parts. The watches that Tempus made were constructed so that if one of them was only partly assembled and he had to put it down, it fell apart and had to be reassembled. Thus, if Tempus got a phone call before a watch was finished, he had to start all over.

Hora's watches were just as complex as Tempus's, but they had been. designed so that they could be put together using subassemblies of 10 parts · each. Ten of these subassemblies in turn could be assembled into a larger subassembly, and ten of the larger subassemblies could be assembled into the 1000-piece watch. Whenever Hora was interrupted, then, he lost only a small portion of his work.

This seemingly slight difference in strategy produces a startling effect: if there is one chance in a hundred that either watchmaker will be interrupted when he adds a part to an assembly, then it will take Tempus 4000 times as long to assemble a watch as it will take Hora.

This parable's crucial implication for our concern with organizing is its suggestion that the time required to create a large organization from simple components depends critically on the numbers and distributions of potential intermediate stable forms. This is a vast simplification, but it does give us a tool to use in comprehending complexity. Organizations do fall apart, do need to be reaccomplished; the vital question for us is, what do they fall back on? When people go home at night and the organization is interrupted, what does it fall back to? What are the stable subassemblies of which it is composed? If an organization undergoes stress and breaks down into components, what is the size of those stable building blocks—that is, the interact, triad, department, or tribe? The presumption throughout this book is that the stable component in organizational growth and decay is the double interact.

The notion of stable subassemblies implies that when sets of subassemblies are aggregated, there will be strong ties within the subassembly and weaker linkages between subassemblies. The bonds among most subsystems, in most organizations, should be relatively loose. This means that both stability and adaptation are achieved with less interdependence, less consensus, less mutual responsiveness than we usually assume. Simon (1962) has given this possibility the stature of a hypothesis that he calls the *empty world hypothesis:* Most things are only weakly connected with most other things. He argues that in any organization we should see that there is a higher frequency of interaction within and between small portions or subsystems of the organization and less frequent interactions between larger sets of subsystems or larger systems. Concretely, what this would argue is that executives at the top of the organization are responsible for large sets of separate subsystems. If this is the case, the executives should have longer interactions when those interactions do occur, but also that the average interval between their interactions should be greater at the higher levels in the hierarchy than at the lower levels. This would be expected from the argument that long but infrequent interactions are an example of loose ties, whereas frequent but short interactions exemplify tighter ties.

DOUBLE INTERACTS AND LOOSE COUPLING

It is possible to expand on implications of the empty world hypothesis by using Glassman's (1973) discussion of persistence and loose coupling. Loose coupling occurs either when two separate systems have few variables in common or when the common variables are weak compared to the other variables that influence the system. Two systems that are joined by few common variables or weak common variables are said to be loosely coupled. What loose coupling means practically is that if one of the variables is disturbed, the disturbance will tend to be limited rather than to ramify (Weick 1976). Or if it does ramify, it will take a long time to affect the other variables and/or the effects will be weak.

Consider the problem of forgetting. Glassman's general formulation is that systems that are loosely coupled to other systems will tend to persist. Memory and forgetting are loosely coupled to one another because some items persist while others disappear quickly. Glassman's argument is that we shouldn't bemoan the fact that we forget things because forgetting may be functional in maintaining behaviors that have proved adaptive in the past and in eliminating behaviors that have not survived this test.

> An important part of our capacity to cope with reality is our ability to form generalizations. The tendency to do so may well be facilitated by the fact that we recall best only those items of information which are repeatedly encountered; that is, information arising from the existence of a given condition in the external world is loosely coupled to our behavioral repertoire, both in the sense that we learn about it only after repeated encounters and forget about it only after long absence (Glassman 1973, p. 88).

Elections provide another example of loose coupling. Elected officials generally remain in office for their full term even though the people who voted for them may disapprove of their actions at any given time during that term.

Even though the elected official has to display a certain amount of responsiveness to the needs of his electorate, the fact that he serves for a definite period of time means that he has some leeway to serve these needs over a long run and does not have to respond to every momentary whim of his electorate.

When people interact in stable social groups there is considerable loose coupling visible in the behavior between individuals. In any group that survives for a reasonable period of time, it's common to hear members say that they "like each other for their own sake." What they mean by this is that they maintain a persistent relationship with the other individual by limiting their responsiveness to and intolerance of temporary annoyances and outbursts in that other individual. Each person essentially takes a running average of the behavior of the other individual, and in this sense responsiveness to someone else is only loosely coupled to the precise things the other individual does.

What is common to these examples is the fact that a system maintains persistent behavior in the face of variables that would normally disturb the behavior. The group survives because members overlook specific annoyances, the elected official continues to serve because policy is not set by the day-to-day whims of that person's constituency, the individual is not overloaded by having to recall every single event that occurs in every single moment in time. With regard to the situation of forgetting, for example, it is not the case that the environment changes so rapidly or so radically that we have to remember all the details of what occurs. On the rare occasions when there are massive and durable changes, the memory process is usually adequate to handle it. The point is that weak ties can promote persistence of behavior and can produce some insulation from continual minor changes in events.

The combination of stable subassemblies composed of double interacts and of loose coupling among double interacts is attractive when pondering organizations because it suggests conditions under which evolution can occur quite rapidly, adaptation can be preserved, and adaptability can also be maintained. Subassemblies and loose coupling provide the potential for flexibility as well as stability. Since double interacts are suitable candidates for stable subassemblies, and since sets of double interacts are suitable candidates for loosely-coupled structures, the fit among the concepts appears fortunate.

Let's examine how double interacts become assembled into processes.

RULES FOR ASSEMBLING DOUBLE INTERACTS

We noted earlier that processes are recipes, and the full force of that observation comes to bear at this point in the argument. Either by design or by accident, numerous interlocked behavior cycles form within organizations (e.g., Graen 1976). It is these cycles that are the stable forms within organizations, and it is these cycles that are assembled into larger subassemblies in the interest of stabilizing equivocal displays and transforming them into information, enacted environments, and cause maps.

Assembly rules are inferred recipes that influential organizational members appear to be using when they create a process. Assembly rules can be viewed as procedures, instructions, or guides that members use to mobilize several double interacts into larger processes that are directed at inputs. The content of these recipes and the degree to which they have the force of regulations vary among organizations. We suggest that any process contains two elements: assembly rules and interlocked behavior cycles. Assembly rules are recipes for assembling the process out of the total pool of interlocked cycles that are perceived to exist within the relevant portion of the organization at the moment of assembly (e.g., McKelvey, in press). Some examples of assembly rules include:

1 *Effort:* select those cycles whose completion requires the least effort.

2 *Frequency:* select those cycles that have occurred most frequently in the past.

3 *Success:* select those cycles that have been most successful in removing equivocality.

4 *Permanence:* select those cycles that will produce the most stable change in the input.

5 *Duration:* select those cycles that can be completed in the shortest period of time.

6 *Availability:* select those cycles that are not currently engaged in other activities.

7 *Personnel:* select those cycles that are manned by more experienced people.

8 *Relevance:* select those cycles that most closely resemble the assumed content of the input.

9 *Reward:* select those cycles that the members regard as most rewarding.

10 *Disturbance:* select those cycles that will cause the least disruption in the ongoing system.

11 *Uncertainty:* select those cycles that communicate conclusions rather than premises.

12 *Obligations:* select those cycles that incur the fewest future obligations.

13 *Precedent:* select those cycles that set the fewest precedents.

14 *Absorption:* select those cycles that absorb the activities of the greatest number of people.

15 *Enhancement:* select those cycles that enhance the input.

16 *Mutilation:* select those cycles that do the least damage to the input.

This list suggests some rules that might be employed; it is not intended to be exhaustive. The important point is that we are hypothesizing the existence of rules by which processes are constructed. We assume that there are several such rules, and that each of them contains a criterion for selecting, from the pool of all possible interlocked cycles, the specific subset of cycles that will be applied to some raw data input.

We further assume that there is a general pattern that relates the way in which the process is constructed to the perceived equivocality present in the display to which that process will be directed. Just as human actors within the organization appear to choose which assembly rules will govern the composition of a process, so too do they appear to make these choices of rules dependent on their perceptions of how much equivocality they face.

Specifically, we presume that actors use the following metarule (a rule about how to choose rules). The greater the perceived amount of equivocality present in the input, the *fewer* the number of rules used to compose the process. Conversely, the smaller the perceived amount of equivocality in the input, the greater the number of rules used to assemble the process. If an input is judged to be highly equivocal, there is uncertainty as to exactly what it is and how it is to be handled: this makes it more difficult to judge what the appropriate cycles would be or how many should be applied. As a result, only a small number of rather general rules are used to assemble the process. However, if the input is judged to be less equivocal, there is more certainty as to what the item is and how it should be handled; hence a greater number of rules can be applied in assembling a process to deal with this input.

To understand how equivocality may be temporarily reduced by assemblages of double interacts, we must discuss the cycles that are actually selected for inclusion in the process. But before discussing cycle selection, it is important to remind the reader that cycles consist of double interacts and processes are sets of double interacts. The following is a hypothetical description of six double interacts that might be appropriate for assembly into a selection process. Remember: a selection process is composed so that it can transform equivocal raw data into information. This transformation is variously described as separating figures from a ground or labeling streams of experience.

The six cycles described in Table 4.1 have the following characteristics: Each consists of a double interact. The person performs some action, which is reacted to by a second person, after which the first person makes some consummatory response to what the second person did.

This three-step sequence is the basic influence sequence proposed by Hollander and Willis (1967) as necessary to distinguish conformity, independence, anticonformity, and uniformity. In the second and third stages of each cycle there are choice points. For example, in cycle 1 the other person can

TABLE 4.1

Act	Interact	Double interact
Action by person	Response by other person	Readjustment by first person
1. Isolates a portion of the input for closer examination	Accepts, rejects, or modifies this choice	Abandons, revises, or maintains the chosen portion
2. Selects interpretation for application to input	Accepts, rejects, or modifies interpretation	Abandons, revises, or or maintains interpretation
3. Constructs new interpretation	Accepts, rejects, or modifies construction	Abandons, revises, or maintains construction
4. Differentiates an existing interpretation, bringing out a new component	Accepts, rejects, or modifies differentiation	Abandons, revises, or maintains differentiation
5. Assembles a set of nouns for application to input	Accepts, rejects, or modifies assemblage	Abandons, revises, or maintains assemblage
6. Assesses reasonableness of interpretation applied	Accepts, rejects, or modifies assessment	Accepts or rejects the acceptance or rejection

accept, reject, or modify the choice of an input property, and after he has done so, the first person can either accept or reject what the other person has done. The four types of influence are outlined in Table 4.2.

Since there are two choices within the cycle (as portrayed by Table 4.2), the ties among the people in this cycle are variable. It is these variabilities that decrease over time as the cycle develops and occurs repeatedly, and it is in this sense that the cycles become a stable collective structure. If, in the initial execution of cycle 1, the other person accepts the designation of a relevant input and the first person maintains this designation, then the next time this cycle is activated this same pattern is even more likely to occur. The same intensification apparently occurs for all the cycles that are listed.

Note also that each cycle is directed toward reducing equivocality. Some of the cycles are more directly involved in this removal than others. For

TABLE 4.2

Act	Interact	Double interact	Type of influence
Affirm A	Affirm A	Affirm A / Affirm B	Uniformity / Anticonformity
Affirm A	Affirm B	Affirm A / Affirm B	Independence / Conformity

example, differentiation of a new interpretation from an existing one (cycle 4) contributes indirectly to removal, whereas the cycle involving the assessment of reasonableness (cycle 6) more directly manages the equivocality.

Any *process* consists of two or more interlocked cycles. The actual set that constitutes the process at any one time is a function of the number and kind of assembly rules that are applied to the pool of all salient cycles at the time of assemblage. The relationship between rules and cycles is assumed to be the following: The number of cycles that are assembled and applied to an input depends on the number of assembly rules that are activated. The greater the number of rules used to select the cycles, the smaller the number of cycles that will be assembled into a process. Conversely, the fewer the number of rules that are used to select cycles, the greater the number of cycles that will be assembled.

This relationship may sound inconsistent with the argument that assembly rules determine the cycles that will be selected. But to think in this way is to miss the nature of assembly rules. If you reexamine the rules, you will note that any *one* rule is rather gross. If it were used, it would select a large number of cycles. For example, if the frequency rule alone were used to assemble the process, then all cycles that have occurred frequently in the past would be assembled.

Suppose now that two rules rather than one were employed. Suppose that frequency *and* duration were the rules used to compose the process. Now the frequency rule would select all cycles that had occurred frequently in the past, *but* this population would be further reduced in number because only those cycles that were completed in the shortest possible time would be retained. Thus the actual number of cycles assembled would become smaller.

ASSEMBLING A PROCESS

With these tools in hand, we can now describe the stages that occur whenever a process is assembled. First, a member judges how much equivocality is present in an input; this judgment conditions that person's further judgment as to the number of rules that will be used to build the process. This is the most crucial part of the formulation that is beginning to emerge. Any input to any process is presumed to have its initial impact on the *rules* by which the process will be assembled. The exact relationship between perceived equivocality and the number of rules used to assemble a process is assumed to be an inverse one. The greater the perceived amount of equivocality, the fewer the number of rules; the smaller the perceived amount of equivocality, the greater the number of rules.

The next important relationship is the one between the number of rules activated and the number of cycles selected for application to the input. If the number of rules is small, a large number of cycles will fulfill these primitive criteria and will be included in the process. However, as the number of rules increases, the number of cycles that will fit all the rules descreases. Stated more precisely, the relationship between number of rules and number of cycles selected is also an inverse relationship.

The third important relationship is the one between the number of cycles applied to the input and the perceived amount of equivocality that remains in the input after the cycles are applied. The relationship between cycles and perceived amount of equivocality is assumed to be inverse. The greater the number of cycles applied to the input, the smaller the perceived amount of equivocality that remains. The fewer the number of cycles applied to the input, the greater the perceived amount of equivocality that remains. What are we saying? If an equivocal input is handled by a large number of separate cycles, then it is more likely that its equivocality will be reduced than if it is handled by a small number of cycles.

At the conclusion of this step the process completes itself, becoming a closed loop, and the perceived state of the input at this final stage—whatever it may be—is the state it's in when the next process is applied to it. A graphic presentation of these stages in a process is found in Fig. 4.11. The notation on the lines connecting the various stages is read in the same way as the notation used in Fig. 3.4.

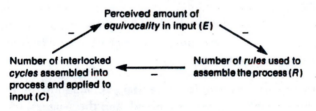

Fig. 4.11 Sequence of a process.

Conclusion

Change rather than stability is the rule in any organization (Weick 1969), and this means that people continually live within streams of ongoing events. If change is too continuous, it becomes difficult for any one person to make sense of what is happening and to anticipate what will happen *unless* that person is able to freeze, break up, or recycle portions of this flow. If a person wants to make the world more predictable, then that person has to carve out events that have boundaries and that are repeated. The person has to segregate and stabilize some portion of the ongoing events. But in an interdependent world crowded with people, it is difficult to produce the acts of closure alone (Sampson 1977). The behaviors that are more likely to produce closure in a series of changing events are behaviors that person A emits that are valuable to person B, and which in turn lead B to produce behaviors that benefit A. Once a set of these interlocking behaviors has been established, a collective structure exists.

These collective structures, variously referred to as interlocked behavior cycles and double interacts, are the elements of organizing. Organizations are built of and fall back on these stable subassemblies.

Crucial information about organizational functioning, given the prominence of interlocked cycles, resides in variables such as these:

1 The number and kinds of cycles that are salient when a process is assembled.

2 The perceived level of equivocality.

3 The degree to which cycles assembled into a process are independent (e.g., cycles assembled could counteract one another and enhance rather than reduce equivocality).

4 The speed with which cycles unfold (faster cycles could have a disproportionate effect on the disposition of the input).

5 The number and diversity of rules that are acceptable within the organization and that can be invoked by people located at different positions within the organization.

6 The extent of tension within any double interact sequence (the postulated tension levels would be anticonformity highest, conformity moderate, and independence and uniformity least).

All of these variables provide potential explanations for what happens when sets of double interacts are assembled, and they suggest leverage points for those who wish to change the ways in which organizations function.

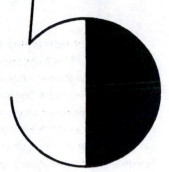

Organizing processes resemble closely the three processes commonly associated with theories of natural selection. Quasi-evolutionary ideas are quite abundant in organizational theory (e.g.,

natural selection and organizing

Kaufman 1975; McKelvey, in press; Jantsch and Waddington 1976; Ruse 1974; Freeman 1974; Bennett 1976; Alexander 1975; Aldrich and Pfeffer 1976; Dunn 1971; Stebbins 1965; Bigelow 1978). In this chapter we will present first an outline of the ideas concerning natural selection that inform our metaphorical use of it in the organizing formulation, and then we will present the outlines of the metaphor itself. More detailed discussion of each portion of the metaphor will continue in the remaining chapters.

A surprisingly rich introduction to theories of evolution can be obtained with a simple deck of playing cards. If the deck is shuffled repeatedly, it is clear that there is continual change as the cards become rearranged, but does the deck evolve? It all depends. Some people are willing to accept any rearrangement of parts as evolution, whereas others would say that some order must occur out of chaos before it can be said that evolution is occurring.

Lewontin (1968) notes that if you keep shuffling the cards they might become grouped by suits or by ascending sequences. In both cases we would say that order has been created, *but* that's only because we had some preconception of what order is (that is, it is numbers that are relevant, not the thickness of each card). Furthermore, a chance grouping of the shuffled cards by suits is no less probable than any other arrangement. If order must be created for events to exemplify evolution, this suggests that evolution is neither a fact nor a theory, but simply a way to organize knowledge. What occurs is simply that an observer watches events happen, imposes on these happenings some preconception about order, and this preconception then allows the observer to watch the changing instances, compare them, and see whether there is a progression toward orderliness in those portions being observed. If there is, evolution has occurred.

These considerations suggest that we can view evolution either as raw change or as change in the direction of order, the latter position requiring that we be explicit about what our preconceptions are concerning order.

Throughout this book we will emphasize themes that establish that ambivalence is the optimal compromise, loose coupling promotes adaptation, ignorance is functional, everything flows, adaptation can preclude adaptability, and things keep falling apart. The degree of "orderliness" implicit in each of these concepts is modest, and these concepts portray the adaptive value of a decrease in order quite as much as they portray the value of increases in order.

Thus, inevitable and irreversible movement from chaos to order is not considered by us as a necessary feature of organizational growth. Instead, we argue that the current state of any system is the result of continuous change away from some original state, but these changes need not be in the direction of increasing orderliness.

Although we assume that change is a characteristic of organizations, we also assume that those forces which produce continuing changes are themselves relatively *un*changeable laws.

> The processes of natural selection and mutation that can be seen occurring in the organic world today are assumed to have been operative forces in all the past history of life. Moreover, since such forces are operating at present, it must be concluded that evolution is still going on. A commitment to an evolutionary viewpoint represents a commitment to the instability of the present order as well as the past. In its simplest and irreducible form, evolutionism is the doctrine that change of state is an unvarying characteristic of natural systems and human institutions and that such change follows immutable laws (Lewontin 1968, p. 203).

The obvious correspondence between this view of evolution and the process imagery presented in Chapter 2 should indicate why we prefer this weaker form of evolutionary theory (evolution as change) to a stronger form (evolution as change toward order). The more one delves into the subtleties of organizations, the more one begins to question what order means and the more convinced one becomes that prevailing preconceptions of order (that which is efficient, planned, predictable, and survives) are suspect as criteria for evolution (Vickers 1967, pp. 67-84; Weick 1977).

Returning to the example of the deck of cards, there is a rather tidy fit between what happens in card games and what happens in natural selection, an analogy first suggested by Charles Saunders Peirce. If a limited number of players with limited funds play a card game long enough, all the players but one will go broke. That's not mysterious as an outcome—it's simply a matter of probability and the rules of the game. And natural selection is no more mysterious than the decreased probability of going broke in the card game as you get more funds. Notice also that in the card game you can't predict every individual event in the game, but that doesn't affect your ability to invoke the principles to explain why one or another player goes broke, or why some organizations go bankrupt (Ghiselin 1969, p. 69).

The card game illustrates other features of natural selection. Sometimes natural selection is thought to mean that chance plays a major role in evolution. The limit of this suggestion is found in the fact that it *is* chance that any specific individual in the card game wins all the money, but it is *not* chance that such an event happens. The card game is also relevant to the notion of progress, a notion that we explored earlier. In card games players progressively go broke and one finally wins. This may resemble progress, but it does so only in a crude sense. The odds are heavily against any one player being the winner, and it is hard to see how these odds represent progress or demonstrate improvement in structure. One person may progress in some sense, but that progress will be at the expense of most others who are eliminated.

This point was well appreciated by Darwin, who held most consistently that progress is not inevitable and that evolution often leads to degeneration (Ghiselin 1969, p. 70).

The deck of cards, as shuffled by Lewontin and as put into play by Ghiselin, serves to demystify the process of natural selection. This stripping is useful because it supplies us with a set of tools that we understand more clearly.

The concept of natural selection seems unsatisfactory simply because it is intelligible by reason. It is no more impressive than the fact that the more fit players—those who in poker, for example, usually fold on a low pair—tend to accumulate money. One wonders how long it will be, if ever, before laws of nature lose their metaphysical pathos, and are looked upon as no more impressive than sound advice on how to win at cards (Ghiselin 1969, p. 69).

More recently, Ghiselin compared evolution to games in general, and his powerful images again help to demystify the aura surrounding evolutionary theory:

Many kinds of games are possible, and we run grave risk of error if we mistake one for another. Actually, evolution has no rules at all, in the sense of those that govern gentlemanly sport. The best we can say is that there are various ways to cheat and that some kinds of cheating are hard to get away with. And just as there are no rules, there is no criterion of victory. Organisms play the game because, and only because, their ancestors did not lose. We can keep score in terms of "fitness" or mortality, but we must not assume that the organisms are striving to gather what we consider points. If we do not know the "rules," we may be unable even to identify the "players." Many who have written on the "reproductive strategies" have been concerned not with the actions of individuals but with the good of the species, for no more basic reason than the tendency to view the struggle for existence as a contest between "teams" rather than "athletes." If there is any truth in this earlier work, as we should admit there may well be, it will not be discovered until we have some way of knowing what kind of spectacle really lies before us (1974, p. 41).

Having described the outlines of evolutionary ideas metaphorically, we now shift to a more detailed exposition of these ideas, relying heavily on the writing of Donald Campbell.

The reader should understand that it is processes of evolution, *not* outcomes of these processes, that we are interested in. We are not interested in what is evolved, but rather in how evolution occurs. Furthermore, the processes are not assumed to be lodged in particular parts of the organization. An individual or a group may engage in all the processes, or different groups may perform different processes. In all likelihood, formal organizations are characterized by the latter possibility, but that is not crucial to the argument.

The Sociocultural Evolution Model

Donald T. Campbell (1970, 1972, 1974a) has been perhaps the most vigorous contemporary exponent of an evolutionary model adapted to social behavior, and this section relies heavily on his thinking. The following excerpt provides an overview of the evolutionary form of analysis.

> For an evolutionary process to take place there need to be variations (as by mutation, trial, etc.), stable aspects of the environment differentially selecting among such variations and a retention-propagation system rigidly holding on to the selected variations. The variation and the retention aspects are inherently at odds. Every new mutation represents a failure of reproduction of a prior selected form. Too high a mutation rate jeopardizes the preservation of already achieved adaptations. There arise in evolutionary systems, therefore, mechanisms for curbing the variation rate. The more elaborate the achieved adaptation, the more likely are mutations to be deleterious, and therefore the stronger the inhibitions on mutation. For this reason we may expect to find great strength in the preservation and propagation systems, which will lead to a perpetuation of once-adaptive traits long after environmental shifts have removed their adaptedness (1965a, pp. 306-7).

The essential ideas in the preceding quotation are: (1) three processes — variation, selection, and retention — are responsible for evolution; (2) variations in behaviors and genetic mutations are haphazard, and those variations are selected and retained that enhance, momentarily, adaptation; (3) the processes of variation and retention are opposed; (4) resort to a concept such as *plan* or *external guidance* is unnecessary to explain the course of evolution; (5) moderate rates of mutation are necessary for survival and for evolutionary advantage; (6) in complex systems, the majority of the mechanisms activated at any time tend to curb rather than to promote variations; (7) any order that appears is due to the hindsight of a selection system and not to foresighted variations; (8) evolution is essentially opportunistic—current advantages outweigh long-run disadvantages in determining survival; (9) characteristics are judged adaptive, in biological evolution, if they increase the reproductive chances of the possessor; and (10) evolution can be thought of as a winnowing model. To gain a more complete understanding of evolution, we will briefly discuss each of the three processes.

Variation is perhaps the most obvious feature that characterizes sociocultural as well as biological evolution. Variations at the sociocultural level can occur between social groups, between members within a single group, or across the different occasions when a single group acts. In general, it is assumed that "the more numerous and the greater the heterogeneity of variations, the richer the opportunities for an advantageous innovation" (Campbell 1965b, p. 28). Unjustified variation, as opposed to rational variation, is emphasized in evolutionary theory (Campbell 1974b). The emphasis on *unjustified* makes a subtle point. An unjustified variation is one for which truth has not yet been established, but one for which truth is not precluded. Justification comes after a belief has been generated and tested. While it might appear that intelligent, preadapted, informed variation is to be preferred, such variations are restricted largely to wisdom that has already been achieved. A person can intelligently suggest some innovation that he has encountered before, but since his experiences are limited, this form of variation is also limited. Note that the occurrence of unjustified variation provides a plausible explanation for the finding that groups often seem to be "wiser" than any of their members (Kelley and Thibaut 1969). In biological evolution, selection creates novelty by compounding various genotypes. Similarly, by combining different portions of responses produced by different members, it is possible for a group to reinforce and establish solutions that no one member was capable of producing by himself.

A final point that must be emphasized concerning variation is that a response must occur at least once before it can be available for selection. This apparently obvious fact has sizable implications. The argument is stated this way: "the entire repertoire of an individual or species must exist prior to . . . selection but only in the form of minimal units" (Skinner 1966, p. 1206). The response does not necessarily have to be emitted in its completed form, but something must be made available that can be shaped over time into an adaptive response.

The importance of this argument lies in the idea that all the forms of behavior we observe in a surviving system, regardless of their present apparent value, were at one time emitted in some more primitive form and then gradually shaped into their present form. The contingencies in the environment that shaped a response are the crucial ones for explaining its origin. In a real sense the response is under the control of those stimuli responsible for the shaping, rather than the stimuli that now make it appropriate. What this means, then, is that the response is apt to be quite resistant to change. It would extinguish very slowly if the present stimuli that reinforce it were removed. To speed up extinction, it would be essential that all the associations between the response and all stimuli *responsible for its shaping* also be removed (Rohde 1967).

The *selection* process is considerably more complicated than variation. It is so complex that many researchers think it cannot be applied to groups. Their objection is that "selection" can occur in so many ways that the concept does not explain very much of what happens. It is easy to attribute everything that occurs to some kind of selection, and for this reason the explanation loses its power. There is also the danger of circular thinking. We observe the outcome of a supposed selection process and "explain" the existence of this outcome by saying that it was selected. But to the question, "How do you know it was selected?" the answer often is, "Because it is there." It is there because it was selected, it was selected because it is there. Thus one must be very careful to specify the selection system and its outcomes independently, and avoid the temptation to infer the selection system from the outcomes it produces.

Campbell discusses selective systems and selective criteria separately. He suggests that there are at least six selective systems that can be observed in sociocultural evolution.

1 *Selective survival of complete social organizations.* This is the most direct parallel between biological and social evolution. This is the situation in which entire societies or large portions of them may have been eliminated because they were unfit for efficient collective action.

2 *Selective diffusion among groups.* This selection system is the *least* direct parallel between biological and social evolution, because borrowing is impossible in gene systems. The essence of this system is that behaviors characteristic of prosperous groups are borrowed by groups that are less prosperous.

3 *Selective perpetuation of temporal variations.* As a group performs different actions over time, different memories of pleasure and pain will be associated with these actions, and pleasurable actions will be repeated more often than painful ones.

4 *Selective imitation of interindividual variations.* Just as groups may imitate other groups, members within one group may imitate the actions of other members of that same group. The psychological processes of conformity and imitation describe this form of borrowing.

5 *Selective promotion to leadership roles.* A further mechanism by which certain variations may be singled out for perpetuation is the promotion mechanism. The group singles out persons who vary customary practices in ways that appear more adaptive, and then the group elevates these persons to positions of authority.

6 *Rational selection.* Societies do plan, forecast, and anticipate. For the sake of completeness we will include this form of selection, noting that people differ strongly in the importance they attribute to this mechanism.

The selection process contains one or more of these six mechanisms. They are the media through which selection criteria operate.

Selection criteria appear to be almost infinite in number. In the case of organizations, one can think of numerous decision premises (Simon 1957) that serve as selection criteria: accept that which brings pleasure, reject that which brings pain; accept prompt responses, reject slow responses; accept a novel response, reject a conventional response; accept the rational, reject the irrational. But even though criteria are abundant, one need not assume that an infinite number are used. Furthermore, it is probable that criteria exist in hierarchies, so that some are more important and applied more frequently than others. There is general agreement that the environment, including the environment composed by other organizations, imposes criteria for selection, but not necessarily on entire organizations. When environmental factors impose selection criteria, these criteria frequently can operate on particular structures and behaviors within organizations and modify or eliminate them.

Furthermore, decision makers in organizations intervene between the environment and its effects inside the organization, which means that selection criteria become lodged more in the decision makers than in the environment. What the decision makers attend to and enact, the cues they use, why they use those cues, their patterns of inattention, and their processes for scanning and monitoring all become more influential as sources of selection criteria. Reality as perceived by the members becomes more the source of selection within the organization than does reality as perceived by some omniscient, less involved observer.

The final evolutionary process is *retention*. Despite the fact that retention appears to be a straightforward storage process, it has more importance for human organizations than may be realized. For example, it was noted earlier that one would:

> expect the greatest rigidity, the greatest demand for conformity, [in] . . .
> those societies with the more elaborate adaptive systems, particularly when
> these systems demand restraint on individual hedonistic impulse (Camp-
> bell 1965b, p. 34).

The reason for this prediction is that elaborate adaptation systems are vulnerable to mutations; they are held in place by complex forces that can easily be
destroyed, and one of the principal threats is persons acting in terms of self-
preservation rather than in terms of group preservation (see Campbell 1976).

Retention systems are not simply repositories for interpretations that have
been selected. They affect subsequent actions; they are frequently edited; they
are protected in elaborate ways that may conflict with variation and selection;
they are coercive only to the degree that members are informed of their
contents; and they contain items that frequently are opposed to the self-interest
of persons who must implement these items.

Retained contents can also be internally inconsistent. This point is crucial.
The selection system operates in terms of contemporary inputs, a psychological
here and now, and items which are selected for retention may contradict items
that were stored previously and were valid for an earlier here and now. Thus
to understand the working of evolutionary processes within organizations, it
may be necessary to posit internal reorganization in the retention system, even
though such reorganization is not given central attention in biological versions
of evolutionary theory.

Subtleties in the Natural Selection Model

Before we introduce the modified evolutionary model associated with organizing we want to mention some intriguing puzzles for organizational theorists
that are implicit in ideas about natural selection.

ADAPTATION AND SELECTION

A frequent assertion in evolutionary theory is that the progression from simpler
forms to more complex forms was made in the interest of improved adaptation
and selective advantage. However, there are numerous instances in which
selected items are *non*adaptive. For example, Skinner interprets the existence of
superstitious behavior as an indication that selection and adaptation do not
necessarily coincide:

> Behavior may have advantages which have played no role in its selection.
> The converse is also true. Events which follow behavior but are not neces-
> sarily produced by it may have a selective effect. . . . All current character-
> istics of an organism do not necessarily contribute to its survival and

procreation, yet they are all nevertheless "selected." Useless structures with associated useless functions are as inevitable as superstitious behavior. Both become more likely as organisms become more sensitive to contingencies (1966, p. 1207).

The circumstance of superstitious behavior arises when an organism, receiving reinforcement at fixed intervals (every 30 seconds, for example), typically repeats the pattern of behaviors present before the reinforcement is produced, whatever the pattern may be (e.g., jumping, turning around, walking away from the food, and so on).

An analogous situation occurs in groups in the form of confounded feedback (e.g., Mithaug and Burgess 1968; R. L. Hall 1957; Zander and Wolfe 1964). Whenever the different members of a group contribute portions of a finished product, and the group is given feedback about performance only in terms of the group product (e.g., it is acceptable, it is unacceptable), individual members have no way of knowing how adequate their *individual* contributions were. If the outcome is judged acceptable, this could mean that individual members will repeat their actions even if they were actually irrelevant or detrimental to the outcome (Cohen and March 1974, pp. 200-1; March and Olsen 1976, pp. 17, 57, 150). Thus we would have yet another instance in which certain behavior was selected (reinforced due to the success of the group) without any relation to adaptation.

Note the final sentence in Skinner's quotation. It says that as sensitivity increases, there is greater likelihood that superstitious behavior will develop. Or stated in another way, the greater the sensitivity of the actor to contingencies in his environment, the greater the likelihood that his selected behaviors may be nonadaptive or irrelevant to adaptation. In the case of human actors this should be a persistent problem. In terms of the notion of retrospective meaning, when an actor attempts to determine what has occurred and why it has occurred, his explanation may well be erroneous and he may persist in his nonadaptive responses. The point we wish to make here is simply that selection processes are not infallible, and that selection can hinder adaptation as well as promote it. This point can be appreciated only if we free ourselves from the notion that selection is for environmental advantage.

EVOLUTIONARY PROCESSES AS VARIABLES

There is the intriguing possibility that the three components of evolution (variation, systematic selection, and retention) *seldom* concur, or if they do, that they differ sizably in their relative strengths. It may be rare, rather than common, to have all three components operating at the same time. One reason for this incomplete functioning is simply that at least the processes of variation and retention operate at odds. The success of one is the failure of the other.

But of even more interest for organizational theorists is the fact that as the environmental conditions change, the presence of one or more of these evolutionary components may be affected. Campbell notes, for example, that crystal formation occurs only rarely and only when all three requirements of variation, selection, and retention are present:

> Extreme heat, such as to liquify or vaporize salt, will increase the variations component, but destroy the retention system by continually producing energy inputs that exceed the disruption threshold. Extreme cold will remove the variation component. It is only when these two are in a compromised balance that the selective-retention ... process of crystal formation can take place (Campbell 1974b, p. 145).

The interesting possibility implied is that one reason we may find it difficult to apply evolutionary theory to organizations is that we deal with a situation where one or more components of evolution are absent. For example, mergers may remove both variation and retention. Mergers destroy unique solutions to the problem of organizational survival. Like hybrids in plants, they undercut the wild stock. Mergers may also be consequential because they introduce contradictions into retained wisdom, thereby destroying it.

Therefore, we might be wise to treat evolutionary processes as a dependent variable and ask, under what conditions will various combinations of evolutionary components be visible and functioning? If we continually suspect that partial evolution is the rule, then we might detect more of the forms in which quasi evolution actually occurs in organizations. It is possible that most of the changes and discontinuities we observe in organizations can be understood in terms of the number and kind of evolutionary components that are in operation when they occur.

FORMS OF SELECTION

Biologists sometimes distinguish between *r* and *K* selection. These two letters stand for two different kinds of evolutionary strategy: the *r* strategy involves a heavy species commitment to reproduction, whereas the *K* strategy involves a heavy commitment to longevity. The *r* strategy is described in this way:

> Suppose that a species is adapted for life in a short-lived, unpredictable habitat, such as the weedy cover of new clearings in forests, the mud surfaces of new river bars, or the bottoms of nutrient rich rain pools. Such a species will succeed best if it can do three things well: 1. Discover the habitat quickly, 2. Reproduce rapidly to use up the resources before other, competing species exploit the habitat, or the habitat disappears altogether, and 3. Disperse in search of other new habitats as the existing one becomes inhospitable (Wilson 1975, pp. 99-100).

A species adapting a *K* strategy

> characteristically lives in a longer lived habitat—an old climax forest, for
> example, a cave wall, or the interior of a coral reef. Its populations, and
> those of the species with which it interacts, are consequently at or near
> their saturation level K (carrying capacity of the environment). No longer
> is it very advantageous for a species to have a high r (rate or increase of
> births minus deaths). It is more important for genotypes to confer competi-
> tive ability, in particular the capacity to seize and to hold a piece of the
> environment and to extract the energy produced by it (Wilson 1975, p. 100).

Although the distinction between *r* and *K* selection is controversial, it is of
interest to organizational theorists because some biologists feel that the theory
of natural selection was formulated primarily with *r* selection in mind. In other
words, most principles of natural selection may be suitable for understanding
those species whose mortality was often catastrophic and nondirected, whose
intraspecies competition was often lax, whose lifetimes were short, and
whose social behavior involved weak social bonds such as are found in
schools, herds, or aggregations.

If we think analogically then, it could be argued that if members of organizations confront environments similar to those associated with *r* selection, the
theory of natural selection will be helpful. Thus, the theory of natural selection
should tell us something about success and failure in organizations that build
discos, market rock stars, design faddish restaurants, cater to a seasonal trade,
create high fashion, collect and disseminate news, speculate, handle emergencies,
trade currency (Edwards 1978), and exploit fads (e.g., the pet rock company).
But as organizational environments resemble more closely cave walls or climax
forests (e.g., utilities), the propositions of natural selection may be less appropriate.

LOSS OF VARIANTS

Natural selection takes time. Therefore, one must ask why variations in
organizations do not get lost before natural selection has had time to derive
from them what potential advantages they might present. If mutations occur
too frequently or are too short-lived, they'll get lost in the process of natural
selection. Thus it is not routine for all variations that "represent an improvement" to be selectively retained. Instead it may only be those mutations that
are stabilized long enough for sluggish selection to occur that have any chance
of being retained. Notice that the additional requirement of persistence until
natural selection can operate may shrink drastically the pool of mutations
available in any system.

Organizing as Natural Selection

When organizing processes are assembled they seem to resemble the processes of natural selection. We intend to capitalize on this resemblance and to model organizing after those processes presumed to produce natural selection.

The four elements of organizing are ecological change, enactment, selection, and retention.

Ecological change   Within the flows of experience that engage people and activities there frequently are changes or differences. The flows exhibit discontinuities (Steinbeck 1941), differences (G. W. Bateson 1972), or other variations that engage attention (Slack 1955). These differences may provide the occasion for attempts at equivocality removal and attempts to determine the significance or triviality of the differences. Ecological changes provide the *enactable environment*, the raw materials for sense-making. Ecological changes normally would be said to be *the* source of raw materials, except that past experience in the form of previously enacted environments often provides sufficient materials by itself for sense-making. This portion of the organizing process is dubbed ecological *change* to capture the fact that people normally are not aware of things that run smoothly. It is only the occasion of change when attention becomes active.

Enactment   Enactment is to organizing as variation is to natural selection. The term enactment is preferred over variation because it captures the more active role that we presume organizational members play in creating the environments which then impose on them. Enactment is intimately bound up with ecological change. When differences occur in the stream of experience, the actor may take some action to isolate those changes for closer attention. That action of bracketing is one form of enactment. The other form occurs when the actor does something that produces an ecological change, which change then constrains what he does next, which in turn produces a further ecological change, and so on. I move items on my desk, which then makes it necessary for me to readjust my writing position, which further rearranges the items in my working area, which then further rearranges me. Or being a musician, I generate a series of chords which are sent back to me by my accompanists, which chords in turn rearrange my solo, which in turn rearranges their accompaniment (see Sudnow 1978), and so on. The activity of enactment parallels variation because it produces strange displays that are often unlike anything that the individual or the organization has seen before.

Enactment is the only process where the organism *directly* engages an external "environment." All processes subsequent to enactment work on edited raw materials and whatever episodes have been extracted by enactment. The external environment literally bends around the enactments of people, and much of the activity of sense-making involves an effort to separate the externality from the action. If I wander into a strange gathering with a chip on my shoulder and people are gruff with me and I leave in a huff, my actions are intertwined with those of the people milling around when I walked in. It remains for the selection activity to untangle how much hostility I generated and how much hostility was there already. Are they to blame for the rude reception, am I, are we both, or are neither? At the conclusion of enactment, this is not known. The enactment, as it becomes linked with ecological change, merely provides the equivocal raw materials which then may be seized or dismissed by the selection process.

Selection Selection involves the imposition of various structures on enacted equivocal displays in an attempt to reduce their equivocality. These imposed structures are often in the form of cause maps that contain interconnected variables, these maps being built up out of past experience. When these maps, which have proven sensible on previous occasions, are superimposed on current puzzling displays, they may provide a reasonable interpretation of what has occurred or they may confuse things even more. These maps are like templates that reveal configurations that may make sense or may not.

Think of any enacted equivocal display as a *potential* figure-ground arrangement. The activity of selection involves both the differentiation of alternative figures from the ground (equivocal displays by definition can be read in a variety of ways) and stabilization of that figure-ground arrangement or that limited set of arrangements that provides reasonable clarity and allows the continuation of living. Rather than select individuals or behaviors, selection processes involved in organizing select schemes of interpretation and specific interpretations. They select schemes of interpretation in the sense that some cause maps repeatedly prove helpful in reducing the equivocality of displays, whereas other maps add to the equivocality. Those maps that are helpful tend to be selected, and those that aren't helpful tend to be eliminated. In addition, the specific interpretations of the specific equivocal display also are selected and are retained for possible imposition on future situations that look the same.

Retention Retention involves relatively straightforward storage of the products of successful sense-making, products that we call *enacted environments*. An enacted environment is a punctuated and connected summary of a previously equivocal display. It is a sensible version of what the equivocality was about, although other versions could have been constructed. We have used the terms *enacted environment* and *cause map* to refer to retained content. Each phrase captures a slightly different nuance of what is retained.

We have used the label *enacted environment* to emphasize that meaningful environments are outputs of organizing, not inputs to it. The enactment process itself segregates possible environments that the organization could clarify and take seriously, but whether it actually does so is determined in the selection processes. Boundaries between organizations and environment are never quite as clearcut or stable as many organizational theorists think. These boundaries shift, disappear, and are arbitrarily drawn. We don't take them very seriously. Instead, we argue that environments are created by organizations out of puzzling surroundings and that these meaningful environments emerge quite late in organizing processes. Before the environments have been made sensible and before they emerge from the selection process, organizing processes are directed at externalities that may or may not become environments.

We have used the label *cause map* as a second means to characterize retained content to emphasize that retained content is organized and stored in forms very much like those you used to summarize your group discussion experience (p. 70). These maps consist of variables connected by causal relationships. These maps summarize co-variations between labeled portions of the formerly equivocal display. These maps resemble Schutz's recipes (p. 46) because they allow the person to interpret what goes on in a situation *and* they allow that person to express herself in that same situation and be understood by others.

THE ARRANGEMENT OF ORGANIZING PROCESSES

The four processes of organizing are presumed to be arranged as detailed in Fig. 5.1. A more detailed breakdown of this model will be found in the remaining chapters, but by way of introduction we can note the following properties: (1) ecological change and enactment are linked causally in a deviation-amplifying circuit, (2) enactment is linked to selection by a direct causal relationship, indicating that the volume of enactment will have a direct effect on the volume of selection activity that occurs, (3) likewise selection has a direct effect on retention, meaning that an increase in the amount of selection activity will trigger a corresponding increase in the amount of retention activity, (4) retention affects both selection and enactment and these effects can be either direct or inverse, depending on whether the person decides to trust his past experience ($+$) or disbelieve it ($-$).

The three-stage structure associated with any process (see p. 117) is presumed to be distributed among enactment, selection, and retention as

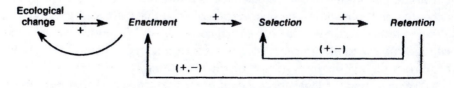

Figure 5.1

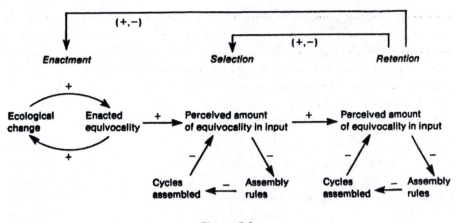

Figure 5.2

detailed in Fig. 5.2. Since enactment produces equivocality instead of reducing it, it is not a process in the same sense as the other two. Enactment is action that produces the raw materials which can *then* be made sensible. Recall that sense-making is commonly retrospective. Sense is made of previous actions, things that have already occurred. Enactment produces the occurrence that can then be made sensible by the selection process.

The specific rules and cycles associated with retention and selection are presumed to be organization-specific. Some examples of these rules and cycles have already been presented (p. 115), others have been implied in this chapter, and more will be suggested when we treat each process separately in subsequent chapters. For the time being, the crucial point is simply that all of these rules and processes are directed toward reducing the perceived level of equivocality judged to be present in enactments that are taken seriously by the organization.

Furthermore, it should be noticed that unless members of the organization are ambivalent toward their past experience, these organizing processes will be unstable, and the entire system will be deviation-amplifying. If members completely trust their past experiences there are six negative signs, and if they completely distrust their past experiences there are eight negative signs—both being even numbers. Only simultaneous trust and disbelief will stabilize the system, a strategy that is explored more fully in Chapter 8.

ILLUSTRATIONS OF THE ORGANIZING FORMULATION

In this section I will show how several different themes already mentioned in this book coordinate with the organizing model.

The basic theme for the entire organizing model is found in the following recipe for sense-making: "How can I know what I think until I see what I say?" Organizations are presumed to talk to themselves over and over to find out

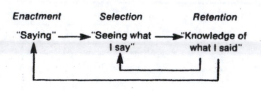

Figure 5.3

what they're thinking. That's basically what this entire book is about. The basic recipe coordinates with organizing in the way outlined in Fig. 5.3. The organism or group enacts equivocal raw talk, the talk is viewed retrospectively, sense is made of it, and this sense is then stored as knowledge in the retention process. The aim of each process has been to reduce equivocality and to get some idea of what has occurred.

A fuller version of the basic sense-making recipe will show how much flexibility it has for addressing organizational issues of all kinds. The revision of the basic recipe detailed in Fig. 5.4 is a kind of do-it-yourself organizational analysis. By picking one element out of each bracketed set in Fig. 5.4, the reader can portray virtually any kind of equivocality reduction that occurs in organizations and can coordinate this with the processes of enactment, selection, and retention. This extension of the basic recipe has the additional advantage of allowing us to specify compactly what organizing is. Whenever a plural pronoun appears anywhere in the sense-making recipe, organizing is under way (e.g., how can I know what I think until I see what *they* say?). If no plural pronouns appear anywhere in the sentence, then no collective sense-making is taking place. This extended version also makes it clear that the organizing model is not confined just to cognition and thinking. Organizing is also built around feelings, actions, and desires and collective attempts to understand them. Insertion of the pronoun *they* allows for such things as external consultants, vicarious experience, reference groups, and conformity as tools for sense-making in organizations.

Other ideas can be adapted to the enactment-selection-retention format. People commonly assert, "I'll believe it when I see it." This bit of wisdom probably should be turned on its ear so that it approximates more closely the ways in

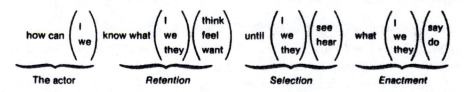

Figure 5.4

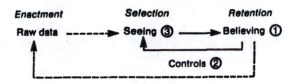

Figure 5.5

which people actually act: "I'll see it when I believe it." Beliefs are cause maps that people impose on the world after which they "see" what they have already imposed. One of the aims of this book is to equip you with lots of beliefs so that you'll see some of what is talked about here, or at least you'll see enough that you'll be able to amend the mistakes that inevitably must litter any attempt to understand human beings. "Believing is seeing" maps across the organizing process as shown in Fig. 5.5.

Represented as it is in Fig. 5.5, we see once again the circularity involved in most sense-making. Believing does control seeing, but, as the diagram illustrates, the seeing in turn conditions further beliefs, which in turn constrain seeing, and so on. The tightness of this linkage is one of the reasons why we argue repeatedly that people create the environments which then impose on them. Beliefs put portions of the environment in place, and they put different portions in place for different people. Those who talk about *the* environment determining *the* organizational structure introduce some rather severe simplifying assumptions that we are eager to erase (and replace with other severe simplifying assumptions).

Clifford Geertz describes man with a turn of phrase which is quite compatible with the analysis that pervades this book: "man is an animal suspended in webs of significance he himself has spun" (1973, p. 5). That world looks like the one shown in Fig. 5.6.

A chronic concern of ours throughout this book is with the question, "Under what conditions does adaptation preclude adaptability?" Organizations that acquire an exquisite fit with their current surroundings may be unable to adapt when those surroundings change. Organizations that hedge against an

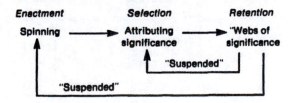

Figure 5.6

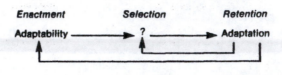

Figure 5.7

exquisite fit may also dissolve when placed in competition with those that do have a better momentary fit. This tension pervades all of organizing and injects the dynamic that keeps organizing decisions consequential. When we say that adaptation precludes adaptability this is just another way of saying that retention precludes enactment. Thus, adaptation and adaptability are coordinated as shown in Fig. 5.7. Notice that the mode of representation detailed in Fig. 5.7 illustrates just how crucial selection is, if anyone had to be reminded. Selection is the means for attempting to accommodate the antithetical pressures generated by that which produces adaptation and that which produces adaptability.

As a final illustration of enactment-selection-retention imagery, Tom Lodahl (personal communication) has suggested that the organizing model portrays organizations in the following way: "Organizations paint their own scenery, observe it through binoculars, and try to find a path through the landscape."

In Fig. 5.8 we again see the centrality of selection activities and we also see how the enactment-selection-retention model, as is true of any model, edits some of the richness in the original observation. Lodahl's observation loses something when it is resorted into the enactment-selection-retention compartments. What we hope is that the inevitable rearrangement required by the enactment-selection-retention model does not also mutilate the original document beyond recognition.

This chapter will conclude with two examples that show a more detailed picture of organizing. The first example will illustrate how the three stages contained *within* the processes of selection and retention may reduce equivocality in an input.

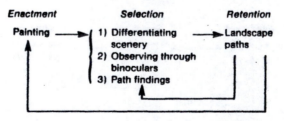

Figure 5.8

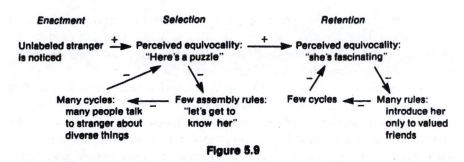

Figure 5.9

Suppose that a stranger wanders into a group, and suppose that people notice her. The noticing is *enactment* that brackets the stranger for further work. To transform the stranger into a known commodity—a *selection* activity—the host and hostess activate a small number of rules to assemble a *selection* process out of the interacts flowing around the gathering (e.g., "See that the stranger is made to feel at home"), many separate interacts are directed at the stranger, and she becomes a known commodity whose "identity" is then stored as someone who should be approached or avoided on subsequent occasions. This sequence, largely composed of selection activities, is detailed in Fig. 5.9.

To see the contrast, imagine that another stranger walks into a group but that she has a known position. Imagine that the stranger is a new colonel unknown to the captains and majors present at the gathering.

It is probable that the colonel is less equivocal since there is shared knowledge concerning how one gets to be a colonel and how colonels are to be treated. It is this information concerning "how colonels are to be treated" that supplies many of the assembly rules that determine how this particular stranger will be "processed." The strange colonel is likely to be the occasion for the organizing in Fig. 5.10 to be built. Notice by examining Fig. 5.10 that the colonel *remains* more of a puzzle at the conclusion of the gathering than does the stranger who comes with no categories attached to her.

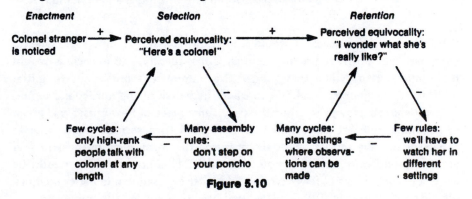

Figure 5.10

The second example is more lengthy and shows the several features of organizations that are given serious attention in the organizing model. The particular organization to be described is an orchestra, and there are many ways in which it resembles other kinds of organizations.

A jazz orchestra, numbering between 17 and 21 members, is a perfect example of a small organization. There is a leader; there are 3 section leaders under him, each of whom is responsible for 3 to 5 men; and finally there are the players within each section. It is a convention within organizational work to have at least three levels represented in one's theory or experiment, and that is what the orchestra has. Demands for coordination within an orchestra are substantial, but these are balanced by equally strong demands for innovation in both solos and section interpretations. Once the group begins to play, there is no turning back. Musicians must somehow complete the number even if this requires extraordinary effort to cover up the errors others make; feedback is swift and comes at the conclusion of a number; responsibility for errors as well as success is oftentimes difficult to place. The quality of the outcome is affected both by cognitive factors and by noncognitive ones such as sheer physical endurance and strength. Negotiating the final interpretation of a number is something that occurs either openly or covertly.

The point of departure for this illustration is a field experiment (Weick, Gilfillan, and Keith 1973) in which 38 musicians in two functioning jazz orchestras rehearsed three compositions written by composers whose attributed credibility was presented as either high or low. Composer credibility is of potential importance in musicmaking because it is thought to influence the amount and kind of effort a musician will put forth to comprehend a new piece of music. Meyer has argued that efforts to comprehend new music are mediated by the "presumption of logic."

> Without faith in the purposefulness of, and rationality of art, listeners would abandon their attempts to understand, to reconcile deviants to what has gone before or to look for their *raison d'etre* in what is still to come (1956, p. 75).

We predicted that musicians would find it difficult to presume logic when a composer was portrayed as nonserious. Consequently, the musicians would make more errors when they played that composer's music due to initial indifference or doubts, would downgrade the worth of the music, and would forget it sooner. However, when the *very same* piece of new music was given to a comparable orchestra and was attributed to a serious composer, we expected that the musicians would presume the music was purposeful and would expend more effort to comprehend it. This greater effort would be evident in such things as fewer errors and higher evaluation and better memory for the tune relative to its fate when attributed to a nonserious composer.

The predicted difference in errors occurred on the first play-through of the new music but disappeared on the second play-through, due to a combination of additional nonserious rehearsing plus direct observation that the composition itself was purposeful (the three selections were written by two established jazz composers, Alf Clausen and Don Piestrup). The predicted difference in evaluation did not occur, but when assessed by a recognition test, the compositions given as written by serious composers were remembered significantly better 24 hours after the rehearsal.

These data suggest that the attribution of credibility can be self-confirming. Closer attention to the work of the credible composer resulted in fewer errors and a better-sounding performance relative to the work of the noncredible composer, thereby confirming the credibility prophecy. When the musicians believed that the music was of higher quality, they generated, by their own heightened attentiveness, a better-sounding tune, which then constrained their subsequent playing.

Viewed more broadly, any orchestra rehearsal where musicians process new music is an ideal setting in which to observe the ways that a strange piece of music is made more sensible. There are numerous sources of equivocality when new music is rehearsed (Gilfillan 1977). The music itself is equivocal because it is unknown, it contains some amount of musical complexity, it contains certain amounts of calculated or intentional disorder, many of its performance characteristics (such as the tempo where it plays well) have to be established, it is equivocal relative to the style in which the band prefers to play, and the tune shows a greater or lesser departure from convention in music. These and other questions are what an orchestra tries to resolve when it rehearses.

The environment that the orchestra members face is not simply the composition placed in front of them, but rather what they do with that composition when they play it through for the first time. The musicians don't react to an environment, they *enact* the environment. In the credibility study the environment available to the musicians after their first play was an undifferentiated "soup." As observers, we might label this soup with nouns such as "sounds," "tempos," "themes," "shading," and "errors." The first play-through of the composition could be made sensible by participants in a variety of ways. The crucial point is that the play-through, not the sheets of music, was the environment the musicians tried to make sensible.

Once musicians enact an environment, they then break that environment into discrete events that are available for relating (e.g., "those 12 notes are thrilling," "those six bars are impossible," "that portion is ugly," "the notes are hard to read," "the tempo at which we start seems to be crucial"). Essentially, the musicians label the stream of enacted music with reasonable nouns and then try to relate or connect the nouns in a reasonable manner.

Once a musician breaks the stream of experience into a set of variables, he is able to make the inference that some of these variables co-vary. When one of the variables changes its value, one or more other variables also move, and these movements may be in the same or opposite directions. Based on these movements, the observer then infers a connection among the variables and may also infer, in the case of temporally separated but co-moving variables, a relationship of "causality."

Musicians who perform music by high- or low-credibility composers might sort this enactment into seven variables: (1) attributed credibility; (2) playing effort exerted; (3) tolerance for errors; (4) attention to notes; (5) willingness to reconcile deviant notes; (6) willingness to suspend judgment; and (7) quality of tune when judged retrospectively. These seven variables are specified solely to illustrate the argument. It should be apparent that we can maintain consistency in our argument only if these variables are specified by the participant, *not* by an observer.

Given these seven variables, it is possible for the musician to connect them causally. For example, on the basis of repeated experience he might note that as credibility decreases, playing effort and attention to notes decrease and tolerance for error increases; when effort decreases, this decreases both the judged quality of the tune and the attention that the musician pays to the notes; when the tolerance for errors increases, this serves to decrease the attention to the notes, the willingness to reconcile deviant notes, and the willingness to suspend judgment about the tune; and finally the musician may note that all of these relationships may decrease the perceived quality of the tune, which then leads to a further lowering of credibility. If these connections are summarized graphically, then we would obtain the set of causal connections shown in Fig. 5.11. This is a *cause map*, it summarizes those variables and connections that are inferred by a person after repeated exposures to a stream of experience.

We assume that musicians, as well as people in general, retain cause maps in their minds. These maps, in the case of musicians, are superimposed on flows of experience that involve music-making. What the maps do in part is suggest which variables can be labeled in that flow of experience (e.g., "I should single out from the flow of experience the amount of effort I am exerting because this is a significant portion of this experience"). These maps also suggest which variables are connected with which other variables. Notice that the map in Fig. 5.11 is an overlay or a template that the individual imposes on a stream of enacted experience to separate portions of that display into a figure-ground relationship.

It is an interesting property of superimposed structures that they are often self-validating structures. To see this, reexamine the cause map (Fig. 5.11). It

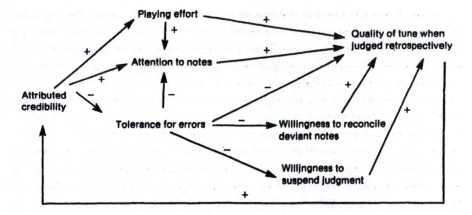

Fig. 5.11 Cause map. (From Staw and Salancik 1977, p. 294.)

contains several loops by which one can start with the variable "attributed credibility" and trace a path that returns to the starting variable. The interesting property of each pathway is that it is a positive feedback loop. For example, if credibility decreases this causes an increase in the tolerance for errors, which causes a decrease in the judged quality of the tune, which causes further decrease in credibility, and so forth.

A musician who imposes this particular structure on his music-making will generate self-fulfilling prophecies that reinforce the map and confirm the initial attribution of credibility. If we treat "presumption of logic" as a variable, this means that a musician may find it easier or harder to presume that the composer is credible and that the composition will be serious or reasonable. If the musician increases the presumption of logic, then he raises the level of attributed credibility, and through the imposition of the cause map produces the higher-quality tune—which confirms the initial presumption. If, however, he doubts the presumption of logic, then this lowers the level of credibility and *through the very same cause map* produces the lower quality tune which confirms the initial doubts about credibility.

The point is, the cause map in Fig. 5.11 may *be* the orchestra. If we then ask *where* that orchestra is, the answer is that the orchestra is in the minds of the musicians. It exists in the minds of the musicians in the form of the variables they routinely look for and the connections they routinely infer among these variables. These maps are then superimposed on any gathering where the announced agenda is music-making.

So far, most of the points made deal with processes that take place in the minds of solitary actors. Within the orchestra it is true that the cause maps differ among 38 musicians and it is also true that any individual musician has his own doubts about the stability of some of the labels and connections he imposes. These differences and doubts suggest two things. First, there should be residual equivocality even after individuals impose their own idiosyncratic versions of what has happened. Second, coordination will be problematic until some agreements can be reached among the participants as to what has happened and what should be done about it.

As we stated in Chapter 4, equivocality removal is essentially an interpersonal process and involves at least two members interlocking some behaviors to accomplish this removal. Using the ideas already presented, we can state more precisely how interlocked behaviors remove equivocality. The crucial collective act in organizations may consist of members trying to negotiate a consenses on which portions of an enacted display are *figure* and which are *ground*. More specifically, members collectively try to reach some workable agreement as to which portions of elapsed streams should be designated variables and which connections among which variables are reasonable.

Thus, when we assert that equivocality is removed by interlocked behavioral cycles, we mean that members negotiate over specific issues of identifying variables (e.g., "I don't think that the temperature of this room is important, but you seem to think it is") and issues of connection (e.g., "We seem to agree that temperature is crucial to our performance, but I think we play better when we are warmer and you think we play better when we are cooler"). Once members can reach some agreement as to what is consequential and what is trivial in their elapsed experience, and once they can get some kind of agreement as to the nature and direction of the connections among these consequential elements, then the elapsed experience becomes more sensible. That is, there is more overlap in the separate maps that are stored in the minds of the musicians when they leave the rehearsal and there is a greater likelihood that they will interlock their activities of music-making more tightly when they confront new music at subsequent rehearsals.

The crucial point is that equivocality removal is both a social and a solitary process. What we are trying to specify is precisely what in that social process is crucial for what is basically a private, singular, and solitary activity. Sensemaking is largely solitary in the sense that structures contained within *individual* minds are imposed on streams of *individual* elapsed experience that are capable of an infinite number of *individual* reconstructions.

To recapitulate, musicians *enact an environment* when they first play through a piece of music, and the outcome of this first play-through is an *equivocal display*. Based on previous experiences in processing new music, the musicians impose a *figure-ground structure* on this undifferentiated enacted display. This *imposed structure*, which is in the form of a *cause map*, sorts the display into a set of variables that are *connected* by means of *reasonable causal* linkages. The act of superimposing a cause map involves *retrospecting* elapsed experience. Although an imposed cause map makes the equivocal display more sensible for an individual musician, there remains the problem that the labels and connections are both uncertain within individuals and different between individuals. Cause maps are approximations and deal with likelihoods, not certainties. Since residual equivocality remains after individual cause maps are superimposed, it is necessary to gain some consensus among musicians as to what the orchestra is confronted with and how it is to be handled. Members activate *sets of interlocked behavior cycles* to deal with this residual equivocality. Initially, they try to *negotiate* a consensus on which portions of the display are figure and which are ground. When people collectively try to shrink the possible meanings attached to an equivocal input, they essentially are negotiating issues of naming and connection (e.g., "What did we or the composer do that caused that horrible chord?"). Having consensually made the enacted environment more sensible, the members then store their revised and presumably more homogeneous cause maps for imposition on future similar circumstances.

Conclusion

The primary difficulty one has when invoking the organizing model is brilliantly summarized by Mozart's description of how he composes music:

> First bits and crumbs of the piece come and gradually join together in my mind; then the soul getting warmed to the work, the thing grows more and more, and I spread it out broader and clearer, and at last it gets almost finished in my head, even when it is a long piece, so that I can see the whole of it at a single glance in my mind, as if it were a beautiful painting or a handsome human being; in which way I do not hear it in my imagination at all as a succession—the way it must come later—but all at once as it were. It is a rare feast. All the inventing and making goes on in me as in a beautiful strong dream. But the best of all is the *hearing of it all at once* (James 1950, vol. 1, f.n. p. 255).

Even though the enactment-selection-retention model is depicted in a linear, sequential fashion, this depiction may be misleading. The image of a field may be more appropriate (Lana 1969, chap. 5). At any given time more than one piece of information is being processed, the various pieces are at various stages in the organizing processes, the various inputs affect one another in the sense that the interpretation made of one can affect the sense made of another, system capacity that is absorbed in the reduction of substantial equivocality in one imput is momentarily unavailable to deal with other equivocalities, and there is a plurality of cycles, rules, cause maps, enacted environments, doubts, and beliefs that intercept flows of events.

Thus, the meaning of any episode of organizing is massively conditioned by the context or field in which it happens to be embedded, the inputs being processed, the cycles available, and the interpretations that are acceptable and unacceptable at that point in time. Furthermore, the frequency with which ecological changes occur, the magnitude of these changes, and the ease with which these changes can be induced by enactment and in turn constrain enactment will similarly be affected by the context created by the various episodes of organizing all in various stages of their unfolding.

Perhaps the best means to loosen this rigid sequential image and get it closer to what seems to be happening is to use a clever graphic device that William James (1950, vol. 1, p. 283) used. The box-like object of Fig. 5.12 illustrates one way to visualize organizing processes in action. With appropriate substitution in James's description, we can show how this image is to be used. If we make a solid wooden frame with the organizing processes written on the front and a time scale on one of its sides (Fig. 5.12), if we spread flatly over its top a sheet of India rubber on which rectangular coordinates are painted, and slide a smooth ball under the rubber in the direction from 0 to the word *retention*, the bulging of the membrane along this diagonal at successive moments will symbolize the changing of the organizing process's content.

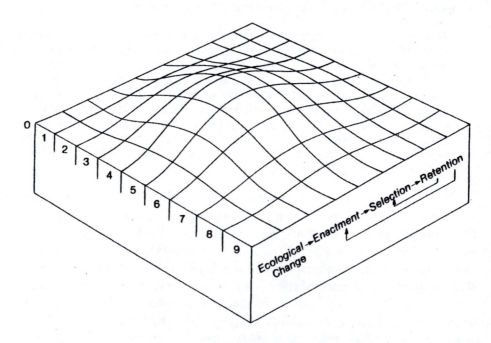

Figure 5.12

The visualization in Fig. 5.12 shows that there is a progression from enactment through selection to retention, *but* also that one process shades into another. More than one process is active at any time. The illustration is even richer because the size of the ball can be varied (signifying greater and lesser equivocality), the speed with which the object moves diagonally can vary (swift passage is associated with routine, unequivocal inputs), pliability of the rubber sheet can be varied (very stiff rubber is equivalent to thick sets of assembly rules that allow inputs to have minimal impacts), spacings of the three words on the front board can be varied, and so on. If you can visualize a stack of these frames, each one having different dimensions, different pliancy of rubber, different-sized balls, and balls located at different positions along the diagonal, then you have a picture of a frozen moment in an organization, and you have an organizational "structure."

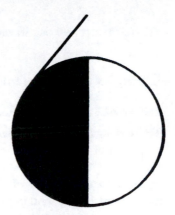

The essence of enactment is found
in these three exhibits:

enactment and organizing

1   "Experience is not what happens to a man. It is what a man does with what happens to him" (Huxley, cited in Auden and Kronenberger 1966, p. 54).

2   "Our so-called limitations, I believe,
Apply to faculties we don't apply.
We don't discover what we can't achieve
Until we make an effort not to try"
(Hein 1968, p. 33).

3   Imagine that you are playing a game of charades, and that you must act out the title of a movie. Imagine that you are given, as your title, the movie *Charade*. As the presenter, you probably would try somehow to get "outside" of the present game and point to it so that the observers would see that the answer is the very activity they are now engaged in. Alas, the observers are likely to miss this subtlety and instead to shout words like, "pointing," "finger," "excited," "all of this," and so forth.

One of the ironies in organizational analysis is that managers are described as "all business," "doers," "people of action," yet no one seems to understand much about the fine grain of their acting. "If we knew more about the normative theory of acting before you think, we could say more intelligent things about the function of management and leadership in organizations where organizations or societies do not know what they're doing" (March and Olsen 1976, p. 79). This chapter is about acting that sets the stage for sense-making. You have already seen exhibits of enactment (Chapter 5) in the activities of saying, doing, spinning webs of significance, adapting, and producing variations. In each case enactment served to bracket and construct portions of the flow of experience. Bracketing and construction are visible in the three comments that begin this chapter.

Examples of Enactment

THE ENACTMENT OF EXPERIENCE

There is no such thing as *experience* until the manager does something. Passive reception of a shower of inputs is not synonymous with having an experience (Simmel 1959). Experience is the consequence of activity. The manager literally wades into the swarm of "events" that surround him and actively tries to unrandomize them and impose some order. The manager acts physically in the environment, attends to some of it, ignores most of it, talks to other people about what they see and are doing (Braybrooke 1964). As a result the surroundings get sorted into variables and linkages and appear more orderly.

William James provides a vivid portrayal of what it takes to build an experience:

> The world's contents are *given* to each of us in an order so foreign to our subjective interests that we can hardly by an effort of the imagination picture to ourselves what it is like. We have to break that order altogether, and by picking out from it the items that concern us, and connecting them with others far away, which we say "belong" with them, we are able to make out definite threads of sequence and tendency, to foresee particular liabilities and get ready for them, to enjoy simplicity and harmony in the place of what was chaos. . . . While I talk and the flies buzz, a seagull catches a fish at the mouth of the Amazon, a tree falls in the Adirondack wilderness, a man sneezes in Germany, a horse dies in Tartary, and twins are born in France. What does that mean? Does the contemporaneity of these events with each other and with a million more as disjointed as they form a rational bond between them, and unite them into anything that means for us a world? Yet just such a collateral contemporaneity, and nothing else, is the *real* order of the world. It is an order with which we have nothing to do but get away from it as fast as possible. As I said, we break it: we break it into histories, and we break it into arts, and we break it into sciences; and then we begin to feel at home. We make ten thousand separate serial orders of it. On any of these, we may react as if the rest did not exist. We discover among its parts relations that were never given to sense at all,—mathematical relations, tangents, squares, and roots and log-arithmic functions,—and out of an infinite number of these we call certain ones essential and lawgiving, and ignore the rest. Essential these relations are, but only *for our purpose*, the other relations being just as real and present as they; and our purpose is to *conceive simply* and to *foresee* (James 1950, vol. 2, p. 635).

These statements summarize the nature of organizational sense-making. First of all, the chaos that is to be decomposed is both flowing and equivocal. People in organizations try to sort this chaos into items, events, and parts which are then connected, threaded into sequences, serially ordered, and related. These are the very same activities that seem to occur when people build cause maps like those you constructed in Chapter 3 of your group discussion experiences. The connections in which James is interested are those connections involving *sequence* and *tendency*. Sequence and tendency are the same sensible threads that occur in cause maps. Furthermore, the assertion that cause maps are inventions rather than discoveries is supported by James's point that when we create serial orders we often find relations that were never presented to the senses at all.

James also emphasizes that these sense-making efforts differ among people. This difference sets the stage for much activity that goes on in organizations: people spending time trying to make their views of the world more similar. What this means practically is that people negotiate over which nouns and verbs should be imposed on the flow and how those nouns and verbs are to be connected. Notice that if there is considerable difference among people's views of an organization, then the organization will be characterized by multiple realities and in all likelihood the resulting unit will appear to be loosely coupled since there is disagreement on what affects what.

James does not say how one knows whether an event is an antecedent or consequent, but this is not crucial because the labels *antecedent* and *consequent* are rather arbitrary distinctions, especially when variables exist in causal loops. As we saw earlier, any variable can be either a cause or an effect, an antecedent or a consequent. It all depends on where you start and terminate a causal loop.

One of the nice things about James's remarks is that they are quite physical. Breaking an order, picking out items, connecting events all suggest sizable rearrangements of the displays that people face. If an individual breaks up chaos so that other forms of order can be created, then it stands to reason that what is eventually available for inspection is something very much of the individual's own making. And the act of breaking itself suggests isolating some portion of the flow of experience for closer attention, which is largely what enactment consists of.

THE ENACTMENT OF LIMITATIONS

Perceptions of personal "limitations," in Piet Hein's view, turn out to be a failure *to act* rather than a failure *while acting*. Limitations are deceptive conclusions but, unfortunately, people don't realize this. What they don't realize is that limitations are based on presumptions rather than action. Knowledge of limitations is not based on tests of skills but rather on an *avoidance* of testing.

On the basis of avoided tests, people conclude that constraints exist in the environment and that limits exist in their repertoire of responses. Inaction is justified by the implantation, in fantasy, of constraints and barriers that make action "impossible." These constraints, barriers, prohibitions then become prominent "things" in the environment. They also become self-imposed restrictions on the options that managers consider and exercise when confronted with problems. Finally, these presumed constraints, when breached by someone who is more doubting, naive, or uninformed, often generate sizable advantages for the breacher.

As a laboratory exercise, Harold Garfinkel (1967) had some of his students go into a department store and offer a small fraction of the list price for some item. The students were apprehensive in advance about doing this, since an explicit rule presumed to exist in most American stores is that things must be bought for the list price. Much to their surprise, the students discovered that once they actually began to bargain for items, they were able to get rather substantial reductions in price. The interesting thing about the list price "rule" is that it seems to have force because everyone expects it to be followed and no one challenges it.

Garfinkel takes that observation and expands it to a more general statement about knowledge based on avoided tests:

> If upon the arousal of troubled feelings persons avoid tinkering with these "standardized" expectancies (in the example above the standardization would be the rule that things must be bought for the list price) the standardization could consist of an *attributed* standardization that is supported by the fact that persons avoid the very situations in which they might learn about them. Lay as well as professional knowledge of the nature of rule governed actions and the consequences of breaching the rules is prominently based on just such procedure. Indeed, the more important the rule, the greater is the likelihood that knowledge is based on avoided tests. Strange findings must certainly await anyone who examines the expectancies that make up routine backgrounds of commonplace activities for they have rarely been exposed by investigators even to as much revision as an imaginative rehearsal of their breach would produce (1967, p. 70).

Even though organizations appear to be quite solid, in fact much of their substance may consist of spurious knowledge based on avoided tests. While Garfinkel does not formulate propositions about avoided tests, it *is* possible to speculate about the form such propositions would take. For example, implicit in his analysis is the suggestion that avoided tests may occur because people fear the experience of failure. Transformed into a proposition, it might be predicted that the greater the fear of failure, the greater the likelihood that a person's knowledge of the world is based on avoided tests.

Notice that if one were to fail while attempting a test, the results might or might not be reversible. In other words, a person might be able to undo the damage or might never be able to normalize the event. This suggests that the greater the difficulty of undoing an outcome, the more likely it is for a person to engage in avoided tests.

There appears to be a cognitive side to the avoidance of tests. So far it has been argued that immediate outcomes of pleasure or pain may control the choice to test or not. Notice, however, that there are subtleties in the interpretation of outcomes. If you go into a store, try to buy a 49-cent toothbrush for 40 cents, fail, and experience some embarrassment, you might interpret that outcome as one of those little stresses in life that "builds character." Thus, if individuals in organizations believe in such things as the cleansing power of suffering, the school of hard knocks, or the saneogenesis proposition that it is too little rather than too much stress that causes breakdown (Scher 1962), then those individuals will be more likely to attempt tests rather than to avoid them.

There is a parallel between avoided tests and the Ziergarnik Effect. An avoided test is like an unfinished task, especially if the person has wondered repeatedly whether a barrier is fictional or substantial. There is a distinct quality of unfinished business in avoided tests. This suggests that people should be more aware of their avoided tests than of their nonavoided tests.

Not very much is known about avoided tests, but it seems likely that they could be the basis for a substantial portion of the knowledge that organizations retain. The question of interest for organization epistemologists would be, "What precedes and is the occasion for an avoided versus an attempted test?"

A variation of the point that the ingenuous shall coopt the environment is the idea that people who seem backward historically are, in fact, privileged (Sahlins and Service 1960). Their privilege lies in the fact that they can benefit from the mistakes and oversights of pioneers. The "backward" group is able to leapfrog the pioneer and employ neglected actions to locate opportunities that prove beneficial. With both avoided tests and privileged backwardness it is inaction (a failure to enact) propped up by the fiction of constraints that erects trappings which, when treated irreverently, vanish abruptly.

A presumption throughout this book is that managers often know much less about their environments and organizations than they think. One reason for this imperfect knowing is that managers unwittingly collude among themselves to avoid tests. And they build elaborate explanations of why tests should be avoided, why one shouldn't/couldn't act within settings presumed to be dangerous. The disbeliever, the unindoctrinated, the newcomer, all being less influenced by a cause map dotted with noxiants, wade in where avoiders fear to tread. Having waded in they find either that the avoider's fear is unfounded or that it is valid, in which case their demise provides vicarious learning for the avoiders.

The point is that the enormous amount of talk, socializing, consensus-building, and vicarious learning that goes on among managers often results in pluralistic ignorance (Shaw and Blum 1965) about the environment. Stunted enactment is the reason. Each person watches someone else avoid certain procedures, goals, activities, sentences, and pastimes and concludes that this avoidance is motivated by "real" noxiants in the environment. The observer profits from that "lesson" by himself then avoiding those acts and their presumed consequences. As this sequence of events continues to be repeated, managers conclude that they know more and more about something that none of them has actually experienced firsthand. This impression of knowing becomes strengthened because everyone seems to be seeing and avoiding the same things. And if everyone seems to agree on something, then it must exist and be true.

If people want to change their environment, they need to change themselves and their actions—not someone else. Repeated failures of organizations to solve their problems are partially explained by their failure to understand their own prominence in their own environments. Problems that never get solved, never get solved because managers keep tinkering with everything *but* what they do.

THE ENACTMENT OF CHARADES

As the final example, Jencks and Silver (1973) provide a perfect description of charades when they call it an "acted out rebus." A rebus is a representation of original words or symbols by means of some other pictures or symbols that sound like the original. For example, ICURYY4me is a rebus for "I see you are too wise for me." Charades involve the same kind of representation. An object is symbolized by other objects that sound the same. According to Jencks and Silver, one of the all-time best (or worst?) solutions for a charade occurred when a person was given the name Salvador Dali and acted out the three words, "saliva," "tore," and "doily."

There are several interesting features of enactment in charades. The person doing the gesturing knows what he is perceived as enacting only after he hears the observers' guesses. That is, the actor produces a soliloquy, the punctuation of which is done by others. The actor produces an enacted environment as an output, but the observers are faced with a display that they can punctuate and connect in numerous ways. The actor imposes meanings on his environment that come back and organize his activities, except that the observers see these implanted meanings as puzzles rather than certainties. If the actor has enacted a puzzling or complicated or subtle environment, that enactment comes back and organizes him in the sense that he has to do enormous work to salvage, patch up, and redirect the observers' efforts to invent plausible constructions for his subtleties.

The image of a rebus is relevant for organizations because it captures the essence of enactment. People in organizations need to act to find out what they have done, and the person enacting a rebus needs to play out his version of the charade to see what he really is conveying to interested observers. The person acting out a charade enacts most of the environment for observers. And what we are arguing is that it isn't that much different in organizations. The environment that the organization worries over is put there by the organization.

CONCLUSION

The reciprocal linkage between ecological change and enactment in the organizing model is intended to depict the subjective origin of organizational realities (Israel 1972). People in organizations repeatedly impose that which they later claim imposes on them. Farmers with heavy tractors enact the packed earth (ecological change), which requires heavier tractors, more fuel, deeper plows, and/or wider tires to work. The presence of elaborate multitrack mixers in recording studios has compelled engineers to produce increasingly elaborate effects on recordings, which leads to demands for even more elaborate mixing equipment, and so on. Many listeners, however, have become fed up with this meddling and are now purchasing direct-to-disc music that bypasses the engineer, his busy hands, his passion for remixing, his elaborate technology, and his precious output (McDonough 1978). Nevertheless, engineers have enacted the environment of contrived music that now organizes and threatens to disorganize their jobs. Physicians, through nonsubtle diagnostic procedures ("hmmm, when did you start holding your head at that angle?"), often implant maladies that *weren't* there when the examination began. Their procedures consolidate numerous free-floating symptoms into the felt presence of a single, more specific, more serious problem. Physician-induced disease (*iatrogenics*) is a perfect example of people creating the environment that confronts them (Scheff 1965). Firemen on steam locomotives enacted the pattern of hot and cold spots within the boiler by their method of shoveling coal into it, which then constrained their subsequent attempts to preserve steam pressure (Withuhn 1975).

Examples like this are plentiful. The point is, much current work on the relationships between organizations and their environments tends to downplay the extent to which the boundaries between the two are blurred (Starbuck 1976, p. 1070) and the extent to which organizations produce their environments. In the remainder of this chapter we will try to remedy this imbalance.

Characteristics of Enactment

ENACTMENT AS BRACKETING

We have described enactment as a bracketing activity. To visualize what this means, imagine that the major input to be processed by employees is either a stock market tickertape with no spaces between symbols, or a teletype machine whose output contains no punctuation into sentences or paragraphs. In the unpunctuated output one does not know where one "story" leaves off and another story begins, or even whether a story is a reasonable unit of analysis. The same thing is true in the case of the unpunctuated stock market tickertape. In both cases there is a mass of data, without any hints concerning their importance. It's the job of the employee to tear off portions of the tickertape or teletype for further study. Those activities of tearing are crude kinds of enactments. Once something has been isolated, then that *is* the environment momentarily for the organization and that environment has been put into place by the very actions of the employees themselves.

To get a feeling for the phenomenon we're interested in, think back to times when you have read the verbatim protocol of some important speech. When these speeches are printed verbatim, the columns of type often continue uninterrupted without any indications of how the speech is structured. When a reader confronts this display of uninterrupted type he wonders such things as, "Where were the good parts?" "What was said that is new?" "What's different?" "What's surprising?" "What's the news?" As you read, these questions become frustrating because you basically have to decide for yourself what's new and different and good without any prompting from commentators. Confronted with an unpunctuated speech, you're in precisely the same position as an employee who confronts a flow of experience and has no one around to coach him on which are the good parts, the bad parts, the interesting parts, and the trivia. Those are all decisions involving bracketing.

When you pull out some portion of the text of the speech from its surrounding context, then the environment that you have bracketed for inspection is a different environment than the original one that contained intonations, facial expressions, and surrounding text. The reader of the extracted portion does see part of herself because her own interests influenced the process of extracting. And this is true whether those biases suggest that speeches are better at the end than at the beginning, or that paragraphs starting with personal pronouns are better than those that don't. The "chaos" of the speech transcript has been dealt with by breaking it into chunks, by ignoring portions of it, and by trying to figure out on the basis of the extracted chunk what kinds of decisions and situations on the part of the speaker would have generated those particular words (in other words, the bracketed portion is analyzed in terms of potential antecedents and consequences).

A suggestion of the way in which bracketing might operate is found in Neisser's (1976) recent discussion of the perceptual cycle. Neisser casts his discussion of perceptual cycles in terms of schemas used to aid interpretation. A schema is an abridged, generalized, corrigible organization of experience that serves as an initial frame of reference for action and perception. A schema is the belief in the phrase, "I'll see it when I believe it." Schemata constrain seeing and, therefore, serve to bracket portions of experience.

Neisser describes schemata as active, information-seeking structures that accept information and direct action. "The schema accepts information as it becomes available at sensory surfaces and is changed by that information; it directs movements and exploratory activities that make more information available, by which it is further modified" (Neisser 1976, p. 54). Neisser notes that schemata are analogous to things like formats in computer programming language, plans for finding out about objects and events, and genotypes that offer possibilities for development along certain general lines. Neisser posits a perceptual cycle to illustrate how schemata operate, and this graphic provides a useful medium to describe enactment.

The perceptual cycle shown in Fig. 6.1 is continuous (Jordan 1968, p. 26). A schema directs the exploration of objects, this exploration samples portions of an object, and these samples may modify the schema, which then directs further exploration and sampling, which then further modifies the schema; this kind of process goes on continuously. Notice that the three components of Neisser's perceptual cycle—schema, exploration, and object—correspond rather neatly to the components of thinking, seeing, and saying in the sense-making recipe, "How can I know what I think until I see what I say?" On the basis of what a person thinks, he sees different things in his saying, and what he sees in this saying then modifies what he thinks and will then single out for closer attention in subsequent saying.

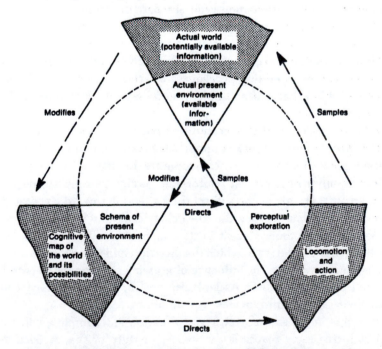

Fig. 6.1 Neisser's perceptual cycle. (From Neisser 1976, p. 112.)

Bracketing is very much like Neisser's sampling. When an object is sampled, only portions of it are pulled out for closer inspection, but these are sufficient to give some indication as to what is going on. Notice that after a sample has been extracted and there is more certainty as to what is being examined, subsequent exploration should tend to confirm these hunches. Perceptual activity seems to move in the direction of self-fulfilling rather than self-defeating prophecies, and it is this bias that is behind much of our feeling that enacted environments are commonplace rather than rare.

While Neisser's formulation describes the directing, sampling, and modification that goes on in just one head, it's important to realize that these activities are dispersed among many people in organizations. Boundary people, for example, are in an ideal position to sample (Aldrich and Herker 1977; Leifer and Delbecq 1978), but their sampling seldom gets communicated vividly or quickly to those people who could modify schemata that bind the interpretations imposed by other people in the organization. The dispersal of the various stages of the perceptual cycle throughout an organization serves as another way to describe what an organization is like and to predict how well it will know the world it enacts.

Examples of schemata in organizations are abundant. They may exist as cognitive maps that members infer from their organizational experience (Axelrod 1976; Bougon, Weick, and Binkhorst 1977).

The most conspicuous example is the standard operating procedure (Allison 1971). A standard operating procedure is a schema that structures dealing with an environment. A standard operating procedure is a frame of reference that constrains exploration and often unfolds like a self-fulfilling prophecy (Martin 1977). The standard operating procedures direct attention toward restricted aspects of an object that, when sampled, seemingly justify routine application of the procedure.

Janis's (1972) description of groupthink has overtones of schema theory. The phenomenon of groupthink is important because it demonstrates some of the dysfunctional consequences when people are dominated by a single schema and this domination becomes self-reinforcing. Having become true believers of a specific schema, group members direct their attention toward an environment and sample it in such a way that the true belief becomes self-validating and the group becomes even more fervent in its attachment to the schema. What is underestimated is the degree to which the direction and sampling are becoming increasingly narrow under the influence of growing consensus and enthusiasm for the restricted set of beliefs. As Janis demonstrates, this spiral is frequently associated with serious misjudgments of situations.

Notice that any idea that restricts exploration and sampling will come to be seen as increasingly plausible by the very nature of that restriction. If a person has an idea and looks for "relevant" data, there's enough complexity and ambiguity in the world that relevance is usually found and the idea is usually judged more plausible. One of the prominent characteristics of schemata is that they are refractory to disproof (Ross 1977, p. 205).

Neisser would argue that schema are not that vulnerable to distortion, and that by and large they pick up real objects. It is our contention that most "objects" in organizations consist of communications, meanings, images, myths, and interpretations, all of which offer considerable latitude for definition and self-validation.

Notice that when we coordinated Neisser's perceptual cycle with the sense-making recipe, the *object* in that coordination was raw talk. It's certainly obvious that saying is subject to numerous interpretations, which means it can appear to support quite divergent schemata. This seeming universal support does not arise from stupidity or malevolence on the part of the actor, but rather from the combination of an intact, reinforced schema and an equivocal object. Actors with bounded rationality presumably are more interested in confirming their schemata than in actively trying to disprove them. Even though people may build up schema anew each time they apply the schemata, they have to start this buildup with something. And it's that something, that assumption, that retrieved portion of the past, that can rather swiftly become elaborated into a schema that is like a previous schema and that has a controlling effect on what people perceive.

ENACTMENT AS DEVIATION AMPLIFICATION

In many instances of enactment there is a deviation-amplifying causal structure that contains an even number of negative signs. The importance of this observation is that minor disturbances, when they are embedded in a deviation-amplifying loop, can grow into major happenings with major consequences. When it is argued that organizations enact their environments, some readers may assume that these enactments have always been present on about the scale they now exhibit. That implication is not intended. The modest origins of consequential enactments are illustrated by efforts to desegregate the schools in San Francisco (Weiner 1976).

In trying to figure out how desegregation should be implemented in San Francisco, a Citizens Advisory Committee consisting of 67 citizens was appointed by the board of education. Over time this committee became increasingly influential in deciding how the desegregation order would be implemented. The fascinating point for our analyses is the differential frequency with which these 67 people attended meetings.

The committee began its deliberations on February 16, 1971, and concluded them on June 2, 1971. During this time they held 70 meetings, or approximately one meeting every two days. This implies the obvious point that all members could not attend all meetings. This minor difference in participation rates soon became amplified:

> Deadlines led to a domination of the decision making process by middle and upper class white women, who had available time during the day because they were not employed and could arrange care for their children, and by other participants whose employers permitted them to devote daytime hours to the decision making process (Weiner 1976, pp. 234-35).

As a result, black members of the committee did not participate actively in developing the desegregation plan. But the issue here is not just one of time. There is the further issue of differential competence produced by differential attendance:

> As high participation rates continue the most active members become a relatively small group possessing a near monopoly position concerning the competencies required in decision making. The joint operation of these factors constitutes a positive feedback loop where activity causes greater competence and greater competence leads to increased activity.... Thus, one effect associated with the sharply increased participation rates by some participants in the choice is that the most active participants gain a much higher share of the competence and experience necessary to deal with the remaining problems. As they become substantially more competent it becomes more difficult for other potential participants to gain access to the decision making process (Weiner 1976, p. 247).

Weiner labels this phenomenon the *competence multiplier*. The participants who show up repeatedly produce an environment of sophisticated analyses that requires more participation from them, which makes them even more informed to deal with the issues that are presented. A vicious circle is created in which the regular participants of the advisory council enact the very sophisticated and subtle issues that their new-found competence enables them to deal with. People who attend less often feel less informed, increasingly unable to catch up, and more reluctant to enter the conversation at the level of sophistication voiced by the persistent participants. The relatively less informed people select themselves out of the decision-making process, and this elevates the level of desegregation planning to an even more detailed and complicated level where even fewer people can comprehend it. Over time the combination of high and low participation rates, a minor deviation in the beginning, changes the issues, plans, and environment that confronts the Citizens Advisory Committee.

The question of desegregation and how to implement it is not an external problem that is handed to the committee for its action. Instead, the issue that gets handed to them is an issue partly of their own making. The density of detail in the solution, the subtlety of the issues addressed, and the interests that are accommodated are all influenced by the patterns of participation at the meetings.

Once again we have a clear example of a deviation-amplifying loop. People with time to spend on a problem transformed that problem into something that only people with time to spend on the problem can manage. The resulting discussion is one from which infrequent attendees become more and more alienated because they understand fewer of its intricacies. Thus the mundane activity of simply showing up at meetings generates an environment that only those who show up at meetings are able to manage and control. Several iterations through the cycle are necessary for this consequence to occur, but again, its plausibility is evident and its relevance to enactment processes should be apparent.

ENACTMENT AS SELF-FULFILLING PROPHECIES

Enactment could be described as efferent sense-making. The modifier *efferent* means centrifugal or conducted outward. The person's idea is extended outward, implanted, and then rediscovered as knowledge. The discovery, however, originated in a prior invention by the discoverer. In a crude but literal sense, one could talk about efferent sense-making as thinking in circles. Action, perception, and sense-making exist in a circular, tightly coupled relationship that resembles a self-fulfilling prophecy (e.g., Archibald 1974; G. W. Bateson 1951; James 1956; Kelley and Stahelski 1970; Henshel and Kennedy 1973; R. A. Jones 1977).

A self-fulfilling prophecy involves

> behavior that brings about in others the reaction to which the behavior would be an appropriate reaction. For instance, a person who acts on the premise that "nobody likes me" will behave in a distrustful, stiff, defensive, or aggressive manner to which others are likely to react unsympathetically, thus bearing out his original premise. What is typical about this sequence and makes it a problem of punctuation is that the individual concerned conceives of himself only as reacting to, but not as provoking, those attitudes (Watzlawick, Beavin, and Jackson 1967, pp. 98-99).

A related phenomenon has been described by music critic Leonard Meyer as the presumption of logic and was noted briefly in Chapter 5. Meyer assumes that the presumption of logic is important in comprehending new music (that is, an equivocal input). Essentially Meyer argues that whenever individuals try to comprehend new music, their success or failure at this activity depends on their prior belief in the seriousness, purposefulness and logic of the artist, and the work:

> The presumption that nothing in art happens without a reason and that any given cause should be sufficient and necessary for what takes place is a fundamental condition for the experience of art. . . . Without this basic belief the listener would have no reason for suspending judgement, revising opinion, and searching for relationships; the divergent, the less probable, the ambiguous would have no meaning. There would be no progression, only change. Without faith in the purposefulness and rationality of art, listeners would abandon their efforts to understand, to reconcile deviants to what has gone before or to look for their raison d'etre in what is still to come (Meyer 1956, p. 75).

Notice that the presumption of logic resembles a self-fulfilling prophecy. The listener presumes that the music about to be played will have made sense, exerts effort to make the music sensible, postpones premature judgments on whether it makes sense or not, and thereby makes his own contribution toward inventing a sensible, complete work of music. The presumption of logic is slightly more content-free than is a self-fulfilling prophecy. Self-fulfilling prophecies typically contain specific content such as the expectations that students will be bright or stupid (Rosenthal and Jacobson 1968), that people will like me or dislike me (James 1956, pp. 23-25), that the bank is about to become insolvent (Merton 1948), or that this is a fatalistic world (G. W. Bateson 1951). Each of those prophecies is quite explicit, whereas the presumption of logic is more general (a metaprophecy) and says essentially that there *is* an order of some kind there and that it's simply up to the listener to extract/create that order.

When managers confront equivocality and try to reduce it, they too often operate on the presumption of logic. They assume that their views of and actions toward the world are valid, they assume that other people in the organization will see and do the same things, and it is rare for the managers to check these assumptions. Having presumed that the environment is orderly and sensible, managers make efforts to impose order, thereby enacting the orderliness that is "discovered." The presumption of nonequivocality provides the occasion for managers to see and do those things that transform the environment into something that is unequivocal.

A clear exhibit of self-fulfilling prophecies in organizations has been described by Warwick (1975). In July 1965 Deputy Undersecretary of State for Administration William Crockett launched an attempt to reorganize the State Department along three lines: reduce the number of hierarchical layers, increase the autonomy of decision-making, and decentralize key functions. The Foreign Service Officers, one group within the State Department, did much to undermine the success of this change. Their undermining was not intentionally malicious, but simply illustrated the inevitable outcomes when events are linked together as self-fulfilling prophecies.

The Foreign Service Officers are an elite corps within the State Department. Members hold many of the key policy-making positions in Washington, and they serve as the chiefs and deputy chiefs of the embassies. They pride themselves on being substantive generalists, astute political reporters, and adept negotiators. The norms of this group are traditional and elitist; they rely heavily on a diplomatic approach to problems, which means that they value subtlety, skill in negotiation, cultural sophistication, and good manners. The pinnacle of this career hierarchy is to be an ambassador.

Given the self-contained, almost guild-like nature of this unit, it should not be surprising to learn that whenever newcomers who are political appointees enter the State Department they see these officers as insular, aloof, and uncooperative. The officers, in turn, worry about the newcomers being uninformed, unappreciative of subtleties in diplomacy, and likely to underestimate the importance of Foreign Service Officers.

Given this background it is easy to see how the Foreign Service Officers enact their own hostile environment. Newcomers, facing the closed ranks of Foreign Service Officers, conclude that these officers produce little that is creative or progressive. Once the new top leaders make these assumptions, they avoid involving the officers in any plans or programs for change. The Foreign Service Officers, in turn, become offended when they are excluded from planning and become more suspicious of ideas or suggestions that impinge on areas in which they have some expertise. As a result, members of the Foreign Service cling even more tightly to the key element in their self-definition within the agency: the traditional concept of diplomacy. When the Foreign Service Officers behave defensively, this simply confirms the newcomers' initial impressions, in which case they pay even less attention to the ideas of the officers.

Using the conventions of Chapter 3, we can diagram the vicious circle as we have done in Fig. 6.2.

This example is a classic case of a self-fulfilling prophecy. If we view this situation from the standpoint of the newcomers, they prophesy that the

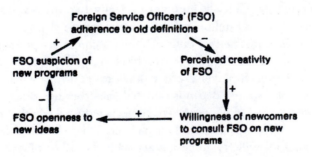

Figure 6.2

Foreign Service Officers will be defensive, protective, and traditional. Having assumed this they exclude them from all crucial activities, which produces a protective and defensive response on the part of the Foreign Service Officers, thereby confirming the newcomers' prophecy.

If we view the same situation from the vantage point of the Foreign Service Officers, they presume that the naive leaders won't appreciate the nuances of diplomacy and will sabotage these activities. Based on these assumptions the Foreign Service Officers close themselves off from the new appointees and conduct business as usual. This leads the newcomers to conclude that the diplomats themselves are naive and old-fashioned, which conclusions simply confirm the original fears of the Foreign Service Officers that their newly appointed leaders have only the most superficial understanding of how the State Department "really" works.

Each subgroup enacts its own hostile environment and finds itself constrained by the very naivete and bungling that it projected in the first place. Each subgroup enacts the incompetent environment that it faces. Each subgroup can argue self-righteously that it would be more effective were it not for the incompetent people through whom its intentions have to be mediated. What will not get noticed is the fact that this incompetence that confronts each subgroup in fact was put into place by that subgroup.

A particularly good experimental example of self-fulfilling prophecies obtained under more carefully controlled conditions is the study by Kelley and Stahelski (1970) of differences in the style of interaction between cooperative and competitive individuals. The striking finding of this study is that a competitive person's anticipations of how other people will behave tend to have a self-fulfilling aura that transforms those other individuals, regardless of their preference for cooperation, into competitors.

People were put into a standard prisoners' dilemma game that resembled the game of chicken. "Chicken" derives its name from the game occasionally played by young drivers who, on a dare, race toward each other on a highway both straddling the center line in order to see who will "chicken out" first and give way to one side. Chicken involves basically two moves: pulling off the road (response Y), or not pulling off the road (response W). Whoever pulls off the road (Y) loses, but if neither pulls off, the outcomes are poor (see Fig. 6.3). If we use the language of Chapter 4 it can be seen that there is direct conflict in this game and that each player exerts behavioral control over the other one. Each person's best response depends on what the other one does.

Before they started to play chicken, subjects were asked what they wanted to achieve in the relationship with their partner. Their choices were between a cooperative goal ("I will try to cooperate with the other player and will be concerned with my own score and the other player's score") or competitive ("I will work for myself against the other player and will be concerned only with

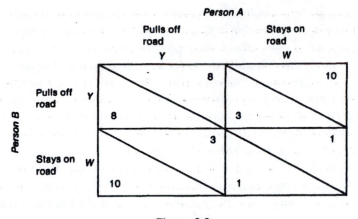

Figure 6.3

my own score"). People were then paired off so that a cooperator was paired with a competitor, and the two people played for a series of trials. After several plays they were interrupted and asked to judge what the goals of their partner were. Errors in these judgments were rampant, and the most common error was the judgment by the competitor (the subject who chose the competitive goal) that his cooperative partner was also a competitor and had chosen a competitive goal. Essentially what happened during the game was that the competitor behaved in such a way that he shifted the cooperator's initial cooperative behavior toward his competitive style even though he didn't realize that *he* had caused his partner to do this.

On the basis of these studies it was suggested that competitive individuals tend to believe that other people are always competitive, whereas cooperative individuals believe that other people are heterogeneous and may be either cooperative or competitive. Kelley and Stahelski (1970) have represented this asymmetry in the form of a triangle hypothesis which is depicted in Fig. 6.4.

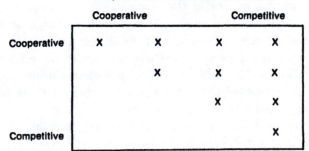

Fig. 6.4   The triangle hypothesis. (From Kelley and Stahelski 1970, p. 77).

The triangle hypothesis (Fig. 6.4) simply summarizes the fact that cooperators and competitors develop different views of what other people are like.
And in the case of competitors, their presumption that other individuals are
universally competitive leads them to act in such a manner that they produce,
in cooperative individuals, that competitiveness that they assume was there all
along. The competitive players simply don't see cooperative overtures in the
beginning. Instead, they act in such a way that the cooperative players modify
their efforts and become competitive, thereby fulfilling the original competitor's definition that all people are competitive.

The important point in this sequence of events is that there is a grain of
truth to the competitor's sweeping assertion that everyone is competitve. What
the competitor doesn't realize is that the grain of truth has been planted by
personal actions, which produced the competitiveness in another individual
who otherwise would have been cooperative. Thus, the competitor's claim that
it's a dog-eat-dog world is a perfectly accurate reflection of what seems to have
happened. But what the competitor underestimates is the extent to which he
enacted that world.

The frequency with which self-fulfilling prophecies occur may be underestimated because of the inflated image implied by the phrase *self-fulfilling
prophecy.* The image of a prophecy suggests something that is a major activity
preceded by considerable fanfare and, consequently, rare. The more appropriate
image would be that in everyday/anyday life people expect, anticipate, fore-
see, and make mundane predictions all the time. (For instance, I predict that
when I turn the page there will be some print.)

ENACTMENT AS SOCIAL CONSTRUCTION OF REALITY

The concept of an *enacted environment* is not synonymous with the concept of
a *perceived environment*, even though citations of the concept would suggest
that it is. If a perceived environment were the essence of enactment then, as
Lou Pondy suggested, the phenomenon would have been called enthinkment,
not enactment.

We have purposely labeled the organizational equivalent of variation
ena*ct*ment to emphasize that managers construct, rearrange, single out, and
demolish many "objective" features of their surroundings. When people act
they unrandomize variables, insert vestiges of orderliness, and literally create
their own constraints. This holds true whether those constraints are created in
fantasy to justify avoided tests or created in actuality to explain tangible
bruises (Simmel 1959).

People have talked for some time about the fact that reality is constructed
(e.g., McLeod and Chaffee 1972; R. A. Jones and Day 1977; Berger and
Luckmann 1967; Ball 1972). These views stress that reality is selectively perceived, rearranged cognitively, and negotiated interpersonally. In most cases it

is assumed that something tangible is the target of these efforts and that what is required to locate this target is that one be clever enough to choose both a good partner and a good procedure to uncover this underlying order. Analyses of the social construction of reality emphasize that actors attain at least a partial consensus on the meaning of their behavior and that they look for patterns that underlie appearances, actions, events. These patterns are assumed to have an existence independent of the interpretation procedures (e.g., Goffman 1974, pp. 1-2; Gonos 1977).

A more extreme position is that the social order exists precariously and has no existence at all independent of the members' accounting and describing practices (e.g., Mehan and Wood 1975). The organizing model is based on the view that order is imposed rather than discovered, on the grounds that action defines cognition. The basic sense-making device used within organizations is assumed to be talking to discover thinking. How can I know what I think until I see what I say? In that sequence, the action of talking is the occasion for defining and articulating cognitions. When it is argued that organizational members spend much of their time uttering soliloquies, we are describing a crucial feature of enactment. The soliloquies are action soliloquies because it is action that leads and defines cognition. G. W. Bateson uses a similar image: "an explorer can never know what he is exploring until it has been explored" (1972, p. xvi).

The notion that reality is a product of social construction does have some connotation of action conveyed by the word *construction*. But this construction is usually thought to involve activities of negotiation between people as to what is out there. Less prominent in these analyses is the idea that people, often alone, actively *put* things out there that they then perceive and negotiate about perceiving. It is that initial implanting of reality that is preserved by the word *enactment*.

Concepts such as the negotiated environment and the social construction of reality share a presumption that knowledge is acquired with the flow going from an object to a subject:

$$\text{Object} \longrightarrow \text{Subject}$$

The object is perceived, worked on cognitively, variously labeled, and coupled with various remote or distal events. Less attention is given to the possibility that understanding also moves in the opposite direction:

$$\text{Object} \longleftarrow \text{Subject}$$

The potential effect of the subject on the object signifies that knowledge is an activity in which the subject partly interacts with and constitutes the object

(Gruber and Vonèche 1977). There is a reciprocal influence between subjects and objects, not a one-sided influence such as is implied by the idea that a stimulus triggers a response. This reciprocal influence is captured in the organizing model by the two-way influence between enactment and ecological change.

Another distinguishing feature of the enacted environment is that it is treated as an output of organizations, not as an input. Conventional treatments of the perceived environment argue that it is current personal definitions of the situation, not a material world, that influences the organization.

The enacted environment, being an output of organizing activities, is in some ways an anachronistic, dated, belated stimulus. The enacted environment is a sensible rendering of previous events stored in the form of causal assertions, and made binding on some current enactment and/or selection. There is a definite time lag and a definite tinge of retrospect to the definitions of the situation that are taken seriously within the organizing model.

The further stipulation that these environments are stored as cause maps and have their influence via imposed causal networks is also not found in discussions of the social construction of reality.

Implications

Investigators who study organizations often separate environments from organizations and argue that things happen between these distinct entities. This way of carving up the problem of organizational analysis effectively rules out certain kinds of questions. Talk about bounded environments and organizations, for example, compels the investigator to ask questions such as "How does an organization *discover* the *underlying* structure in *the* environment?" Having separated the "two" entities and given them independent existence, investigators have to make elaborate speculations concerning the ways in which one entity becomes disclosed to and known by the other. But the firm partitioning of the world into the environment and the organization excludes the possibility that people *invent* rather than discover part of what they think they see.

It certainly is the case that organizations bump into things and that their bruises testify to a certain tangibility in their environment, even if that tangibility can be punctuated in numerous ways. The enactment perspective doesn't deny that. But it also does not accept the idea that organizations are most usefully viewed as reactive sensors of those things that happen outside. It can be argued (Heider 1959) that with any pair of items one is more internally constrained, more tightly coupled, and more thing-like than the other. The more tightly coupled object is the equivalent of a thing; the more loosely coupled object corresponds to a medium whose properties are rearranged by and resemble the more coherent thing.

This simply means that any organization examined relative to any environment may be more or less internally constrained than that environment. If the organization is more internally constrained, then it can rearrange the environment more readily than the environment can rearrange the organization. Student activist groups on campuses are often more tightly coupled internally than are the faculties toward which they direct their appeals. As a consequence, these activist groups frequently are the thing-like environment to which a more loosely coupled faculty accommodates. Those same student groups, however, built on temporary alliances, multiple loyalties, and short attention spans, are loosely coupled relative to many labor unions. The activist groups are less able to enact an environment among union personnel than they are among faculty.

The important point is that solidarity is not an absolute judgment. In any situation where it is argued that an environment coerces organizational responses, it is crucial to assess which of the two entities being compared is the more tightly coupled. The more tightly coupled body is apt to be a constraint on the body that is less tightly coupled.

Organizational size undoubtedly affects whether enactment is a major or minor contributor to the environments that an organization faces. As an organization becomes larger it literally becomes more of its own environment and can hardly avoid stumbling into its own enactments. Campbell makes a related point:

> Adaptive evolution is a negative feedback steering device, and therefore works best when the evolving social organization is a small part of the total environment, so that variations in the social organization did not substantially change the selective system, that is, the overall environment. It is on these grounds that one might well doubt that any adaptive social evolution is going on at the level of nations today. Major nations are so few in number, and so much the dominant part of each other's environment, that each variation initiated by one nation may fundamentally change the overall system, thus altering the selective system in creating something closer to a runaway positive feedback rather than a stabilizing negative feedback (1975b, p. 1106).

Unless an evolving organization is a small part of the environment, its actions will change the selection system implied by that environment. As an organization increases in size it becomes its own selection system and quite literally does impose the environment that imposes on it. It should be apparent that distinction between organization and environment becomes hopelessly obscured under these conditions.

Industries with dense technology should find their enactment has to cope with and bend around some rather substantial pieces of hardware (Klein 1976).

Technology may alter the processes of enactment, but to argue that enactment decreases as the density of technology increases is to forget that it is not machinery but information that is processed by organizations. Technology generates a great deal of raw data, a process that places even greater demands on the organization to bracket those raw data so that they can be made manageable.

R. H. Hall (1977, p. 61) suggests that enactment varies according to the level of the person within the organization, a suggestion also implied by Child (1972). People in different positions have differential access to power, which means they have differential success in imposing their enactments on other people both inside and outside the organization. People who have the ear of powerful people and who gather information for them (e.g., congressional committees) also should produce binding, persuasive enactments.

Nevertheless, we should not be lulled into thinking that there is a simple linear relationship between height in a hierarchy and pervasiveness of one's enactments. The power of lower participants, mentioned in chapter 1, implies the potential for their enactments to be influential. Restrictions of output by lower participants are powerful enactments for higher participants (and they also remove equivocality from variable material inputs and variable co-workers). Binding enactments follow the lines of power within organizations and these lines often do not correspond to those implied by a formal depiction of ranks and positions.

A major caution implicit in this chapter is that analysts should be wary of asserting that they know what *the* environment consists of and should be eager to assert that environments are plural and that there is always *an* environment. Environments are multiple, exist in the eye of the beholder, and are more prone to breakage and reassembly than is often realized. A reasonable questions is, "So what?"

Whenever an organization tries to position itself to "see" the environment better, those actions should be examined from a different standpoint. The question should be, in positioning itself to see the environment, "What is the organization doing that might create the very displays it will see?" When an organization wants to see things, it usually positions itself so that in seeing things it is also seen. The environment that "knows" it is being watched is thereby rearranged and gives off different raw data than if it were blind. Under these conditions it is obvious that the organization sees much of itself when it wades into a data collection effort.

The enactment perspective implies that people in organizations should be more self-conscious about and spend more time reflecting on the actual things they *do*. If people imagine that the environment is separate from the organization and lies out there to be scanned so that effective responses can be produced, then they will spend their resources outfitting themselves with the equivalents of high-powered binoculars to improve acuity. If people recognize that they create many of their own environments, then all of that effort to improve acuity is irrelevant. The organization concerned about its own enactment needs to discover ways to partial out the effects of its own interventions from effects that would have happened had the observer never obtruded in the situation in the first place. An organization that is sensitive to the fact that it produces enacted environments will be less concerned with issues of truth and falsity and more concerned with issues of reasonableness. If environments are enacted then there is no such thing as a representation that is true or false, there simply are versions that are more and less reasonable. Thus, endless discussion of questions about whether we see things the way they really are, whether we are right, or whether something is true will be replaced by discussions that focus on questions such as What did we do? What senses can we make of those actions? What didn't we do? What next step best preserves our options and does least damage to our repertoire? What do these bruises mean? How did we ruin that equipment?

Organizations enact, adapt to, and survive amidst an environment of puns. A significant portion of their success or failure in managing the equivocalities

selection and organizing

associated with puns is due to the selection process. How that process works and what it works on are implied in the following examples.

Puns and Organizing

PUNS IN EVERYDAY LIFE

Organizational puns are everywhere. Car buyers frequently run into pun-like information when automobile makers raise their prices and at the same time give large discounts. Given a particular price for a car, is the car cheaper or more expensive than it was last year? The answer is nonobvious, and mulitple meanings exist. When department store buyers view the latest designs of famous fashion designers, they often applaud some of the exhibits. That applause is equivocal, however, because many buyers never clap for the creations they like best because they don't want their competitors to know what they will order (Goffman 1969, p. 16). A man said he was disappointed to find there was no suggestion box in the office because he wanted to put a suggestion in it about having one. A banker will lend you money only if you can prove you don't need it. When an analyst says, "The groups were broken down by sex," does he mean that the groups were partitioned into males and females or into more exhausted and less exhausted?

Military officers often receive equivocal directives. Field commanders get their inspiration from two doctrines: the chain-of-command doctrine which says follow orders, and the local-autonomy doctrine which says a commander is the chief in any region. Austria's highest military decoration is given to people who follow *both* doctrines. The Order of Maria Theresa is reserved

171

exclusively for officers who turned the tide of battle by taking matters into their own hands and actively disobeying orders. Of course, if things went wrong, they were not decorated but were court martialed for disobedience (Watzlawick 1976, pp. 24-25).

PUNS AND PARANOIA

The world of counter-intelligence and espionage consists of nothing but equivocal information. Consider what happens when an intelligence agent is turned:

> When, say, the British discover that one of their diplomats is a Russian spy and imprison him for forty-two years, and then five years later he escapes, what are the Russians to think? Is he their man and the information he gave them reliable? Was he all along a double agent, feeding them false information and then imprisoned briefly to give false assurances that he had not been working for the British? Was he loyal to Russia but discovered by the British and, unbeknownst to himself, given false information to feed to the Russians? Has he been allowed to escape so that the Russians would wrongly think that he had really been working for the British and therefore that his information had been false? And the British themselves, to know what import the Russians gave to this spy's information, must know whether indeed, the Russians think their man was really their man, and, if so, whether or not this had been known from the start by the British (Goffman 1969, p. 64).

The questions seem endless, and that is often the case with equivocal information. The potential corruptibility of all cues in intelligence work produces chronic puzzles. The day before the attack on Pearl Harbor, for example, an American naval attache informed Washington that he did not think there would be any surprise attack by the Japanese fleet because they were still stationed at their home base. He made this judgment because he observed that large crowds of sailors were walking in the streets of Tokyo the day before Pearl Harbor. What the attache did not know was that those sailors were actually soldiers *dressed* as sailors to deceive the Americans and conceal the departure of the fleet on its mission (Goffman 1969, p. 62).

The attache had looked for a fool-proof cue as to the behavior of the naval forces, but in doing so he became more vulnerable to exploitation.

> The very fact that the observer finds himself looking to a particular bit of evidence as an incorruptible check on what is or might be corrupted, is the very reason why he should be suspicious of this evidence; *for the best evidence for him is also the best evidence for the subject to tamper with.* However many moves the observer thinks he is ahead of the subject in an expression game, he ought to feel that it is just this sense of being ahead that the subject will find of maximum use in finally trapping the observer. The harder a spy must work to obtain startling secret information, the

more confidence his masters may put in his findings; but the very fact that masters do behave in this way provides the best reason why the enemy should be careful to leak false information only to those who have worked hardest to get the true facts, or insist that "turned" agents put up a show of having to work hard for the information planted with them . . . when the situation seems to be exactly what it appears to be, the closest likely alternative is that the situation has been completely faked; when fakery seems extremely evident the next most probable possibility is that nothing fake is present (Goffman 1969, pp. 62-69).

Lest it be thought that these examples have no bearing on organizations, it's important to realize that organizations have adversaries, compete for scarce resources, and mislead their competitors. Emery and Trist (1973) argue that organizations use decoys in *disturbed reactive environments*—environments that contain goals and noxiants that are clustered, rather than randomly dispersed, over space. This clustering means that some calculation and strategy is appropriate to attain good locations, which would not be the case when goals and noxiants are randomly dispersed. A disturbed reactive environment also has more than one organization of the same kind in it; the significance of this is that what one organization knows about the good and bad spots in the environment can also be known by the other organizations. This means that everybody wants to move to the same place.

Knowing this, they will wish to improve their own chances by hindering the other, and they will know that the other will not only wish to do likewise, but will know that they know this. . . . one has not simply to make sequential choices of actions (tactical decisions) such that each handles the immediate situation and yet they hang together by each bringing one closer to the strategic objective; instead one has to choose actions that will draw off the other organizations in order that one may proceed. The new element is that of choosing not only your own best tactic, but also of choosing which of someone else's tactics you wish to invoke. Movement towards a strategic objective in these environments seems, therefore, to necessitate choice at an intermediate level—choice of an operation or campaign in which are involved a planned series of tactical initiatives, predicted reactions by others and counteraction (Emery and Trist 1973, pp. 49-50).

PUNS AND MANAGING

Puns are everywhere (Crosbie 1977). People in organizations disregard that fact at their own peril. Having selected and imposed a single meaning on any display in front of them, people often discover with regret that additional meanings are just as plausible. If we simply extrapolate from the fact that most events in the world are overdetermined, and that more things operate on an event than are really necessary to produce it, then it follows that the significance of any event is plural. There are, of course, degrees of clarity, and some displays are more equivocal than other ones. But any organization that pays close attention to multiple indicators (any one of which could be corruptible or corrigible), that has a decent retention system which contains numerous possible images to be superimposed on enactments, that is active and stirs up the world in which it operates, and that is neither so large that it is its own environment nor so powerful that it can control all of the resources on which it is dependent, can expect a steady stream of puns to be singled out of its stream of experience.

Numerous formulations assume that organizations work on uncertainty (Duncan 1972; Downey and Slocum 1975; Manning 1977), ambiguity (Lerner 1976; Upton 1961), and other forms of indeterminacy. We have chosen to avoid this terminology and to use the idea that organizations try to manage equivocality for specific reasons. To understand these reasons consider the noun *equivoque.*

An equivoque is a pun, a term with at least two meanings, two disparate strings of thought tied together by an acoustic knot (Koestler 1978). Things that are equivocal do not lend themselves to definite classifications. They can always be classified as indications of two or more different objects and meanings. Equivoques are indeterminate, inscrutable, ambivalent, questionable, and they permit multiple meanings. It is important to realize that an input is not equivocal because it is devoid of meaning or has confused meaning (both of these connotations are associated with the words *ambiguity* and *uncertainty*). Instead, equivocal inputs have multiple significations. They are difficult to classify and manage precisely because they fit numerous classifications and might be indications of any one of several states of the world.

Thus, when we assert that organizations confront equivocality, we mean that organizations live in an environment of puns. The image we want to capture is not that of an environment that is disordered, indeterminant, and chaotic. Instead, we want to capture the image of an environment that is rich in the possible connections that could be imposed on an equally rich assortment of possible punctuated variables. We feel that equivocality is the term that most accurately preserves these nuances. It is the richness and multiplicity of meanings that can be superimposed on a situation that organizations must manage. An important characteristic of a pun is that its multiple meanings cannot be compromised. The meanings originally are distinct, they remain distinct, and the only way they can be managed is for some of the meanings to be suppressed or ignored or for the organization to alternate among its choices of various meanings.

Organizations often confront dilemmas (Aram 1976). The important point about the two horns in a dilemma is that those horns are distinct, cannot be merged or compromised, and whenever one horn is resolved the other one remains to haunt the organization. There are close resemblances between dilemmas and puns. The multiple meanings in a dilemma simply don't go away, nor do the multiple meanings in a pun go away. The organization must deal with those multiple meanings if by nothing more than ignoring or denying the existence of them. We are concerned with ways in which organizations make sense out of the world and of the fact that they spend the majority of their time superimposing a variety of meanings on the world. It is virtually impossible for one meaning to be imposed on the stream of experience and exhaust all of its possibilities, and it is for that reason that we assume equivocality is a prominent component of an organization's existence.

The Nature of Selection

In the formula "How can I know what I think until I see what I say?" selection is seeing. Selection is the organizational process that generates answers to the question "What's going on here?" The selection process selects meanings and interpretations directly and it selects individuals, departments, groups, or goals indirectly. The selection process houses decision-making, but it is crucial to remember that decision-making in the organizing model means selecting some interpretation of the world and some set of extrapolations from that interpretation and then using these summaries as constraints on subsequent acting.

The selection process is one of the most difficult to understand of all the processes associated with natural selection (Buckley 1967, p. 495). Selection often seems like a black box. One input to that black box is enacted raw data that potentially point to more than one feature of some ecological change. Another input is enacted interpretations that have worked in the past. Out of the black box comes an enacted environment and a moderately stable interpretation of what the person has recently been up to. What we will try to develop is one version of what might occur inside that black box.

To recapitulate quickly, the organizing model asserts that members of organizations initially generate and/or bracket such things as words, actions, and happenings, all of which are equivocal. These equivocal inputs become more sensible through transformations performed on them in the selection process. The selection process, by means of various interlocked cycles, selects meanings that are imposed on these equivocalities. Selection occurs in the sense that many of the possible meanings that are tried simply fail, either because they are not useful or because the present data are inconsistent with them. The meanings that are tried come both from previous experience (signified by the causal arrow from retention to selection) and from patterns implicit in the enactments themselves (signified by the causal arrow from enactment to selection).

ARTIFICIAL SELECTION AND ORGANIZING

To appreciate the unique form that selection takes in organizing, we must reexamine the nature of selection in biological evolution. Domestic animals exist in bewildering variety, and some of this variety is produced by people who select and breed stock with desired attributes. Through the breeder's acts of volition and interventions to keep desirable individuals from breeding with less desirable ones, groups develop that are characterized by novel selected properties. If an intelligent agent making choices were not present, could the same shaping process occur?

It was Darwin's genius to demonstrate that differential reproductive success is a natural selection device that acts much like a breeder who makes methodical interventions (Darwin 1844, in DeBeer 1958). In its simplest form, Darwin's argument was this:

> Organisms differ from one another. They produce more young than the available resources can sustain. Those best suited to survive pass on the expedient properties to their offspring, while inferior forms are eliminated. Subsequent generations therefore are more like the better adapted ancestors and the result is a gradual modification, or evolution. Thus the cause of the evolutionary adaptation is differential reproductive success (Ghiselin 1969, p. 46)

To talk about selection in organizations is to reach back beyond Darwin's *natural selection* and revive the image of *artificial selection*. The modifier *natural* implies that features of the environment differentially favor the reproduction of some mutations and the destruction of others. All of this fitting, failing, mutating, and reproducing is said to be unguided, essentially random, or at least underrationalized.

Events in organizations are somewhat different. Selection is guided less by caprice than by the intention of people to be methodical, deliberate, and plausible—to act, in short, like breeders rather than dice players. Intentions commonly fail (Salancik 1977), and for this reason organizational selection often exhibits the same haphazard quality that is associated with natural selection. But haphazard moments in organizations are byproducts of bounded rationality applied by fallible rationalizers. Ideas and interpretations, as much as things, exert selective forces in organizations. If perceptions are important in the functioning of organizations (D. Silverman 1971), then there has to be a mechanism whereby perceptual environments confer differential advantage on people, positions, or pluralities. And it is the enacted environment imposed on action and interpretation by selection and retention that supplies this mechanism. The enacted environment is artificial rather than natural in the sense that it is laced with preferences, purposes, idiosyncratic punctuations, desires, selective perceptions, and designs. It is the environment of the breeder.

ENACTED ENVIRONMENTS AS SELECTION MECHANISMS

When people in organizations select actions and interpretations, they try to be reasonable in making these selections, even if they have only modest success doing so. What people impose in their attempts to be reasonable are previous interpretations of causal sequences that have worked—that is, cause maps of previously enacted environments. When current equivocalities are filtered through these prior enactments, some things go unnoticed while others are labeled as familiar, strange, relevant, and so on. In all cases the enacted environment is acting as a surrogate for the natural environment. And it is enacted versions of reality that supply the rocks, pools, edges, nutrients, shade, and enemies amongst which people with equivocal power and equivocal positions fit with varying degrees of success.

The enacted environment substitutes for the natural environment only when it is unequivocal and credited, only when people who are trying to understand a current equivocal input compose a selection process using many rules and few cycles and treat the incoming input as a known rather than unknown commodity. Or, in the case of the enactment process, crediting of an unequivocal enacted environment results in the person literally doing what he has done before, regardless of the current ecological changes. Credited enactment will appear stereotypic, routinized, and will bear a close resemblance to a standard operating procedure. Crediting of past enacted environments can readily undo, reverse, or modify ecological changes. It is this sense in which enacted environments can dominate "objective" environments in organizing.

This portrait of selection is conservative and suggests one set of reasons why organizations show inertia and slowness to change. Actions and interpretations accommodate to enacted environments, not to current natural environments. People try to fit novel interpretations and actions into what they've known all along. And when something doesn't fit with the past, it's often discarded or misread. That suggests why newcomers, entrepreneurs, marginal men, outsiders, hatchet men, and other anomalies (Rickards and Freedman 1978) are crucial sources of innovations.

Members of organizations can also introduce their own anomalies by partially discrediting their enacted environments (chapter 8). Members entertain systematic, chronic doubt concerning the validity of past enactments. In this way they can avoid being victimized by their stand-in for the natural environment, by their parochial volition, and by their bounded methodicalness.

SELECTION IN ORGANIZATIONAL THEORY

To conclude this introduction, we will examine quickly the views of three investigators who comment on the nature of environmental selection in organizations.

John Child (1972) suggests that environmental influences may not exert an overwhelming constraint on organizations because decision makers are often loosely coupled with environments. Just like volitional animal breeders, decision makers can (1) select among several structures, all of which are appropriate in their present environmental niche, (2) choose the type of environment in which they will operate, (3) reshape the environments in which they exist, and (4) improve the accuracy of their perceptions of the environment, thereby enhancing their chances to control it. In all of these cases, an unmediated environment is not the major source of selection criteria, or if it is, this influence can be softened.

If decision makers intervene between the environment and its effects inside the organization, then selection criteria become lodged more in those actors than in the environment. What the actors attend to and enact, the cues they use, their reasons for using those cues, their patterns of inattention, and their processes for scanning and monitoring all become selection criteria.

The question of whether enacted reality or "objective" reality contains more compelling selection criteria is handled by Aldrich and Pfeffer:

> If the organization is severely constrained by the environment, as in a very competitive market, then perception is not important. The personnel in the organization will operate and perceive effectively or else it will soon go out of existence. Perception becomes important to the extent that the organization is insulated from or immune to environmental effects. To the extent that the organization is not tightly constrained, variations in perceptions of organizational reality have more importance in understanding organizational structures and processes (1976, p. 89).

Finally, Starbuck (1976) has written insightfully about evolutionary ideas and has also emphasized that environmental determinism shouldn't be over-estimated. "The constraints imposed by environmental properties are not, in general, sufficiently restrictive to determine uniquely the characteristics of their organizational residents" (1976, p. 1105). Environments change continuously, as do competing firms, so consistent environmental properties are unlikely to exist. Furthermore, given the loose coupling between environments and organizations, it is likely that a variety of behaviors will enable the organization to survive in the same setting. Starbuck goes even further and raises the interesting possibility that "organization environments are themselves largely composed of other organizations that are all changing at the same time, so that both organizations and their environments are evolving simultaneously *toward better fitness for each other*" (1976, p. 1106; emphasis added).

Before taking a closer look at equivocal inputs to selection, one additional nuance of selection criteria should be noted. Social systems commonly use two types of selection criteria: criteria relevant to the internal functioning of the system, and criteria relevant to the external functioning of the system with its environment. It is rare for equal attention to be given to both sets of criteria, even though both are instrumental to survival. Even more crucial is the fact that actions which satisfy internal selectors may provide the illusion that all is going well (the system is humming) when in fact virtually no attention has been paid to the changing environment and the placid group is in imminent danger of bankruptcy.

These deceptive internal criteria focus mainly on the stability of the system. Habit-meshing is an example:

A process of habit meshing takes place within any organization, in that each person's habits are a part of the environment of others. Encounters which are punishing tend to extinguish [the habit]. . . . Rewarding encounters increase the strength of behavioral tendencies on the part of both parties. Thus any social organization tends to move in the direction of internal compatibility, *independently of increased adaptiveness* (Campbell 1965b, p. 33; emphasis added).

If this discussion of habit-meshing is placed alongside the earlier discussion of interlocking, it can be seen that successful interlocking (habit-meshing) can occur without any necessary increase in the productivity or viability of the system.

Inputs to Selection

The raw material fed into selection consists of equivocal enactments and cause maps of varying equivocality; the purpose of this section is to say more about the nature of these materials. The justification for this enlargement is that the nature of the materials dictates the nature of the process that must be posited if these materials are to be transformed into sensible outputs.

Initially we need to distinguish equivocation from a closely related communication hazard, noise. In standard depictions of communication (e.g., B. Mc. Johnson 1977), some source sends a message along some transmission channel in the direction of a recipient, and that message eventually reaches the recipient as an output from the system. Noise is present when, knowing what the input is, you cannot predict what the output will be when it reaches the recipient. The same input can generate a variety of outputs because noise is added during the time of transmission and one can never be sure what will eventually be received. Noise is like a second communication. It introduces messages into the channel which neither the original source nor the destination can predict. The noise implied here should not be confused with noises like static on a radio, because that kind of noise is a fixed distortion and can be filtered out if necessary. The noise being depicted here has variable effects on the transmission; consequently, filtration is more difficult.

The prediction problem with equivocation is just the opposite of the prediction problem with noise. We now take the vantage point of the receiver and look back toward the person who sends the message. The problem of equivocality for a recipient is that, given an output, the receiver can't decide what input generated it. Two or more possible inputs are implied in that single output message, and the recipient faces the question of which of those possible meanings are the appropriate ones. Frick (1959) represents these differences in Fig. 7.1.

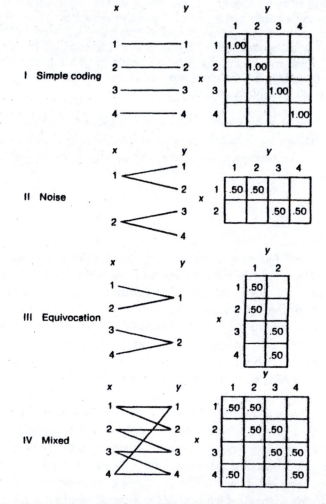

Fig. 7.1 Schema of the possible correspondences between the inputs (x) to a channel and the outputs (y). The right-hand figure in each case represents the conditional probability matrix; cell entries are the probability of y, given x = $p_x(y)$. The conditional probabilities indicated for Cases II, III, and IV are arbitrary. (From Frick 1959.)

A good example of an equivocal output is a figure-ground reversal (Teuber 1974; Jordan 1968; Kahnemann 1973). With these figures it is difficult for the observer to know what input generated the display, because more than one input appears to be present. A figure-ground reversal, like a pun, has two or more meanings that can't be compromised.

One of the best examples of a figure-ground reversal is Miller and Buckhout's description of the Mach-Eden illusion:

> Take a strip of paper about 2 inches wide and 8 inches long and fold it three times as shown in [Fig. 7.2]. Place it on the table resting on the two folds, with the outside flanges sticking up. Now close one eye. Imagine that the two corners labeled *x* in [Fig. 7.2] are not down on the table, but are actually standing up above it, as if they were on the top edge of a standing screen. (A similar reversal is more easily achieved while looking at the two-dimensional drawing in [Fig. 7.2], but with a little persistence you can also reverse the three-dimensional object.) When you have succeeded in getting the reversal to occur, slowly move your head to the left and right. If your perception of the paper is reversed, you will see it tilt and twist in a surprising way. Once again, moving your head moves the world.
>
> This phenomenon can be made to seem even more dramatic if you will hold the paper, one end in each hand. Now, with the figure reversed, rotate your hands toward your body. The paper almost feels alive as it twists in the opposite direction! (1973, p. 133).

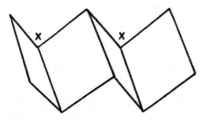

Fig. 7.2 The Mach-Eden illusion. Fold a strip of paper as shown and examine it with one eye. Imagine that the corners X, which in fact lie on the supporting surface, are on the top edge of a standing screen and that the illumination comes from the opposite side. While the three-dimensional figure is reversed, head movements produce apparent movements in the object itself. (From Miller and Buckhout 1973.)

Fritz Heider (1958, pp. 35-37) has developed a related analysis of equivocality that enables us to portray more accurately some of the problems organizations confront when they encounter noise and puns. Organizations typically prefer the situation in which a specific sign is connected back to a specific property ("simple coding" in Fig. 7.1). In this case people only have to learn specific connections between signs and things and to memorize a vocabulary of these connections consisting only of nouns. A person perceiving one of these signs simply reacts as if also perceiving clearly the more distant object. A raised eyebrow signifies that a person is *always* suspicious, a sudden drop in criminal activity is always a sign of a pending revolution within a country, a sudden increase in miles traveled by company aircraft is always a sign of the company being reorganized, appointments of an insider to key positions in the company would always indicate that the company's performance will improve, and so on. If the world was like this, there would be no problem of equivocation.

Obviously, enactments complicate this picture considerably. The patterns in nature are offered to us less often in the form of unequivocal nouns and more often in the form of ambiguous words, synonyms, and adjectives. These ambiguities are illustrated in Fig. 7.3, adapted from Heider.

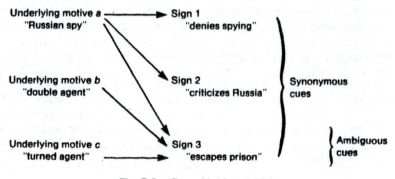

Fig. 7.3 (From Heider 1958.)

In Fig. 7.3 it can be seen that there is a direct parallel between an ambiguous cue and equivocal enactments. An ambiguous cue can be coordinated with two or more original events. In the example drawn here, Sign 3, escaping from prison after five years, could be caused by the fact that this is a real Russian spy escaping to go home, a British spy "escaping" to improve his chances of infiltrating deeper and getting better intelligence, or a real Russian spy who, during his imprisonment, was given asylum, recruited into British espionage work, and "released" to get additional information. The meaning of the escape is equivocal to employees of both the Russian and British intelligence communities.

Heider argues that the placement of equivocal items into a context is one of the better ways to clarify them. Just as ambiguous words become more clearly defined when they're placed in sentences, the equivocality of cues is reduced when they are embedded in the total situation. Meaning is suggested only when one takes account of surrounding stimuli. To take account of more stimuli may require that observation of equivocality be extended over time so that sequences of events can occur and be observed. In a description that fits neatly into Neisser's perceptual cycle, Heider says of himself and equivocal objects,

> I often have to watch the object taking part in events, interacting with other objects, or I have to handle it to perceive its causal possibilities. I may have to bend a wire in order to cognize its pliability or to scratch a stone to cognize its hardness. In examining a machine, I may move some parts to see with what other parts they are connected, and in testing a car, I must at least drive it. Then the causal possibilities are mediated to me through *events*. As we have seen, however, a look at the static object often tells us much about the way it would perform. It is probably fair to say that the stimulus fields basic for person perception are usually *more extended in time* than those relevant to thing perception (1958, p. 39).

The fact of embeddedness and the need for context to shrink the population of puns and the meaning of puns reiterate themes found in previous chapters. When retained cause maps are superimposed on enactments, equivocality is reduced because those enactments are embedded in the past and they are also differentiated into a figure-ground relationship in the present.

Two final examples will simulate the nature of equivocality as it is experienced by people in organizations. First, here's a word: *teralbay*. If you arrange the letters of that word they spell an everyday English word. What is that English word?

Given that output, it is extraordinarily difficult to predict the input. The input might have been *tearably*, *trayable*, or *rateably*, except that none of those are English words. Notice that in managing this equivocality, people may use relatively few rules to form a quasi-selection process and may try several interpretations that fit those rules. For example, people might try a simple rule: alternate consonants and vowels. That simple rule will lead to a large number of cycles applied to the input, and people who do this should generate more possible answers than people who try to solve this "scientifically" using lots of rules that allow for few interpretations. The important point about this example is that it illustrates an equivocal state of the world. Given an output, there are numerous possibilities that could have produced that scrambled word.

Figure 7.4 contains a second example of equivocality, an example that should reinstate pleasurable childhood activities (mild equivocality can be pleasurable). Given the output in Fig. 7.4 of 342 numbered points, it is difficult to reconstruct the original solid figure which produced that pattern of dots.

As simple as those two examples may seem, they contain most of what is found in equivocal information processed by organizations. Organizations run into strange words like *teralbay* every day. And when made less equivocal, those words prove to be consequential. Swiss watch-makers run into strange words like *digital*, *Seiko*, and *chip* and are never the same again. Kodak runs into the unfamiliar word *Ilfex* and discovers that this manufacturer is rapidly reversing Kodak's dominance in the field of photographic paper. Polaroid sees a strange phrase, *The Handle*, and finds that the input which produced that label is competition for the instant camera market.

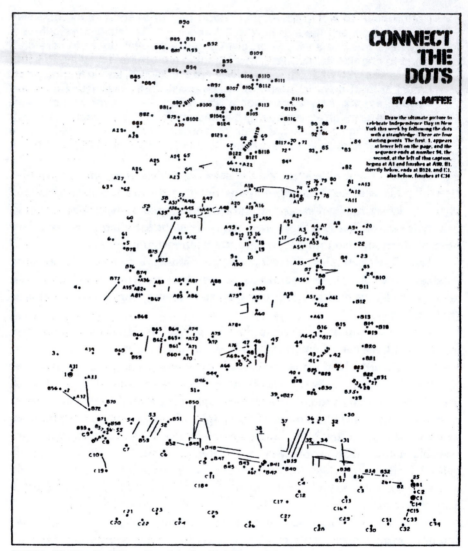

Figure 7.4

Organizations similarly see the equivalent of strange drawings, piecemeal divestitures, strange acquisitions ("Kaman: How to Bring Aerospace Know-how to the Guitar Industry," 1978), nonrational personnel shakeups (Metz 1978), and in each case try to figure out what inputs produced those puzzling outcomes. And usually, when faced with such equivocalities, through one assemblage or another, there will usually be a *betrayal* of the answer and a resolution of the equivocality.

ENACTMENT → SELECTION

Frequently it is difficult to distinguish between enactment and selection because some sense-making occurs in both. A tangible example of this is the fact that Neisser's perceptual cycle fits as readily into this chapter (schemas select meanings, are superimposed, resemble cause maps) as into the enactment chapter (sampling is acting).

In the formula "How can I know what I think until I see what I say?" saying (enactment) can itself be clearer or more opaque. Depending on the soundness of sentences when one says something, what can be seen in that saying will vary dramatically. Once we recognize that enactment can produce variable raw materials for selection to process, then it is clear that some material can already be sensible by the time it is intercepted by a selection process where many rules and few cycles will be applied to it.

Enactments often consist of trial-and-error behavior, but it remains for the processes of selection to impose on those earlier struggles the interpretation that trial-and-error was underway. If unlabeled fitting occurs during enactment, this means that one way in which prior actions can be interpreted *is* in terms of their fittedness. Fittedness, then, is one way retrospectively to make sense of earlier activities. Fitness is a judgmental label that is superimposed on data generated by enactment processes after-the-fact.

The ecological changes present when trial and error is undertaken seem to favor certain forms of action, forms that have been variously described as structural looseness (Bidwell 1965), loose coupling (March and Olsen 1976; Weick 1976b), plasticity (Gould 1975), and defenses in depth (G. W. Bateson 1972). McAdams describes ecological changes that dominate in social environments, noting in particular that there is a high premium

> on the capacity of a social system to make rapid, large scale adaptive shifts in order to cope with unanticipated conditions. There would also appear to be a premium on structural fluidity and ambiguity that would permit alternative, even opposed, adaptive strategies to co-exist. From this point of view there are selective advantages accruing to human social systems that foster and protect innovation, pluralistic differentiation, tolerance of divergence, skepticism toward received wisdom and tradition, dissidence with respect to institutionalized leadership, and even alienation (1976, p. 351).

Whatever people do during enactment, whether it be operating without goals, misplacing personnel, operating a technology that no one understands, improvising instead of forecasting, dwelling on opportunities, inventing solutions rather than borrowing them, cultivating impermanence, arguing, or doubting, if those "strange" actions promote rapid adaptation to shifting conditions, they're likely to persist, be enacted repeatedly, and to be frequent inputs to the selection process.

By their very nature these contradictory, hypocritical, disorganized, casual actions are the epitome of equivocality even as they are also the epitome of adaptability. This creates problems because as selection processes remove equivocality from these underorganized enactments, those same processes may also inadvertently remove adaptability from these enactments.

Our concern about the difficulty of preserving the basic equivocality of loosely coupled enactments is not idle, because one of the most common perceptual errors is that people overestimate the amount of unity, orderliness, and clarity that is present in an input. This tendency has been known for a long time and is preserved in Bacon's *Idols of the Tribe*, the first of which reads: "The human understanding, from its peculiar nature, easily supposes a greater degree of order and equality in things than it really finds" (cited in Campbell 1959, p. 5).

The problem with adapting in organizations is that structurally loose enactment is apt to be misread and "tightened" during the reflection and perception that occur in selection. The perceiver will imagine that a more orderly action was responsible for his adaptive success than in fact was the case. At least perceptually, the problem for organizations is *not* one of entropy and the loss of order, it's just the opposite. Orderliness is overestimated and erroneously given credit for adaptive success. Having been credited, orderly actions are implemented again in the future, perhaps tightened even more, and suddenly (Moore 1964) the organizations finds itself out of touch with changes that are occurring and finds itself saddled with an antiquated, tight structure.

This speculation about the processes by which organizations stagnate is consistent with the mechanics by which the selection process is assembled. If an equivocal input to selection is misread and treated as orderly, then more rules and fewer cycles are applied to it, which means it is sealed off from discussion, treated as an understood procedure, and people forego the opportunity to learn precisely how their loosely organized actions are helping—not hindering—them. Their success in the environment will seem to be due to the orderliness, not the disorderliness, of their procedures. Since these procedures are mistakenly treated as unequivocal, little further attention is given to them, residual equivocality persists, and, over time, people in the organization develop even less understanding of themselves and what they are doing. This alienation develops because people treat that which is loosely structured and equivocal as orderly and known.

To summarize, when it is asserted that selection is partially constrained by enactment, the following is implied:

1 Enactment (saying) and selection (seeing) both generate plausible interpretations of equivocality, but the interpretations imposed during selection are fuller, more varied, and remove more equivocality.

2 In the case of organizations, ecological changes favor adaptive actions that are flexible, loosely structured, and improvised.

3 Loosely structured enactments are difficult to label and may be destroyed when people treat them as more orderly, unified, and integrated than they actually are.

RETENTION → SELECTION

The other major input to selection comes from the retention process. While retention will be described more fully in the next chapter, the reader needs to have a working acquaintance with it to understand selection. Retention is a reservoir of beliefs, and when we assert that believing is seeing (I'll see it/select it when I believe it/retain it) this is signified by a causal arrow going from retention to selection. If believing *is* seeing, then retention is credited (+), constrains selection, and provides crucial inputs to it.

Most of what is contained in retention consists of enacted environments stored in the form of labeled variables that are causally connected. These enacted environments are fed back to the selection process and act as surrogate environments for the external world in selecting particular interpretations. The enacted environment, when it acts as a constraint on selection, *is* an environment into which events currently being processed and labeled exhibit a better or worse fit. Here the analog of individuals and species fitting into a particular physical environment is instructive. What is being argued is that during selection, organizational members select those labels, explanations, interpretations, and meanings that allow new enactments to be fitted into old, enacted environments. The enacted environment, in other words, acts as a stand-in for the physical environment and does its editing. The physical environment could be said to delegate its selective function to the selection process and to the enacted environments stored in retention.

Given this line of argument, the phrase "survival of the fittest" means in organizing that what "survives" from any confrontation with ecological changes are people, events, and actions which, when labled, find a place in existing cause maps. Survival takes this form if and only if retention is *credited* in selection. If retention is discredited, then people, events, and actions that differ from previously enacted environments will be given greater attention, fresher labels, newer connections, and will have more likelihood of being stored where they will then assimilate and accommodate to whatever content remains in retention.

Thus, (1) the enacted environment rather than the physical environment does the selecting, (2) the typical way in which an organization splits decisions is for retained information to be credited in the selection process and discredited in the enactment process, (3) retention and believing control seeing just as much as seeing controls believing, (4) fit with an enacted environment means that interpretations and labels are consistent with previous enacted environments.

These assertions are plausible because people have a predilection for pattern regularity and unequivocal behavior orientations (Jones and Gerard 1967). Another way that an environment can have an effect is for this effect to be consistent over long periods of time. This consistent effect in organizations is most likely to be exerted by enacted environments that have been edited, revised, and updated through activities in the retention process.

As a final point, it should be apparent that selection always works backward and is behind. The only thing that can be selected and preserved is something that is already there. This simple reality keeps getting lost amidst the preoccupation of people in organizations with planning, forecasting, anticipating, and predicting. Organizations persistently spend time formulating strategy, an activity that literally makes little sense given the arguments advanced here. Organizations formulate strategy *after* they implement it, not before. Having implemented something—anything—people can then look back over it and conclude that what they have implemented is a strategy. The more common (and misleading) way to look at this sequence in organizations is to say that first comes strategy and then comes implementation. That commonplace recipe ignores the fact that meaning is always imposed after the fact and only after elapsed actions are available for review.

A more detailed picture of the retrospective sense-making associated with selection follows.

How Selection Operates

SELECTION AND REQUISITE VARIETY

If equivocal inputs are to be made sensible retrospectively, then most of the equivocality in those enactments must first be registered. This introduces the important concept of requisite variety (Conant and Ashby 1970). The law of requisite variety "states that the variety within a system must be at least as great as the environmental variety against which it is attempting to regulate itself. Put more succinctly, only variety can regulate variety" (Buckley 1968, p. 495). It's because of requisite variety that organizations have to be preoccupied with keeping sufficient diversity inside the organization to sense accurately the variety present in ecological changes outside it.

As an example of the principle of requisite variety, if a photographer has to photograph 20 subjects, each of which is at a different distance from the camera, then his camera has to have at least 20 distinct settings if all of the negatives are to be brought to a uniform density and sharpness. If the camera has fewer than 20 settings it lacks requisite variety and will not register with sufficient detail enough of that environment so that control can be maintained over it. Control in this case means depicting with accuracy.

When applied to organizations the implication of requisite variety is that organizational processes that are applied to equivocal inputs must themselves be equivocal. If a simple process is applied to complicated data, then only a small portion of that data will be registered, attended to, and made unequivocal. Most of the input will remain untouched and will remain a puzzle to people concerning what is up and why they are unable to manage it.

The point that the equivocality of processes must match the equivocality of inputs can also be illustrated in terms of person perception. With respect to the ability of a person to comprehend accurately what another person is like, Allport makes the following assertion:

> As a rule, people cannot comprehend others who are more complex and subtle than they. The single track mind has little feeling for the conflicts of the versatile mind. . . . Would it not follow, therefore, that the psychiatrist, since he deals with intricate mental tangles, should benefit by the possession of a complex personality? If he has neurotic difficulties of his own and manages them well, might they not add to his qualifications? (1961, p. 508).

Restated in the terminology used here, psychiatric understanding improves to the extent that the equivocality in the person who processes information (the psychiatrist) matches the equivocality in the information produced by the patient.

To anticipate a later argument, the inability of people in organizations to tolerate equivocal processing may well be one of the most important reasons why they have trouble. It is their unwillingness to meet equivocality in an equivocal manner that produces failure, nonadaptation, autism, isolation from reality, psychological costs, and so on. It is the unwillingness to disrupt order, ironically, that makes it impossible for the organization to create order. Order consists of data in which equivocality has been suppressed, but equivocality can be suppressed only after processes have first registered that equivocality. Accurate registering requires the matching of processes to the characteristics of their inputs. If people cherish the unequivocal but are unwilling to participate in the equivocal, then their survival becomes more problematic.

INTERLOCKED CYCLES AND REQUISITE VARIETY

In the organizing model, the assembly rules determine the equivocality of the process and the extent to which it exhibits requisite variety. Whenever some difference impinges on people, there is the question, What's up? To answer that question people build a process to handle the difference. If the difference is treated as a familiar difference, then the recipe for building the process is detailed and the resulting process is specific and contains few cycles. If the difference is strange, the recipe is usually brief and the process is sprawling.

A sprawling, equivocal process contains many independent elements that have few internal constraints. Those three properties of (1) many elements, (2) independence of elements, and (3) weak internal constraint are the properties that are associated with a good medium (Heider 1959) that registers accurately the things to which it is exposed. And it is this detailed registering that has to occur if an equivocal input is to be dealt with in all of its variety (Weick 1978).

Said differently, in the organizing model, the potential variety within the organization that can match the variety outside it is contained in the interlocked cycles that are assembled into processes. When few rules are used to assemble these processes, the cycles assembled into them are more diverse and contain more variety. That variety inside the process registers more of the variety in equivocal inputs to the process, and this more accurate registering increases the probability that people can produce an enacted environment that is reasonable, sensible, useful, and cumulative with other experience. When few rules are used to assemble a process, there is more independence among more cycles, a condition that enhances sensitivity.

A graphic representation of the point that registration depends on the number of independent elements that are externally constrained is found in the contour gauge pictured in Fig. 7.5. This gauge is six inches long, holds 180 steel spines, and when this gauge is pressed against some firm object, the outlines of that object are impressed on the gauge and this imprint can be duplicated somewhere else. If the object being registered is equivocal, then this equivocality can be registered more thoroughly as the number of spines in the gauge increases, as the independence among the spines increases, and as there is an increase in the degree to which spines are moved by the object rather than by adjacent spines or imperfections in the bar that holds the spines.

There are numerous examples of gradations in registering. To register wind currents, sand is a better medium than rock. Sand has more independent elements that are under external constraint than does rock. If you put one earring under a piece of burlap and the other earring under a piece of silk, and if you ask a person to feel the earrings through the silk and burlap and describe them to you, silk will be a better mediator than burlap. There are more independent elements that are externally constrained by the earring in the case

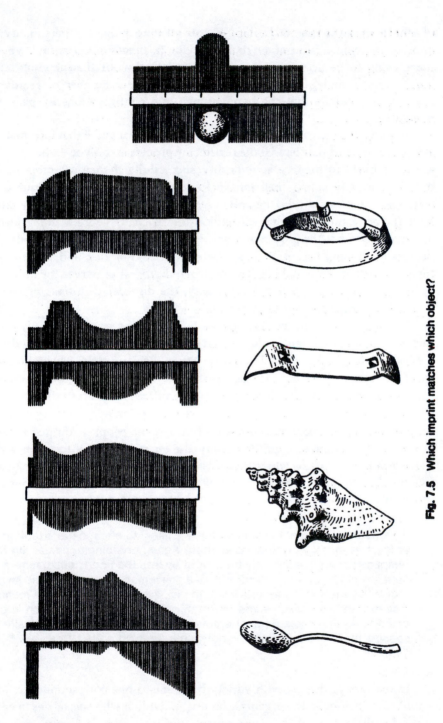

Fig. 7.5 Which imprint matches which object?

of silk than in the case of burlap. If you want to judge the personality of another individual from nonverbal behavior (a precarious pastime), you're more likely to be accurate if you watch facial behavior than if you watch hands, torsos, or legs because the face has a greater number of relatively independent muscles that can be combined into configurations by personal tendencies.

If there is equivocal information in the environment and if that information is most likely to be registered if the registering process is equivocal, then people are most likely to manage equivocality successfully if they assemble many different, loosely constrained interlocked cycles into a process. Equivocal processes are rather untidy, they often work at cross purposes, and they often have the appearance of being wasteful and inefficient. Those seeming ineffi-ciencies testify that the process is *working*, not that it has malfunctioned. The process is working because it has registered discontinuities, and it preserves them for further sense-making. The disordered process preserves the indepen-dence of its sensing elements; in this way, the disordered process preserves more of the fine grain in the enactments.

When faced with the need for requisite variety, there really are only three things an organization can do. First, it can establish a one-to-one correspondence between variety in the controller and variety in the controlled. One policeman would be assigned full-time to each person in the nation, and if that citizen began to depart from what is legal the police officer would restrain him. In a situation of one-to-one correspondence there is perfect requisite variety. Britain, for example, has one policeman for every five hundred people in the population. From the standpoint of requisite variety the question is how to arrange the policemen to win a game where the odds against any individual policeman are five hundred to one. To see the force of the law of requisite variety, consider this point:

> An embattled gang of thugs in a house is likely to engage the attention of *at least as many* individual policemen. Again, one single maniac on the rampage cannot conceivably be caught by less than one policeman—and certainly not by one five-hundredth of a policeman. At this point, the law of requisite variety really asserts itself. In fact, it is very clear that one maniac may turn out to engage *some* of the attention of *every* policeman in the country. As the whole force attempts to generate the variety requisite to sponge up this one criminal's riot-generating potential (Beer 1975, p. 195).

In the case of dealing with variety by a one-to-one correspondence, this would mean having in the organization one individual who specializes in each particular dimension of the environment and who attends to nothing else. Aside from the motivational issues in trying to implement that solution, the solution of one-to-one correspondence makes for extraordinary problems of coordination and piecing together the highly molecular single observations into an understandable whole.

The second way to deal with variety is to reduce it, an option that is open to only the most powerful organizations. Variety is reduced by interorganizational networks, cartels, monopolies, and other agreements among potential competitors in turbulent environments. These arrangements can simplify environments and shrink variety. However, these kinds of solutions are real alternatives to only a handful of organizations. Furthermore, simplifying an enacted environment may also simplify the enactor, which creates the problem of requisite variety all over again.

The third alternative, and the one toward which we are most sympathetic, is to complicate the controller. This intentional complication increases the controller's variety relative to the variety in the inputs that the controller processes. A complicated individual embodies in one place the several sensors implied when there is one sensor assigned to each variable. This embodiment means that the complicated individual can sense variations in a larger environment, select what need *not* be attended to, what will *not* change imminently, what *won't* happen, and by this selection the individual is able to amplify his control variety. He safely (that is, insightfully) ignores that which will not change, concentrates on that which will, and much like the neurotic psychiatrist is able to anticipate significant environmental variation when and where it occurs. Complicated observers take in more. They see patterns that less complicated people miss, and they exploit these subtle patterns by concentrating on them and ignoring everything else.

Our enthusiasm for complication does not blind us to some of the problems it creates. To "manage" several loosely coupled cycles is potentially more difficult, more time-consuming, more prone to inequities than is the case when one has to manage relatively homogeneous tightly coupled units where delegation and giving orders is legitimate and expected.

There is the further danger with complication that openness to equivocality paralyzes action. Conceivably when the equivocality of the world is sensed most fully, the absurdity of any one interpretation or action also becomes sensed fully (Goodwin 1971). That is the danger that faces any person who is open to equivocality and who participates in it in the hope of managing more of it more wisely.

We assume that on the average, complicated organizations survive because they align their actions and beliefs retrospectively and achieve an unequivocal behavior orientation with regard to a greater proportion of the environment than is true for the individual who retrospects an impoverished, shallow version of his acting and his surroundings. No one is ever free to do something he can't think of. That's why requisite variety produces adaptation.

Selection as Retrospective Sense-making

Action precedes thought (Bem 1974; Zimbardo 1969). People continually are rewarded when they act as if the opposite were true, when they try to think before they act. Planners in organizations typically earn more than doers, but favoring those who think before they act is mischievous because you have to do or say something first so that you can then discover what you thought, decided, or did. You'll seldom know what you've been up to until it's too late, until the words have already been uttered or the action is already finished.

The nature of selection becomes clearer if we examine two distinct forms of time: (1) pure duration and (2) discrete segments with spatial and temporal properties.

Pure duration can be described as a stream of experience. Notice that experience is singular, not plural. To talk about experiences implies discreteness and separateness of contents, and pure duration does not have this segmental quality. Pure duration is a coming to be and passing away that has no contours, boundaries, or differentiations (Schutz 1967, p. 47).

The reader may object that his experience seldom has this quality of a continuous merging and melting of phases into phases. In fact, experience as we know it has the quality of being bounded, distinct, episodic, particular. But the only way a person can sense the separateness of experience is to step *outside* the stream of experience and direct attention to it. When a person does this it is only possible to direct attention at what has already passed, not at what is yet to come. All understanding originates in reflection and looking backward.

The nature of the reflective glance is captured in the following quotation:

> When, by my act of reflection, I turn my attention to my living experience, I am no longer taking up my position within the stream of pure duration, I am no longer simply living within that flow. The experiences are appre-hended, distinguished, brought into relief, marked out from one another; the experiences which were constituted as phases within the flow of duration now become objects of attention as constituted experiences. What had first been constituted as a phase now stands out as a full-blown experience, no matter whether the Act of attention is one of reflection or of reproduction. . . . *For the Act of attention*—and this is of major importance for the study of meaning—presupposes an elapsed, passed-away experi-ence—in short, one that is already in the past (Schutz 1967, p. 51).

George Herbert Mead made the same point:

> We are conscious always of what we have done, never of doing it. We are always conscious directly only of sensory processes, never of motor

proceses; hence we are conscious of motor processes only through sensory processes, which are their resultants (1956, p. 136).

Actions are known only when they have been completed.

RETROSPECT AND HISTORICIZING

Much sense-making in the selection process can be viewed as writing plausible accounts, histories, and sequences for enactments. Equivocality is removed when an enactment is supplied with a history that could have generated it.

> In place of the view that decisions are made as the occasions require, an alternative formulation needs to be entertained. It consists of the possibility that the person defines retrospectively the decisions that have been made. The outcome comes before the decision.... The rules of decision making in daily life ... may be much more preoccupied with the problem of assigning outcomes their legitimate history than with the question of deciding before the actual occasion of choice the conditions under which one, among a set of alternative possible courses of action, will be elected (Garfinkel 1967, p. 114).

The enactment process produces outcomes that are interpreted by the selection process as if a decision had been made. A search is made for what that decision might be. This means that the situation is decision-*interpreted*, not decision-guided.

The same line of analysis can be applied to career planning. Careers usually turn out to be a set of actions that are career-interpreted after the fact rather than career-planned before the fact (Weick 1976a). Behavior isn't goal-directed, it's goal-interpreted. In each of these cases the effect precedes the cause, the response precedes the stimulus, the output precedes the input. Effects, responses, and outputs are pretexts to search backward and discover plausible events that could have produced them. In each of these cases the project is made sensible when a history is imputed to it, but the history is constructed after the project is concluded, not before.

Three somewhat novel demonstrations show how historicizing an outcome facilitates sense-making. In each case, when people take an event and place it in the past they describe it more richly than when they take the same event and place it in the future.

To see this for yourself, get a group of people and divide them in half. Privately tell one group, "A professor *will take* a six-week sabbatical trip in Europe; write out his itinerary"; tell the other group, "A professor *took* a six-week sabbatical trip in Europe; write out his itinerary" (Bavelas 1973). The only thing that differs is whether the sabbatical will occur or has occurred. If it's easier to write histories about past events than future events, and if events with histories are more understandable than events without them, then people who write itineraries for the completed trip should report that trip in richer detail than do people who describe the itinerary for a trip that hasn't occurred yet. In the case of the trip that will occur, presumably there is less to look back over. Consequently the descriptions should be more fanciful, less detailed, less sensible, and shorter, which is what Bavelas found.

Webb and Watzke (undated) conducted a series of experiments comparing prospective and retrospective modes of thinking. The first experiment conveys the pattern that was followed in the remaining studies as well as the nature of the outcomes. The Super Bowl game in 1970 was played on January 11 between Kansas City and Minnesota. On Friday, January 9, two days before the game, 108 male students enrolled in a graduate business course at Stanford were given one of two experimental conditions. *Condition A:* "Imagine that it is Saturday, January 10. Kansas City and Minnesota will play tomorrow in the Super Bowl. Please write down the score of tomorrow's game. What will happen during the game?" *Condition B:* "Imagine that it is Monday, January 12. Kansas City and Minnesota played yesterday in the Super Bowl. Please write down the score of yesterday's game. What happened during the game to account for the outcome?"

There were no differences between the two conditions in the accuracy of the prediction. People who described the game that happened, however, wrote more detailed descriptions of the game. There was also more variance and more fanciful thinking in the descriptions of the event that will happen in the future, the event that was unanchored, rather than the event that happened in the past.

The assertion that the placement of an event in time affects the sense made of it can be illustrated in a different way. Again two groups are necessary. One group is told, "An accident *happened* on Route 89; describe it"; the other group is told, "An accident *will happen* on Route 89; describe it." Both accidents are equally hypothetical; the only difference is that one has occurred and the other has yet to occur. Despite the modest difference in time perspective, the sense made of these two events differs rather dramatically.

Here's what one person wrote about the accident that *happened:* "The light turned red. Car number 1 slammed on the brakes. Driver in car number 2 hit the brakes—the car skidded into the rear of car number 1. The baby in car number 2 fell forward underneath the dash. The child in the back seat hit the floor. Fortunately only the driver of car number 2 was slightly bruised. There were no other injuries."

When asked to describe the accident that *will happen*, another person wrote this: "The traffic light will fail tonight at the intersection of county road 8 and route 69 [*sic*]. A car will go through the intersection and be hit from the side. There will be a pileup of cars coming around the curve before the intersection—a series of rear end collisions."

These two stories differ in many ways, including explicitness of detail. In the accident that happened two cars are singled out, the specific inhabitants of the cars and their fate are detailed, and the entire accident is brought to a close—"there were no other injuries." The feeling one gets is that of a specific accident whose history, uniqueness, and resolution are visible.

In contrast is the accident that will happen. It is a very general accident, rather like "everyman's" accident in which we have a standard chain reaction crash with a pileup of cars and a series of rear-end collisions. There is no mention of the inhabitants, what happened to them, or the extent of the injuries. The description consists of a nonevaluative, general incident of cars bumping cars. Notice that the car that goes into the intersection is hit from the side, whereas in the accident that happened we find the actual precipitating factors stated in more detail: "Car number 1 slammed on the brakes, car number 2 hit the brakes and skidded into car number 1." Were there any brakes applied in the accident that will happen, any skidding? Nothing is mentioned. The question becomes why there is a difference in detail when the only difference involves placement in time. While the following answer is speculative, it is consistent with previous arguments about retrospective sense-making.

Consider the statement X causes Y. If we want to quiz someone about the XY relationship we can ask two questions: Here is X, what do you expect? Or, here is Y, how did it happen? The question "What do you expect?" seems more difficult. Why? When asked what you expect, you first have to specify some outcome, the point where you want it to come out, and then you have to write a plausible history that will get you there. In essence, you have to think in the future *perfect* tense. When asked the question "What will happen?" you can answer only if you imagine an accident that will *have* happened. To do that, you have to locate the accident in some specific future time while simultaneously trying to describe something that hasn't yet been settled. The net result of these dual pressures is a cryptic, undetailed report. Nothing gets fixed in your thinking long enough for it to serve as a stable outcome about which a history can be written.

Consider now the accident that happened and the writer who thinks about this event in the past tense. He has fewer problems with location. When he hears that an accident has happened, he treats the event as fixed in time and works backwards from that to write a history for producing that outcome.

RETROSPECT AND FUTURE PERFECT THINKING

The accident that will happen has a further twist, one of interest to organizational planners. To write about an event that has not yet occurred one has to think in the future perfect tense. To describe an accident that will happen, you must view it as the accident that *will have happened*. Managers' success or failure invoking this complicated linguistic form will have much to do with the success of their planning.

A more complicated picture of future perfect thinking is suggested by Schutz:

> The actor projects his action as if it were already over and done with and lying in the past. It is a full blown, actualized event, which the actor pictures and assigns to its place in the order of experience given to him at the moment of projection. Strangely enough, therefore, because it is pictured as completed, the planned act bears the temporal character of pastness. . . . The fact that it is thus pictured as if it were simultaneously past and future can be taken care of by saying that it is thought of in the future perfect tense (1967, p. 61).

If one is able to treat a future event as if it's already over and done, then presumably it's easier to write a specific history based on past experience that could generate that specific outcome. The future event is more sensible because you can visualize at least one prior set of means that will produce it. The meaning of that end *is* those means that bring it about. Furthermore, when one imagines the steps in a history that will realize an outcome, then there is more likelihood that one or more of these steps will have been performed before and will evoke past experiences that are similar to the experience that is imagined in the future perfect tense. When the past is imported into the present resemblances are noted; the future is put into one kind of context, and thereby becomes more familiar and meaningful.

Consider these two sentences:

a I will describe future perfect thinking.

b I will have described future perfect thinking.

The phrase "I will describe . . ." leaves me wondering whether what I am writing right now is contributing to, detracting from, or irrelevant to my effort to describe future perfect thinking: am I now describing it or will I start to describe it five minutes from now or will I describe it after I get feedback from the publisher or will this whole description be thrown in the wastebasket? All of those possibilities are equally plausible when I think about the open-ended future.

But if I change my language and say, "I will have written about future perfect thinking," then something has changed. Somehow the things I'm doing right now are more readily understood as working on/in the future perfect tense. There is less of a question about whether my current efforts are sensible. Instead I have the feeling that this writing is contributing to the future perfect discussion because it's taken for granted that that's what's being produced. What I will have written is not an open-ended question, it's an assertion. It is harder to transform it into the question, "Will I write a description?" "I will have written" sounds as if the matter has already been decided and I am simply going about the business of producing that uneventful, inevitable outcome.

Future perfect thinking is especially appropriate for executives because they are often rewarded for their ability to forecast the future (Ascher 1978). They spend much of their life planning, forecasting, and thinking in the future tense. They wonder about whether the economy will go up or down, whether markets will expand or shrink, whether employment will rise or fall, whether regulations will increase or decrease, and so on. However, the simple future tense is a difficult tense to work with because any possible outcome might occur. Future *perfect* thinking, on the other hand, can make speculation more manageable by focusing on single events. If an event is projected and thought of as already accomplished it can be more easily analyzed.

While the idea of future perfect thinking may be difficult to grasp, you might try this technique. Suppose that you're trying to write a five-year plan for your department and you get stalled. You experience what some people would call a "writer's block." One way to handle that block about the five-year plan is to imagine that it is *six* years later. Now write yourself a letter from your boss, congratulating you in great detail on how well your five-year plan worked. Be as specific as possible in the congratulatory letter. Although you are writing a letter of congratulations for a set of activities that have not yet occurred, in doing so you may clarify things you want to accomplish in those five years in a way that thinking in the simple future tense won't.

This strategy could be expanded and you could try your own utilitarian daydreaming (Conger 1969; Tullar and Barrett 1976) by writing a fan letter you would like to receive, a review of your unfinished work, a prophetic autobiography covering events starting tomorrow and going for a year, or even an obituary.

Consider retrospect in science. Experimenters might vary substantially in their ability to use future perfect thinking. If this is possible, then it is conceivable that those scientists who were adept at future perfect thinking might have significantly more of their experiments come out successfully than would be true for those who were unable to use future perfect thinking. If, before an experiment were designed or run, an experimenter could think of that experiment as finished, then he might see more clearly what he was trying to do and this in turn might produce a better initial design and cleaner results. To foster this closer look we might ask the scientist to write himself a letter from a journal accepting with enthusiasm the report of the experiment that he is just beginning to formulate. Having received the letter he now learns what these earlier steps mean and to what they are instrumental.

Writing yourself a glowing acceptance letter for incomplete work isn't as strange as it may sound. Something analogous to this seems to have been done by Edison and Pasteur, who "are rumored to have shared the technique of selecting a problem to solve, becoming frozen in incubation, and informing the press that the solution had been made, and scheduling a press conference to announce it; then under the pressure of time that they had arranged for themselves, breaking out of deepfreeze to illumination" (Crovitz 1970, p. 84). While this strategy may hasten solutions by the mere fact of forcing more attention onto the problem more quickly, we prefer to entertain the added possibility that rehearsing what one will have said to the press clarifies what one is now doing, what it is instrumental to, and what might be instrumental to some other outcome the press would find more interesting.

As a final example of outcomes (reviews, obituaries, biographies, testimonials) clarifying that which precedes them, consider the fascinating problem of strange conversations. You start to interact with someone, get partway through the discussion, have no idea what you're talking about, but you keep talking. One reason you keep talking is because the eventual outcome, whatever it may be, may tell you what you have been talking about all along and, by implication, what the specific puzzling talk of this very moment is "about." Garfinkel describes this historicizing of conversations:

> For the sensible character of an expression, upon its occurrence each of the conversationalists as auditor of his own as well as the other's productions has to assume as of any present accomplished point in the exchange that by waiting for what he or the other person might have said at a later time the present significance of what had already been said would have been clarified. Thus many expressions had the property of being progressively realized and realizable through the further course of the conversation (1967, p. 41).

The person is able to understand an event only after imputing both a history and prospects to the puzzling enacted display. Thus in the case of a conversation that contains abundant enactment which cannot be punctuated, more enactment is accumulated so that the odds increase that something punctuable can be found. If more talk is allowed to transpire, then that puzzling segment may be more capable of yielding a history. The person later on will be in a better position to take this current puzzle and punctuate both its history and its consequences given the serial order of the conversation.

RETROSPECT AND SELECTION

Much organizational sense-making consists of writing histories. A history is a kind of cause map that depicts sets of events in sequences that may be repeated (Zaret 1978; Hexter 1962). Retained histories can clarify either a tangible present outcome or a future outcome that has to be imagined. When an event yet to happen is treated as if it's over, this aids sense-making because that imagined completion can be related more easily to similar cause maps that have already been enacted. When something is thought about as ongoing and changing, it's harder to match it with something known in the past than if the event is thought of as completed and fixed.

Reaching into the past to extract history that matches the present is precisely what happens when retention influences selection. Retention provides an enacted environment that has been produced and labeled previously. An enacted map selects among various future perfect histories that are hypothesized to make sense out of imagined outcomes.

We presume that selection is the site where these retrospective sense-making activities occur. And it is the raw materials served up by the enactment processes, raw materials that may be clearer or more cloudy, toward which these retrospective processes are directed.

History in hand, people who select interpretations for present enactments usually see in the present what they've seen before. This recognition imposes a figure-ground construction on equivocal enactments. The ground, in this case, consists of that residual which is strange, unfamiliar, resistant to typification. The size of that ground, as well as the speed with which it changes, affects the fate of people in the organization. As that ground enlarges unnoticed, people who still see what they've seen before and still write the same old histories are seeing less and less of what is there and are becoming more vulnerable to a figure-ground reversal. When such reversals occur, they create panic because nothing makes sense. When ground becomes figure there is nothing retained in cause maps that looks/behaves anything like what is now visible. Sense-making starts all over if the organization hasn't disintegrated when confronted with the reversal. Frequent discrediting and reconsideration of enacted environments seems to be an effective means to keep figure-ground relationships proportional and reasonable given the ecological changes that are occurring.

Conclusion

In 1972 Bobby Fischer confronted Boris Spassky for the chess championship of the world. One of the strangest interludes during that competition was the accusation by the Russians that Fischer was using electronic devices and chemical substances to interfere with Spassky's playing. The Russians were sufficiently serious that they summoned a chemist and an electronics engineer to examine the site. No evidence was found to support the accusations. Nevertheless, there remains the intriguing question of where those charges, a classical instance of enacted equivocality, came from.

Many people at the chess competition had observed that Spassky was behaving in a strange manner. His symptoms (Wade 1972) included not behaving like himself, failure to smile, inability to concentrate, and impulsive playing. Given those behaviors there are numerous ways to interpret them — including physiological tampering via electronic devices, fear, paranoia, illness, and so on. The Russian explanation involving electronic devices is interesting because of the fact that the Russian medical literature describes an ailment known as the "asthenic syndrome." The symptoms for this syndrome include weakness, fatigability, depression, antisocial tendencies, sense of fear, impairment of memory and general mental function, and an inability to make decisions. The cause of the asthenic syndrome is said to be low-intensity microwave radiation. It is thought among Russian physiologists that the central nervous system is particularly sensitive to radiation and that when it is radiated it produces the behavioral symptoms listed above.

The important point for selection is that the Russians came up with their explanation of what was happening to Spassky because they had beliefs already available that would consolidate and label that equivocal set of symptoms. Believing *is* seeing. While that same set of symptoms might have been labeled as self-pity or jet lag or excitement, the interpretation imposed on those enactments was a causal sequence previously enacted by the Soviet delegation, which implied that radiation causes weakness, fatigability, and so on.

The imposition of the cause map associated with the asthenic syndrome on those equivocal inputs was the work of a selection process. In the presence of those equivocal symptoms the Russian delegation, technicians, and members of the Icelandic Chess Federation were mobilized to answer the question, "What's going on here?" Numerous cycles were assembled into a selection process, the outcome of which was the discovery of two dead flies in the lighting fixtures.

Several images could be used to summarize what the selection process consists of. Retrospective sense-making is the key metaphor that shows what selection does. The selection process also acts as if it contains solutions in search of problems. Selection activity matches solutions with people, problems, and choices. These solutions are stored in the retention process in the form of enacted environments that are imposed on equivocal enactments to generate understanding.

The image of figure-ground relationships is also a useful means to describe what happens in selection. Selection differentiates a variety of figures from a variety of grounds and then stabilizes one or more of those figure-ground relationships with a combination of nouns (variables) and verbs (connections). The differentiation, labeling, and connecting are presumed to be constrained by enacted environments into which the newer equivocal enactments are assimilated.

If one studies what managers actually do (e.g., Mintzberg 1975; Stewart 1976; Treadwell 1975) it soon becomes apparent why some of their existence is anomic, many of their observations dated, and much of their decision-making conservative. The reason is that selection is abbreviated, reflection is rare, and habitual interpretations dominate. Managers don't have much time for retrospection or for deliberated selection.

Mintzberg (1975) reports findings like this: 50 percent of a chief executive's activities last less than 9 minutes, foremen perform a different activity on the average of once every 48 seconds, managers work for 30 minutes uninterrupted on the average of once every two days, 93 percent of chief executive verbal contacts are ad hoc rather than planned, and so on. Managers prefer live action. This phrase summarizes several complementary observations. Managers gravitate toward activities that are current, specific, well-defined, and nonroutine. They have a definite preference for "hot" information, instant communication, gossip, speculation, hearsay, odds and ends of tangible detail, information about events, and "trigger" information (information in the form of concrete stimuli). Mintzberg summarizes this point by arguing that the manager works in an environment of stimulus-response. Unfortunately, this puts the manager at odds with most of the information systems in his organization. He seeks trigger, speculative, current information but the formal system gives him largely aggregated, precise, historical information. The manager demonstrates a thirst for external information whereas formal systems provide largely internal information.

Given the arguments in this chapter, the pace of managerial activity implies one or more of the following outcomes:

1   Managers chronically work amidst enduring puzzles because abbreviated selection leads to minimal removal of equivocality.

2   Managers do what they are told, exhibit goal displacement (R. A. Scott 1967), and enforce organizational routines because this reduces variety in the environment (the customer or client must standardize his request or be ignored) and also shifts lingering equivocality to someone else (supervisors handle odd cases).

3   Avoided tests are common because there isn't time to interpret equivocal enactments that would come from attempted tests.

4   Habit, tradition, and total crediting are invoked as often as possible for as long as possible to accommodate demands for selection with the limited time available for selection.

5   Because they deal with smaller scraps of data at any one time—each input gets an immediate response—managers may be able to preserve a sense of

sorts because small-scale enactments can only show small-scale equivocalities, and when puzzles are small, they are dealt with swiftly.

6 Those people who do have time to reflect on occurrences and interpret
them control the labels and definitions imposed by those who don't.

7 Since equivocality is functional as well as dysfunctional (e.g., Kursh 1971;
Bailey 1977; Schneider 1962) it is tolerated by everyone, which means no
one has a big selection problem.

8 Equivocality does exist, but effective managers develop substantial skill at
managing it in whatever time they do have available.

Groups within organizations, as well as managers, can be categorized
according to which of the preceding approximations to selection they assemble
as their problems vary.

Retention is less prosaic than people think. The following three comments show why.

retention and organizing

1 "One of the problems of knowledge is that it is a property of individually deteriorating systems. I understand from my biological spies that we lose about 100,000 neurons a day over our lives, so that each one of us has a depreciating stock of marbles and there is nothing we can do about this, at least up to now, as individuals. We start off with 10 billion at birth, so that even at my age, you still have a lot of marbles left. But I once reckoned that if you lived to be about 273 they would be all gone. There is a very fundamental biological phenomenon here—that knowledge from the social point of view has to be transmitted from deterioratng old minds into deteriorating young ones every generation and that if the transmission process is inadequate or breaks down, or if the transmission of error, on the other side, is very efficient and effective, this may make the difference between deterioration or appreciation of the total system" (Boulding 1971, p. 21).

2 "All of you will probably remember the disaster that took place in Florence with the floods and the great damage that was done to those stored art works. I had very mixed feelings about it. I thought, from a certain point of view, that it could well be regarded as good rather than bad; that is—yes, it's an occasion for mourning, but on the other hand, it also makes room. You know, there can be only so many masterpieces in the world, quite apart from the physical space in which they're stored, and new masterpieces must be produced, ones whose relations to your old masterpieces are perhaps hard to understand. Gregory [Bateson] lifted up the blackboard eraser. You can't live without this" (M. C. Bateson 1972, p. 310).

3 "Man must remember if he is not to become meaningless, and must forget if he is not to go mad" (McGlashan 1967, p. 5).

Drawing by D. Fradon; © 1977 The New Yorker Magazine, Inc.

If an organization is to learn anything then the distribution of its memory, the accuracy of that memory, and the conditions under which that memory is treated as a constraint become crucial characteristics of organizing. If knowledge is packaged in the mind of one individual, presumably the organization will unfold in a different manner than if the memory is housed in a committee or a set of committees with different interests. Furthermore the organization's usage of its retained interpretations will also be affected by whether that memory is placed in files, rule books, or on computers and how much of that information the organization admits to.

As March and Olsen state:

> The patterns of exposure to events and the channels for diffusing observations and interpretations often obscure the events. In situations where interpretations and explanations are called forth some time after the events, the organizational "memory" (e.g., files, budgets, statistics, etc.) and the retrieval-system will affect the degree to which different participants can use past events, promises, goals, assumptions, behavior, etc. in different ways. Pluralism, decentralization, mobility, and volatility in attention all tend to produce perceptual and attitudinal ambiguity in interpreting events (1976, pp. 62-63).

Levinson suggests that when people examine the usefulness of an organization's acquired knowledge, they should inquire about its accuracy, availability, and comprehensiveness. Accuracy concerns questions such as the proportion of knowledge that is factual, the proportion of detail that can be trusted, and how much of the information is speculative. Questions of availability concern where the information is stored, how it is filed, the ease with which it can be checked out, the people to whom it is accessible, and whether it can be used on repeated occasions. Assessment of comprehensiveness is concerned with questions like whether the knowledge is based on thorough or incomplete data, whether the knowledge is annotated, and whether it contains errors and bias (1972, pp. 214-15).

Retention does have a straightforward connotation: "retention means *liability* to recall, and it means nothing more than such liability. The only proof of their being retention is that recall actually takes place. The retention of an experience is, in short, but another name for the *possibility* of thinking it again, or the *tendency* to think it again, with its past surroundings" (James 1950, vol. 1, p. 654). Behind that straightforwardness, however, lie some fascinating problems as we've already seen. File folders do not contain just innocent actuarial displays (e.g., Garfinkel 1974; Zimmerman 1974); standard operating procedures and prominent content in retention systems can fuel international crises (Allison 1971); control over the writing of meeting minutes can be a powerful influence tactic in organizations (Cohen and March 1974, p. 215), and it is only through feedback from the past that people can be free from the immediate pressures of the outside world and make autonomous, self-determined, freely willed choices (Deutsch 1963, p. 203).

The issue of retention takes on added interest if we review the sense-making recipe, "How can I know what I think until I see what I say?" The relevant modification for retention is, "How can I know what I think because I forgot what I said?" The only way the sense-making recipe works is if you can remember the things you've said so that they're available for reflection. Typically, this should be no major problem.

Untypically, individuals do have memory problems. Consider this example witnessed by Warren McCulloch:

I have seen a man over 80 years of age walk into a meeting of a Board of Directors and for 8 hours work out from scratch all of the details necessary for the sale of a complete railroad. He pushed the other men so as to get every piece of evidence on the table. His judgement was remarkably solid. The amount of detail involved in the transaction was enormous, and it actually took over 6 hours to get all of the requisite details on the map. He summarized that detail at the end of the meeting, in a period of a half hour, very brilliantly, and when he came out he sat down, answered two letters that were on his desk, turned to his secretary, and said, "I have a feeling that I should have gone to a Board of Directors Meeting." He was not then, or at any later time, able to recall one iota of that meeting, and he was in that state for nearly a year before he died. This is the picture of what we call "presbyophrenia." In that state, whatever our memory organ is, we are unable to make any new record in it (1965, pp. 88-89).

If saying is distributed among a variety of people in the organization, all of whom are at different loosely coupled positions, then it is more likely that people will forget what someone said. The transmission of saying among people located at distances from one another can foster forgetting and remembering (Krippendorf 1975). So if saying is prolonged, complicated, distributed over space, heterogeneous, or elliptical, then forgetting may be more probable, guidance by past wisdom less likely, and anomie inevitable.

This chapter will be subdivided into two sections, the nature of retention and the nature of discrediting. Under the heading of retention we will discuss a model of memory proposed by deBono as well as samples of assembly rules and cycles associated with retention. In the discussion of discrediting, we will examine the ways in which enacted environments influence selection and enactment and the reasons why people must consistently doubt those things they presume to know.

The Nature of Retention

To visualize the retention process think of it as a memory surface, a surface such as photographic film that is capable of registering a recognizable image. There are good memory surfaces (such as flat film) that register perfectly, and bad surfaces (such as folded, crinkled, or bent film) that distort the image. A good memory surface gives you back exactly what you put on that surface, and a bad memory surface gives you back something different. Since we have argued that retention processes reorganize their inputs, this means that retention gives back something different—which could mean that it consists of bad memory surfaces. Which it does. Which is good.

The two ways in which a bad memory surface can be bad are distortion and incompleteness. Distortion means that things are shoved around, emphasis is changed, relationships may be altered. Incompleteness means that some things are just left out. Paradoxically, this is a tremendously important deficiency, for when some things are left out there must be some things which are left in. This implies a selecting process. And a selecting process is the most powerful of all information handling tools. It is quite likely that the great efficiency of the brain is not due to its being a brilliant computer. The efficiency of the brain is probably due to its being a bad memory surface. One could almost say that the function of mind is mistake (deBono 1969, pp. 54-56).

In organizing, the imperfections that distort inputs to retention are supplied by previously enacted environments. These environments provide the blots on an otherwise smooth surface that shove things around and change their emphasis.

THE JELLY MODEL OF RETENTION

To see more clearly how past patterns organize present inputs, we need some kind of model in which a pattern put on a surface will leave a permanent trace that will affect the next pattern that is put on the surface. Modifying a suggestion of deBono (1969, pp. 97-102), we can construct a jelly model.

Take a shallow dish and on the bottom of it lay kernels of field corn in a pattern that depicts some organizational structure that interests you (see Fig. 8.1). Then cover the kernels with ordinary table jelly. The flat jelly surface is the virgin memory surface that surrounds each person located at some position in the organization, or it could symbolize one person's surface. Since we have said that believing is seeing, the unmarred jelly could also symbolize the beliefs in terms of which people see the world. Depending on their beliefs, some individuals will be more influenced by inputs than others.

Patterns of data that influence this surface are supplied by hot water spooned onto the surface at different places (e.g., tops down, bottoms up, etc.). While it is still hot the water dissolves the gelatin, and after a short while (duration of exposure is a crucial variable in organizations) the water is poured off, leaving a shallow impression on the surface. A second spoonful of hot water is placed on a different portion of the surface, and so on, until the jelly is sculpted into contours. As channels, depressions, troughs, and peaks begin to form, newer spoonsful of water no longer stay where they are deposited—they flow somewhere else. As water flows into old depressions those depressions deepen.

These flows represent the interpretation and recording of incoming data, recording that may involve a string of images as the fluid moves among people

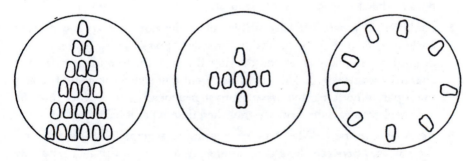

Figure 8.1

having different sets of beliefs (deeper crevices have lower thresholds for activation and represent beliefs that have a significant effect in defining the flow). Flows moving across the memory surface of one individual signify the different images associated with a train of thought, and similar trains of thought can occur when the flow moves across a chain of people, each of whom sees and reports something slightly different (e.g., Bartlett 1932).

Things that happen on this jelly surface illustrate what is presumed to happen in retention:

1 *Identity:* If spoonsful of water are dropped *around* the jelly surface and not in a central depression, the initial depression gets deeper and deeper even though nothing has been placed in it. "This implies that patterns which are linked up to one central pattern will establish that central pattern very firmly. It also means that a pattern may be reinforced by a succession of other patterns that are similar but not exactly the same. It also means that the memory surface can extract one fixed pattern from a succession of overlapping but different patterns". (deBono 1969, p. 99).

2 *Assimilation:* When water is deposited close to an adjacent depression it invariably flows into that depression, showing that it is almost impossible to establish a new pattern which is closely related to an old pattern (recall the privilege of historic backwardness where new lines of inquiry come from newcomers, not oldtimers).

3 *Fixed patterns:* Once patterns become established they are difficult to change, since any new patterns follow, reinforce, and deepen—rather than alter—old contours.

4 *Linked patterns:* If a succession of spoonsful are placed so that each overlaps the other one to form a chain, water always flows completely through the chain to the original position. This implies both that a chain of connected images will always lead back to the original image, no matter how long the chain, and that one pattern can lead eventually to another pattern that seems very remote from it.

5 *Backbone channel:* The jelly surface often develops a deep and narrow backbone channel that connects the various impressions. Since the channel drains from so many areas and the flow through it is so much greater, the channel becomes deep. This could represent a unifying theme that relates the separate patterns, but what is most provocative is the fact that the channel becomes more firmly established than what it is linking up.

6 *Representative part:* When water flows among several linked depressions, the passages between these depressions are narrow, much like a narrow deep-water channel in a harbor. This suggests that only part of a pattern

may come to represent it in a train of images, a part that symbolizes the whole. In terms of sense-making it may be only that part of the pattern which is relevant to the train of images that becomes properly established.

7 *Time sequence:* Suppose that we spoon water onto the same four spots on three separate occasions and all we vary is the sequence with which we pour the water onto the four spots. When deBono did this he discovered that the deepest depressions and the best established pattern never occurred in the same positions. From this demonstration (as illustrated in Fig. 8.2) he concludes that "the memory surface does not accumulate memories by simple addition. Since each memory is processed by the preceding memories, the actual sequence of presentation may make a very great difference to the pattern that is established, even though the individual patterns presented may be the same" (deBono 1969, p. 102).

The beauty of the jelly model is that it demonstrates how incoming information is processed by information that is already recorded. Material that is already recorded tends to interact with newer information in ways that select for and maximize the impact of that which already exists. It is precisely this self-organizing of newer inputs that we presume occurs in the building up of cause maps. New information gets sorted into existing pools (variables) and channels (causal relations) and deepens these pools and channels.

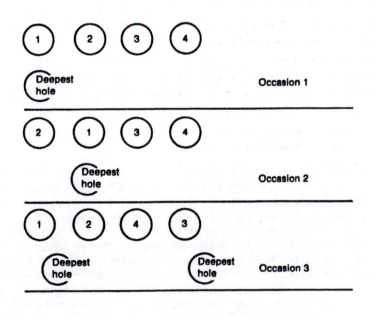

Figure 8.2

Retained material does undergo reorganization. When we talk about retention processes it is important that we not take literally the image of a storehouse. The storehouse is a place where things are put in the hope that they may be found again in exactly the same shape as when they were first stored away. This doesn't happen with cause maps or many other retained items:

> Ordinarily we do not take our experience neat but work it over before we try to store it away. Vivid, detailed, photographic resurrection of the past is not the most efficient way to remember. Every day remembering is more like a syllogism than a photograph: we usually follow a sequence of steps to the past; only rarely do we conjure it up in an instantaneous panorama. An adult uses symbols—usually verbal symbols—to organize his memory so that he can find what he wants in it. We constantly translate our experience into symbols, store them in our memory, and retrieve the symbols instead of the experience itself. When the time comes for recall, we try to reconstruct the experience from the remembered symbols (Miller and Buckhout 1973, pp. 207-8).

Notice that in the jelly model no one person in the organization controls, understands, or sees the entire pattern of dents, even though he makes do with the dents immediately surrounding him. From any individual's isolated position, the world will never make much sense nor will his intentions be realized with much regularity because the full memory surface associated with all the members of the organization is more complicated than any set of them can comprehend (e.g., Campbell 1969). This is precisely the state of affairs that Barnard saw when he tried to explain why people in organizations seem to act in ways that contradict what they say.

Organizations are complex systems containing many interdependent variables, and the only way to describe them is by sets of differential equations. But these equations can be used only if you first measure the variable elements, and to do that with any thoroughness or precision is next to impossible and probably not worth doing anyway. But managers have to describe and try to understand their surroundings somehow:

> The understanding of such systems has to be a matter of judgement almost aesthetic in character and this feeling for the situation to the extent it is attempted to be expressed in words has to be translated into simple cause and effect reasoning or into terms of strategic factors. Such translation is always defective, frequently misleading and not too seldom completely erroneous in practical consequence. . . . Those concerned in the management of business enterprises, or indeed of other kinds of organized activities are almost always concerned with judgement about changes in systems involving numerous interdependent variables. In most cases they cannot measure the factors with which they are concerned and they are unable to express accurately their sense of the changes in combinations resulting from specific action to modify one or another of the variables. It

is to this state of affairs that I think is to be ascribed the confusion and indeed the numerous contradictions in the statements of businessmen and others about what they are doing or proposing (Wolf 1974, pp. 50-51).

The jelly model also shows how the retention process is assembled differently depending on the degree of equivocality present in inputs from selection. Since selection removes considerable equivocality, information that is fed to the retention process should activate many rules and relatively few cycles. Unequivocal inputs are like a spoonful of water poured on one location and touching relatively few points. An equivocal input is more like water that is held in a perforated teaspoon. Water falls through these perforations in an ill-formed mist over a large area of the jelly dish. Many cycles are activated; the troughs and peaks are more numerous and more widespread, it takes a longer time for the water to meander over the surface and collect at one point, but when the water does collect and stop flowing, equivocality has been removed, and the mist has taken form and left its imprint.

RETENTION CYCLES

There is no such thing as cycles devoted exclusively to retention—all people retain portions of their organizational experience and impose it on future occasions—but there are organizational positions that deal with retention activities such as acquisition, storage and maintenance, search, and retrieval (Jennings 1978; Krippendorf 1975). What is perhaps most striking about retention cycles is that they are so diverse. Presumably anything that remembers in any way could be called a retention cycle, even though that's not very helpful (for instance, muscles remember exercises). Because of this diversity in retention behavior we will simply show what it looks like and conclude with that demonstration.

Levinson describes retention in one organization, Arrowhead Tool and Die, and this portrait shows the way retention can occur and be distributed:

The formalized knowledge of Arrowhead Tool & Die is fully known only to the president. Not that he deliberately hides anything, but no one else is left in the organization who started with him. The early experiences and traditions have not been committed to paper. Although the operating committee discusses current production and marketing problems and is aware of the company's financial status from day to day, they are not privy to the details of the offer by Reardon Corp. to buy Arrowhead. The technical designs for Arrowhead products and experiences with them are all filed in the engineering department and available to any of the operating committee who ask, but they are not summarized and discussed with the operating committee as the basis for thinking out new products. Rather, the engineering department is supposed to do this by itself. Only the stockholders are privy to historical financial information. The president informs the operating committee on an ad hoc basis about contemporary issues; each operating committee head does the same. However, none of this is systematically related to previous experiences to maintain a continuous thread and thrust within the awareness of the decision-makers (1972, pp. 216-17).

The portrait of Arrowhead suggests that retention is minimal, highly localized, dated, unwritten, and a modest constraint. The quotation suggests that there is not a great deal of formalized knowledge in Arrowhead Tool and Die and apart from that, there is rather specialized access to that information. It is further apparent that only modest amounts of this retained formalized information are injected into organizational thinking, and not much of it is available on a day-to-day basis to affect decisions.

In describing the nature of memory processes in groups, James G. Miller developed an informative listing of the variables that can be used to describe the process of remembering. This listing and its associated examples illustrate the kinds of interlocked cycles and assembly rules associated with retention.

1. *Meaning of information stored in memory.* Example: The football team stored memories of dozens of plays, any one of which could be retrieved when the quarterback called the appropriate number.
2. *Sorts of information stored in memory.* Example: The family remembered times when they had run out of money, so they put a few lire in a mattress every week.
3. *Total memory capacity.* Example: The ensemble could play together for more than 24 hours without using music and never repeat a composition.
4. *Percentage of information input stored.* Example: During Sunday dinner the family could recall only three of the five points in the pastor's sermon.
5. *Changes in remembering over time.* Example: The students gradually developed a system for sharing the task of remembering the lectures.
6. *Changes in remembering with different circumstances.* Example: The study group at first kept no minutes, but they began to develop such good ideas that they decided to write them down.
7. *Rate of reading into memory.* Example: The group was able to memorize about 100 nonsense syllables during each experimental hour.
8. *Lag in reading into memory.* Example: More than an hour passed before the cast learned the scene's new lines.
9. *Costs of reading into memory.* Example: The conference group paid a secretary ten dollars for tape recording their discussion.
10. *Rate of distortion of information during storage.* Example: The surviving occupants of the presidential car were certain that their memories of what happened during the moments of the assassination of President Kennedy were in no way distorted after three years.

11. *Time information is in storage before being forgotten.* Example: After about a year, the group could no longer remember what they had objected to about the new meeting room.
12. *Sorts of information retrieved.* Example: All three authors searched their memories of childhood to find examples of rope-jumping rhymes to put into the play they were jointly writing.
13. *Percentage of stored information retrieved from memory.* Example: After much hard work, current versions of the first three verses of the old song were put together by the club, but the fourth verse eluded them.
14. *Order of retrieval from memory.* Example: The team remembered all the words concerned with colors first, then the more abstract ones.
15. *Rate of retrieval from memory.* Example: The cheering section spelled out a new letter with its cards every five seconds.
16. *Lag in retrieval from memory.* Example: After the explosion and the prison break everyone's mind went blank for a few seconds, then many details began to be recalled, some by one guard only and some by several.
17. *Costs of retrieval from memory.* Example: The whole story of the accident was finally recalled, but getting the three witnesses to remember it took several hours, during which each lawyer was paid 20 dollars an hour (J. G. Miller 1971, p. 341).

The Nature of Discrediting

Organizations continue to exist only if they maintain a balance between flexibility and stability, but this is difficult to do (Bell 1967).

Flexibility is required so that current practices can be modified in the interests of adapting to nontransient changes in the environment. The organization must detect changes through its enactment and it must retain a sufficient pool of novel actions that these ecological changes can be accommodated to and recognized. The trouble with total flexibility is that the organization can't over time retain a sense of identity and continuity. Any social unit is defined in part by its history, by what it has done and by what it has chosen repeatedly. Chronic flexibility destroys identity.

Stability provides an economical means to handle new contingencies, since there *are* regularities in the world that any organization can exploit if it has a memory and the capacity for repetition. However, chronic stability is dysfunctional because more economical ways of responding might never be discovered; this in turn would mean that new environmental features would never be noticed.

Jones and Gerard describe similar ideas by the concept of *basic antinomy.* The basic antinomy is between openness to change and the desire to preserve

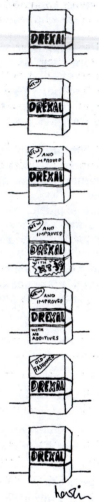

Drawing by Levin; © *1977 The New Yorker Magazine, Inc.*

past wisdom. *Both* processes are necessary for survival. The intriguing point in Jones and Gerard's discussion is their equating of openness to change with predecisional activity, and desire to preserve past wisdom with postdecisional activity. They explain this correspondence as follows:

> Without much strain we may coordinate flexibility and openness to the pre-decisional phase and stability and self-protection to the post-decisional phase. In the pre-decisional phase the person actively attempts to move, through the proper choices, toward the most gratifying outcomes. He is more or less in control; he is the uncommitted chooser; and, as a consequence, he hungers for information that will help him choose adaptively. The less he knows about an alternative, the more he will examine its implications, but his search is not systematically biased by his values or

attitudes. After he has made a committing decision information no longer has the same kind of instrumental value for him. He cannot unmake the decision, so information telling him he should have decided otherwise can only arouse subjective strain or displeasure. Thus, he will bias his search in the direction of information that is likely to support his decision. . . . The critical feature of the pre-decision phase is the prospect that action is possible, and it makes a difference to the actor which course of action is taken. In the post-decision phase action is not possible and the individual is under the fatalistic control of his environment (1967, p. 229).

Given that the preservation of opposed response tendencies in relatively "pure" form is necessary to human adaptation, what implications does this have for theories of information processing?

DISCREDITING AND THE SPLIT DECISION

An organization can reconcile the need for flexibility with the need for stability in several ways: by some form of compromise response, by alternation between stability and flexibility, or by simultaneous expression of both tendencies in different portions of the system. As we will see shortly, only the solutions by alternation or simultaneity make sense. A compromise response typically accomplishes neither flexibility nor stability.

How an organization will fare as it tries to manage these opposed pressures is determined heavily by what it does with enacted environments stored in retention. These bits of memory can be coupled to and can serve as a constraint on selection and enactment. Whether these remembered items actually dominate the assembling of processes is a matter of choice, and two choices are involved: an interpretation choice and an enactment choice.

On the basis of some enacted environment that is retrieved from memory, the *interpretation choice* is this: "Knowing what I know now, should I change the way I label and connect the flow of experience?" This is a choice with respect to the *selection* process. It concerns whether or not the actor should revise the interpretations that he imposes on newer enactments.

The *enactment choice* is phrased this way: "Knowing what I know now, should I act differently?" Where the interpretation choice involves potential revisions in labels and connections, the enactment choice involves a revision in the responses that create or respond to ecological changes.

If a person repeatedly enacts and selects only those things that have been enacted and selected in the past, then this is a case where stability drives out flexibility. Adaptation becomes endangered. When retained content is credited and constrains both enactment and selection, this means that both processes are activated in direct proportion to the amount of material that is retrieved from memory. As more memory is retrieved to guide actions and interpretations, there is more activation of enactment and selection. This direct relationship, signified by a positive sign between retention and enactment and between retention and selection, produces a total of zero negative signs linking the organizing processes (an even number), as illustrated in Fig. 8.3. This implies that the organization has become a deviation-amplifying system and will fly apart unless discrediting occurs somewhere.

This same instability occurs if there is total discrediting of retained content. If nothing is retrieved from memory to guide enactment or selection and if both processes are built from scratch each time an input arrives, these decisions leave the organizing processes linked by two negative signs (again an even number), and again there is a deviation-amplifying system that threatens to destroy the organization. Total discrediting creates the ultraflexible organization, total crediting creates the ultrastable organization, and neither form is adaptive for long. For an organization to survive, it must split its usage of retained content. In either enactment or selection people must act as if memory can be trusted, and in the other process they must act as if it cannot.

SPLIT DECISIONS AND LECTURING

To see what a split decision looks like, consider the case of people who lecture repeatedly in front of audiences. These people often find themselves saying, "If you've seen one audience, you've seen them all." And they conduct their lecturing consistent with that assumption. The effective lecturer probably has an elaborate cause map of what audiences are like and what moves them, but in any setting, if he is to be effective, the lecturer has to both credit and discredit that map. He has to act simultaneously as if this audience is like every other audience encountered and as if this group is like no other audience ever encountered. If those contradictory definitions are managed simultaneously, lecturing will occur, but it will occur in a manner that is sensitive to the idiosyncrasies of the current group.

If the lecturer enacts the lecture as if this group is like every other one, then he can start speaking and can generate actions and responses that he can then interpret retrospectively and adjust to. While these enactments unfold under the direct control of past enacted environments, the lecturer can also discredit these maps by interpreting the current happenings using a novel set of categories

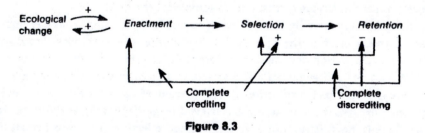

Figure 8.3

that have not been used before. The lecturer interprets this audience in the selection process as though it were unique and acts toward this audience in his enactments as if it were typical. By discrediting his memory in the selection process, the lecturer can thereby sense certain audience reactions that are out of the ordinary. The retained cause map, for example, may suggest that the greater the volume of laughter, the greater the importance of the topic that evokes the laughter. While believing this as he enacts standard jokes and adjusts his topical emphasis accordingly, the interpretations he makes question the linkage between laughter and importance and raise the possibility that laughter may be diagnostic of other characteristics of the audience, that topic importance may be signified by other behaviors than laughing, and that laughter and importance may not even be relevant categories for this group. Thus, while the lecturer is acting partly as if laughter and importance are tightly coupled in a positive direction, the interpretations made of the enactments treat that presumption as problematic. Instead, the lecturer entertains the possibility that his present experience can be labeled differently. It is the split usage of retained content that enables the organization or organism to fit into a particular environment, generate immediate activity, and still detect the necessity for altered actions to improve that fit.

DISCREDITING AND COMPROMISE

The importance of split decisions is the main reason that one piece of advice associated with the organizing model reads "ambivalence is the optimal compromise."

To see the wisdom of this counsel consider that if individuals and groups are to survive over a period of time they have to retain both altruistic and selfish motives. In the interest of adaptation these opposed tendencies must both be exerted strongly and simultaneously.

> If man has altruistic motives, these are certainly mixed with the purely selfish. . . . There is selection both of tendencies leading one man to survive at the expense of another fellow ingroup member as well as tendencies leading one group to survive at the expense of another group. This dual selective system gets ensconced in man as a fundamental ambivalence between egoism and altruism (Campbell 1965a, pp. 304-5).

Both tendencies have survival relevance and if the organism and group are to survive, both must be retained. This means that alternate or simultaneous expression of these opposed tendencies will be more adaptive than will an intermediate or compromise expression.

This point about compromise is important. Whenever a compromise response is fashioned, the adaptive value of the original opposed responses that were altered is destroyed. In the above example mentioned by Campbell, a response that is a mixture of altruism and selfishness furthers neither individual nor group survival. The unfortunate fact is that compromise responses usually dominate everything else since they seem to be acceptable to those with competing interests. The fact of acceptability is not what's crucial here. The crucial point is that, in effecting the compromise solution, important adaptive responses have been selected against and nonadaptive, moderate responses have been preserved. Should it become necessary in a changed environment for the group to ward off threats to its integrity, or should it become necessary for the individual to defend his own integrity, the crucial responses might be unavailable, since only composites have been retained.

This point is relevant to the emphasis in current organizational theory on participation and power equalization as means to gain greater acceptance of decisions that affect organizational members (e.g., Sashkin 1976; Marrow 1975; Forrest, Cummings, and Johnson 1977; Dachler and Wilpert 1978). Our concern based on the adaptive value of ambivalence is that participation may destroy the more polarized responses that aid adaptation. The decision that satisfies both group and individual interests selects against a pure expression of either interest. Should these interests prove to be adaptive in pure form, given a change in the environment, then survival becomes more difficult (Murdy 1975).

There is the further point that participation is usually prescribed as a remedy when there is conflict, frustration, and vacillation present in the group. The expression of ambivalence in a group often triggers a resort to participative techniques. The danger here is that a group's adaptive resources will be weakened. No one questions the reality that if left on its own the group could destroy itself with conflict and ambivalence. Our point is that the presence of conflict does not necessarily indicate that a group is dissolving; it merely signifies that the group retains heterogeneous responses and preferences, all of which may be adaptive under some circumstances (Moscovici 1976). But more importantly, if the conflict appears to be destroying the group, then conflict must be resolved so as to preserve rather than destroy the polarities exhibited in the conflict. A solution that permits alternate expression of polarized responses would be more adaptive than one that produces compromise responses.

Overt conflict in groups is frequently the way in which ambivalent dispositions are expressed. In environments where multiple contingencies arise, responses that are appropriate at one point in time may be detrimental at another. Cause mappings valid at one point in time may be invalid at another. Flexibility to deal with environmental changes is maintained if opposed responses are preserved. If conflict is resolved in such a way that compromise responses replace polarized responses, the ability of the group to adapt to its circumstances may be sacrificed in the interest of group harmony. Internal selectors dominate external selectors, and adaptability vanishes.

DISCREDITING AND DOUBT

To summarize a preliminary understanding of the relationship between retention and discrediting, a common prescription is that organizational actors should "treat memory as an.enemy" (Bartlett 1932, p. 16; Cadwallader 1959; March 1972, p. 427). The present line of argument suggests that we should urge people to *treat memory as a pest!*

Enactment and retention basically work at odds. Organizations need variations so they can deal with changes in.the environment, and they need strong guidance from the past to develop efficiencies. The way to finesse these contradictory demands is to use the past as a *partial* constraint on the present. The argument that organizations should maintain a split usage of their past wisdom accomplishes just that solution, because for either the activity of enactment or selection, the past is trusted, whereas for the other process the past is regarded with suspicion. Both variety and repetition are accomplished. This means that the inherent opposition between variation and retention is rendered more manageable because some variety is constrained when it is put under the control of retention, but the variety in the other process is allowed to unfold in a relatively unconstrained manner, so changes are detected. Whether these changes are detected via novel interpretations or novel actions is immaterial.

The reader should be cautioned that the statement "Organizations must partially discredit what they know" does not mean just that an organization should doubt what it knows for certain. When we argue that organizations need to discredit partially their past knowledge, we also mean that an organization should treat as certain those things which it doubts. To doubt is to discredit unequivocal information, to act decisively is to discredit equivocal information. When things are clear, doubt; when there is doubt, treat things as if they are clear. That's the full and symmetrical meaning of discrediting.

As a final point, the opposite of crediting is not disbelief, but doubt (James 1950, vol. 2, p. 284). The word *discredit* is a strong word typically meaning a refusal to accept as true. By discrediting we do not mean that people treat a retained cause map as wrong and refuse to accept any portion of it. Instead, the nuance we wish to preserve is that there are good reasons to question the accuracy and reliability of enacted environments, that one should be suspicious of any private version of the world, and that the credibility of that enacted environment is not guaranteed. In essence, one acts as if the retained cause map is one version of what may be up in a particular situation, but that it also carries little more.weight than any other version that could be fabricated.

DISCREDITING AND BANKING: AN ILLUSTRATION

James Herndon has written an interesting description of banks:

> The first characteristic of any institution is that no matter what the inevitable purpose for which it was invented, it must devote all its energy to doing the exact opposite. Thus, the savings bank must encourage the people to borrow money at interest. . . . The second characteristic is that an institution must continue to exist. Every action must be undertaken with respect to eternity. This second characteristic is the reason for the first. For unless a savings bank can persuade the people not to save, the savings bank will go broke. But the savings bank must continue to exist, since otherwise the people would have no place to save. . . . Following that argument, we can arrive at a description of an institution: an institution is a place to do things where those things will not be done (1971, pp. 109-10).

Banks have been around for a long time. They have a good history of survival. Why? Herndon suggests that one explanation for this durability is hypocrisy: pretending to be what one is not. The bank champions thrift, but is actually against it. Stated differently, the actions that a bank takes in response to its retained information contradict the interpretations that it makes of its own enactments. The bank does one thing, but what it labels and interprets in its stream of experience is something quite different.

The bank knows what it takes to make profits and hold customers. That knowledge exists in cause maps stored in the retention system. The bank also produces ecological changes, responds to ecological changes, and selects interpretations for these enactments. What's interesting about the bank is that it simultaneously credits and discredits its memory. One portion of the cause map reads, "To make money you have to lend it rather than store it." Having realized this, the bank then acts as if that knowledge is both true and false. It acts as if the statement is true by continuing to select from enacted inputs those occasions where there is an opportunity to lend money at a profit. It acts as if this statement is false by urging customers to be thrifty and use the bank as a repository for the results of that thrift. It is good to save and bad to borrow, it's good to borrow and bad to save. That complicated definition is something a bank must manage as a routine matter.

The bank, as is true for any system, basically incorporates ambivalence. If words and deeds are contradictory and if one perpetuates past wisdom and the other discredits past wisdom, then current functioning should be effective and future adaptation to changed contingencies should be possible. This means that if an organization is to remain both adaptable and maintain its current adaptation, it must show one of two patterns: the organization either has to use old interpretations in the selection process but produce continually novel enactments, or it has to produce routine enactments under the control of tradition and precedent but use continually novel interpretations to make sense of these standard outputs. Either pattern provides simultaneous flexibility and stability.

DISCREDITING AND FIREFIGHTING: AN ILLUSTRATION

Hypochondriacs and people who turn in malicious false alarms pose similar problems for firemen and doctors. If a fireman hears a call from an area noted for false alarms, he knows that the alarm probably means nothing, but he can't ignore it. Nor can he adopt a compromise solution. The compromising fire captain might send the entire company to the presumed false alarm, but at a slower speed. However, that response means that the company is always wrong. If there really is a fire then they've taken the wrong action because of their delay. If there is only a false alarm they've also taken the wrong action because they sent all of the equipment. A better solution would be ambivalent use of retained content. An alarm comes in from an area noted for false alarms, and the company responds just as fast as usual but with less equipment. The company acts as if there is a fire (it sends equipment promptly) and as if there isn't a fire (it doesn't send all of the equipment).

The same solution is used by physicians who treat hypochondriacs: the physician acts as if there is a problem (gives the person a pill) and as if there is not a problem (the pill is a placebo). In all of these instances ambivalence is the optimal compromise. The physicians and firefighters act simultaneously as if there is and is not something to be worried about.

When people act in an ambivalent manner they respond to more states of the world. Whether there is a fire or not, the organization is covered, and if another fire starts somewhere else during the run to the false alarm, they're also covered. In the case of the physician, he is also covered because if there is some real illness it will be presented to him again later and he will be able to falsify one hypothesis (that it was an imagined illness). He will also be able to take more definite medical action without fear of complicated chemical interactions between previous powerful medications and newer ones. When the physician defines a patient simultaneously as both sick and well and acts as if both possibilities are true, then whichever definition eventually is more plausible, the physician remains in a better position to take additional appropriate actions. One-dimensional handling of patients (e.g., give strong medication, not a placebo) makes the resulting data cloudy (if there's a strong reaction to the medication, was it because of the strength, the composition, or the hypochondria?) and subsequent interventions are made more difficult (having loaded a person's body with chemical A, I can't prescribe chemical B because the two interact and produce severe reaction C).

To chide the placebo-giving physician or the stingy fire department is to miss the point that when an organization has to fit its actions into an equivocal world, those fittings must themselves be equivocal. And one way in which an organization produces an equivocal fit with the world is to take ambivalent rather than compromise actions. Partial responses to false alarms of fire and sickness do acknowledge the symptoms while giving the organization leeway to take other kinds of action that may be more appropriate.

The Importance of Doubt

In Broken Images

He is quick, thinking in clear images;
I am slow, thinking in broken images.

He becomes dull, trusting to his clear images;
I become sharp, mistrusting my broken images.

Trusting his images, he assumes their relevance;
Mistrusting my images, I question their relevance.

Assuming their relevance, he assumes the fact;
Questioning their relevance, I question the fact.

When the fact fails him, he questions his senses;
When the fact fails me, I approve my senses.

He continues quick and dull in his clear images;
I continue slow and sharp in my broken images.

He in a new confusion of his understanding;
I in a new understanding of my confusion.

—Robert Graves

Has any organization ever failed to survive because it forgot something important? More likely is the possibility that organizations fail because they remember too much too long and persist too often doing too many things the way they've always done them (Hermann 1963). Organizations seldom fail because their memories fail them.

A good example of this point is Albert Speer's theory of organizational change (Singer and Wooton 1976). Speer, Adolf Hitler's minister of armaments and war, wrote about organizations in his book *Inside the Third Reich.* Speer made strong efforts to debureaucratize his ministry and to create temporary organizational structures that were loosely coupled and that could be assembled and disassembled swiftly. He continually tried to simplify administrative procedures, to do away with a chain of command, and to cut down on requirements for record-keeping by allowing his people to make agreements informally either by phone or orally.

The strategy that seemed most helpful in accomplishing these changes, however, was to take advantage of Allied bombing raids.

These raids were "helpful," according to Speer, because they destroyed the filing facilities, those containers of paper which enable organizations to establish traditions, procedures, and so on, which are mainstays of bureaucracy. Speer was so enamored with the results of these bombing raids that, upon learning of the destruction of his ministry in the Allied air raid of November 22, 1943, he commented: "Although we have been fortunate in that large parts of the current files of the Ministry have been burned and so relieved us for a time of useless ballast, we cannot really expect that such events will continually introduce the necessary fresh air into our work" (Singer and Wooton 1976, pp. 86-87).

Retained information is sacred in most organizations (Grossman 1976), and this means that routines, standard operating procedures, and grooved thinking (Steinbruner 1974) work against the organization being able to discredit its past knowledge. Nowhere is this more visible than in the Kennedy administration's efforts during the Cuban missile crisis to persuade the Navy to conduct a custom-made blockade unlike anything that they had done before. Kennedy's representatives repeatedly ran into the response that the Navy knew how to run blockades and that civilians shouldn't tamper with those routines.

At one point MacNamara asked Anderson (Chief of Naval Operations) what he would do if a Soviet ship's captain refused to answer questions about his cargo (if the naval officers intercepted a vessel and boarded it). At that point the Navy man picked up the *Manual of Naval Regulations* and, waving it in MacNamara's face, shouted, "It's all in there." To which MacNamara replied, "I don't give a damn what John Paul Jones would have done. I want to know what you're going to do, now." The encounter ended on Anderson's remark: "now, Mr. Secretary, if you and your deputy will go back to your offices, the Navy will run the blockade (Allison 1971, pp. 131-32).

The thick layering of routines in most organizations, coupled with the fact that departures from routine increase vulnerability, mean that discrediting is rare. Consider that organizations are said to be accountable and at least in the eyes of their stockholders, banks, and security analysts must continually give the impression that everything is going fine and that the organization *knows* what it's doing. These constituencies impose pressures on organizations to credit and to give evidence that their past definitions are accurate, that they do know what is up, and that they do know what it takes to cope with it. Doubts, hesitance, or reevaluation of past enactments are treated by outsiders as evidence that an organization is unsure of itself rather than as evidence that it is reflecting, preserving adaptability, or preparing for an even more diverse set of circumstances. The moral would seem to be that if you're going to discredit, keep quiet about it.

Anything that heightens commitment in an organization should decrease the likelihood of discrediting (Kiesler 1971; Salancik 1977). Since most managers continually have to justify the existence of their own subgroups when arguing for personnel and money, the commitment that develops as a byproduct of these arguments should work against discrediting, doubting, or suspecting one's view of the world.

Furthermore, the norms in most organizations favor "the school of hard knocks" over vicarious learning. MBA students, for example, are not to be taken seriously until they are seasoned and learn what the "real world" is like. Any organization that values "hands-on," "first-hand" experience should find it very difficult to say of that very same "direct" experience that it may be fallible, unreliable, or misleading.

Another thing that works against discrediting is the gradual buildup of confidence over time. For example, policemen are in the most danger of being killed during their fifth year on the police force. This appears to be the point in their experience where confidence is high, where they believe that most problems have already been encountered in one form or another, and these conclusions tempt the officer to relax just enough to become more vulnerable.

It has also been demonstrated (Dailey 1971) that about two-thirds of the way through judgment exercises, performance will suddenly drop even though it had been improving steadily. The explanation for this is that as confidence increases a person pays less attention to details in the situation, and eventually crucial items go unnoticed and performance drops. In both cases discrediting seems to be at a minimum.

Having described reasons why doubt is difficult, we should balance the picture by describing why it is also desirable. Discrediting makes sense partly because lessons from experience are usually dated. They can't really escape this fate because the world in which they were learned changes discontinuously. Discrediting simply means that every retained experience can be thrown into different figure-ground patterns because it has surplus meaning. A single reading of selected enactments does not exhaust their possibilities. Discrediting is also a crucial internal source of novelty when novelty cannot be borrowed from outsiders (Jacob 1977).

Another reason discrediting makes sense is that the relationships between many variables in a cause map are curvilinear rather than linear. A curvilinear world is the reality to which discrediting makes sense.

Suppose we take the relationship between criticisms received and quality of performance and store this connection in a cause map as a direct relationship: as criticisms increase, the quality of performance also increases. That summary conceals the operation of at least two contradictory processes. As criticisms increase, a person expends more effort to improve performance. The greater the number of criticisms the greater the effort. However, as criticisms increase it also becomes harder to concentrate on playing because the criticisms are distracting. Thus, as criticisms increase, there is a decrease in concentration. When combined, these two relationships begin to cancel one another, as outlined in Fig. 8.4.

As criticisms first start to increase the person exerts more effort, concentration is already quite high, and quality improves. As the criticisms continue to increase there comes a point where the additional increments of effort are now canceled because the person can't concentrate. Beyond this point, the greater the number of criticisms, the lower the quality of performance.

Part of the time criticisms raise quality, and part of the time criticisms lower quality. That's a curvilinear relationship. If it is stored in a cause map as linear and if it is discredited, then a person will act partly as if criticisms help performance and partly as if criticisms hinder it. That split decision applied to an oversimplified summary recaptures the entire range of variation for criticism and quality. It's that sense in which discrediting linear causal sequences promotes adaptation to nonlinear contingencies.

Since curvilinear relationships are complicated to process, remember, and act upon, it is probable that when people build cause maps they build them using linear rather than curvilinear relationships. The act of discrediting linear relationships reintroduces complexity and undoes the simplification, thereby facilitating adaptation.

Discrediting also makes sense because most retained experience contains surplus meaning. Cause maps simplify the fine grain of experience and because of this, any experience can "withstand" considerable discrediting because initial

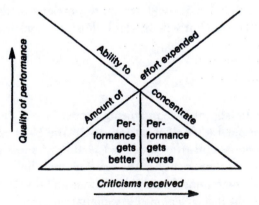

Fig. 8.4 A curvilinear world.

interpretations don't exhaust meanings. Retained experience retains surplus meaning, and it is this sense in which *both* crediting and discrediting are warranted and reasonable. Surplus meaning justifies discrediting, a typified meaning justifies crediting, and both are true at the same time.

A final virtue of discrediting is that it serves to complicate people. Any person who has a view of the world and who also discredits part of that view winds up with two ways to examine a situation. Discrediting is a way to enhance requisite variety and a way to register more of the variety that's present in the world.

Consider a common situation discussed by dissonance theorists (Wicklund and Brehm 1975). Many people believe that the greater the amount of smoking, the greater the likelihood of lung cancer. Those two variables are related strongly in a positive direction. That enacted environment, however, is often discredited when people who believe in it continue to smoke. Such people, we contend, are more complicated than the individual who smokes and disbelieves there's a linkage or who doesn't smoke and believes there's a linkage.

The complication is this: The smoker-believer simultaneously acts as if smoking causes lung cancer and as if it does not. The important point is that both assertions are true. Smoking does cause lung cancer in the sense that high volumes of tobacco intake increase the likelihood of lung cancer. Smoking does not cause lung cancer in the sense that its effects may be overridden by other factors in the environment surrounding smokers. A stream of experience to which are attached the labels *smoking* and *cancer* is an equivocal stream. If smoking is both credited and discredited as a cancer cause, then more of the equivocal world is registered.

It is this sense in which inconsistency promotes adaptability. An environment filled with pollution, chemicals, additives, and lead in drinking glasses simply is not a world in which smoking always produces cancer. A person who holds the theory that it does will see those portions of the world that are consistent with that idea but will overlook those portions that aren't.

Conclusion

A crucial characteristic of the organizing model is that the environment is viewed as an output rather than an input. On the basis of enactments and interpretations people construct a belated picture of some environment that could have produced those actions. The environment that is chosen, however, did not necessarily determine directly the actions and the sense-making. Rather it is instated after the fact as a plausible explanation for why those actions and labels could have occurred.

Once that enacted environment exists it serves as a plausible guide for subsequent actions and interpretations. An enacted environment is a historical document, stored in the retention process, usually in the form of a cause map, that can be superimposed on subsequent activities. Thus in one sense the product of any organization, its chief outcome or "reason" for existence or "goal," is to produce stable interpretations of equivocal displays.

An enacted environment is a cause-effect synopsis of thickly detailed episodes. The cause map of discussion experience that you completed earlier compressed considerable detail into some relatively abstract properties of events. Those abstractions, when retained, are capable of regenerating a more detailed image of the event.

Once environments have been enacted and stored, people in the organization face the critical question of what to do with what they know. These are the consequential moments in organizations. And if the organization is to survive, actions taken during these consequential moments will often look absurd. Throughout this chapter we have described members of adapting organizations as people who oppose, argue, contradict, disbelieve, doubt, act hypocritically, improvise, counter, distrust, differ, challenge, vacillate, question, puncture, disprove, and expose. All of these actions embody ambivalence as the optimal compromise to deal with the incompatible demands of flexibility and stability.

Ambivalent activity bears some resemblance to the process of Janusian thinking defined by Rothenberg (1976) as "actively conceiving two or more opposite or antithetical ideas, concepts, or images simultaneously." This style of thinking, which Rothenberg associates with creative activities, was named after the Roman god Janus, the god with two faces who perceived the world in opposite directions simultaneously. The interesting fact for organizational theorists is that Janus was the god of doorways (read *boundaries* if you prefer), and the two faces

> allowed him to observe both the exterior and interior of a house and the entrance and exit of all buildings. . . . He was the God of "beginnings," presiding over daybreak, and was considered to be the promoter of all initiative. His role as beginner is commemorated in the name January, the month which begins our year. . . . Janus was also considered to be the God of all communication, an extension of his function as God of departure and return (Rothenberg 1971, p. 197).

The rich imagery associated with Janus and Janusian thinking is rendered even more fascinating because of the strange yet elegant piece of tangible technology portrayed in Fig. 8.5. That strange-looking locomotive, which apprehends opposite directions simultaneously, is an actual locomotive named

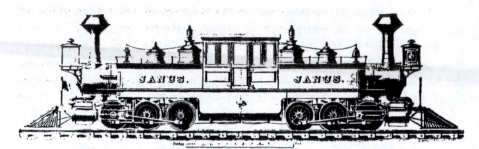

Fairlie Locomotives

WM. MASON, TAUNTON, MASS.

Figure 8.5

Janus built in this country by the Mason Machine Works in 1871 for the Lehigh Valley Railroad (White 1964). It is a fascinating piece of machinery.

Janus belongs to a general category of locomotives called *articulated* (Wiener 1930), and the extreme flexibility of the engine is created by the fact that the driving wheels and cylinders both pivot, so that the engine can go around extremely sharp curves. Since the water and fuel were carried in the center of the engine rather than in a separate car, it adhered better to the track, longer trains could be pulled, and one extra car of payload could be added in place of the normal coal car. Since the engine remained stable on very sharp curves, less steel would be needed to make the curves more gradual.

The stability of this engine's configuration was astonishing, as is illustrated by an incident in the early 1900s on the Mexican Railway between Vera Cruz and Mexico City. A Janus-like engine was used on a 108-mile segment of this 264-mile railroad, a particularly difficult segment that climbed from 2713 feet to 7923 feet. This section has a continuous uphill grade with small curves, some having a radius no larger than 320 feet. In many cases these curves are reverse curves with no straight track between the various swings (ᴠᴠᴠ). The track is steep and curving, and the curves are extremely tight.

Given this strange, demanding environment of track and grades and given the Janus-like configuration of this locomotive, it is interesting to ponder the unexpected value of this ambivalent configuration:

> A curious incident happened here [Cordova] some 30 years ago. One of these locomotives was standing at the top of a long incline, when, owing to its brakes being improperly secured, it started down the grade and ran for no less than 48 kilometers (30 miles) without derailing which is very remarkable (Wiener 1930, p. 137).

> Counting her as one engine, she has nearly double the number of pieces as an ordinary locomotive, and is so much more complex. Counting her

as equal to two, she is more simple in the frame, with less need of pumps and without necessity of counter weights. There are also four less wheels, with their axles, boxes, slides, springs, and equalizers. There is no tender to haul, the equivalent for it aiding her power by additional adhesion. . . . In all cases her motion was so peculiarly soft in comparison with that of the ordinary engine, as to suggest at once a considerable decrease in the item of repairs, both to rolling stock and permanent way. . . . [In using the engine there] would be the saving in engineers' wages, turn-tables, turn-table labor, and turn-table repairs and renewals (White 1964, pp. 177-79).

These comments, which appeared in the March 1870 issue of *Van Nostrand's Engineering Magazine,* suggest some of the unexpected advantages associated with this strange configuration. The engine did not get widespread attention in this country because of its limited fuel-carrying capacity and because of problems of steam leaks caused by the flexible tubing designed to allow pivoting on sharp curves.

What's fascinating about this locomotive is the way it illustrates the nature of simultaneous opposition. The engine is simultaneously a left-moving and a right-moving vehicle, simultaneously a source of power and a carrier of power, a single engine and a pair of engines, the beginning and the end of a train. Janus simultaneously credits and discredits the pattern for a single locomotive. In this ambivalence Janus acquired certain characteristics that enabled it to cope with terrain that defied other configurations. Organizations with multiple actors among whom contradictions and ambivalence can be distributed should be expected to do at least as well.

There is pampleteering; there is inquiry. In so far as an age is bent, a writer establishes equilibrium by leaning (leaning either as his age leans, or in the direction opposite

implications of organizing

to his age)—and this we might call "pamphleteering." A writer will also desire to develop an equilibrium of his own, regardless of external resistances—and this we might call "inquiry." His actual work will probably show an indeterminate wavering between two positions; he himself will not be sure just when he is inquiring and when pamphleteering. And he may not be wholly satisfied by the thought of doing exclusively either.

We recall a book on diet which, though it gave stern precepts against over-eating, went on to suggest that one should glut himself on occasion lest he become so inept at managing large quantities of food that he risk insulting his host at a banquet. And perhaps by a similar discrepancy, though cherishing the ideal of inquiry (or sober eating), we should occasionally dip into pamphleteering (or gluttony) in order that so biologic a weapon (for snatching a livelihood from the jungles of society) be not wholly lost through disuse. Once one has pamphleteered, however, dare he not in revision try, even at the risk of cancelling himself, to transform the contentious into the speculative? (Burke 1968, pp. vii-viii).

In the preceding chapters there is pamphleteering, inquiry, pamphleteering inquiry, inquiring pamphleteering, complicating, spine-counting, Sierra appreciation, and simplification, all of which simply goes to prove that ambivalence is the optimal compromise in theorizing as well as organizing. The nature of that ambivalence for theorists and managers is the topic of this chapter.

Implications for Organizational Theorizing

The person interested in organizational theorizing, and I hope that includes most managers reading this book, can grasp the spirit of our argument by reflecting on Kurt Vonnegut's first exposure to the social sciences:

"At last! I was going to study man."

I began with physical anthropology. I was taught how to measure the size of the brain of a human being who had been dead a long time, who was all dried out. I bored a hold in his skull, and I filled it with grains of polished rice. Then I emptied the rice into a graduated cylinder. I found this tedious.

I switched to archaeology, and I learned something I already knew: that man had been a maker and a smasher of crockery since the dawn of time. And I went to my faculty adviser, and I confessed that science did not charm me, that I longed for poetry instead. I was depressed. I knew my wife and my father would want to kill me, if I went into poetry.

My adviser smiled. "How would you like to study poetry which *pretends* to be scientific?" he asked me.

"Is such a thing possible?" I said.

He shook my hand. "Welcome to the field of social or cultural anthropology," he said. He told me that Ruth Benedict and Margaret Mead were already in it (Vonnegut 1975, p. 176).

Welcome to the field of organizational theorizing. Our reason for blurring the art/science boundary on occasions is evident in Peter Vaill's statement that "art is the attempt to wrest coherence and meaning out of more reality than we ordinarily deal with." Organizational theorists bite off too little too precisely and we've tried to encourage them to tackle bigger slices of reality. And if poetry, appreciation, and the artistry of inquiry need to be coupled with science to produce those bigger bites, so be it.

This entire book is as much about organizational theorizing as it is about organizational theory. It has been written to evoke lines of theorizing from the reader, to serve as grist for the reader's free associational mill, and to release lines of argument that previously may not have been given much attention. To the extent that the volume successfully releases productive lines of free association then it has accomplished its purpose.

The book is about ways of talking about organizations, and it is intentionally focused this way in the belief that as ways of talking and believing proliferate, new features of organizations are noticed. That's why the book is more concerned with metaphors and images than it is with findings. The preponderance of findings currently available in the organizational literature justify, validate, and confirm prior beliefs of investigators about what they would find when they entered organizations (Moscovici 1972, pp. 38-39). While many of those findings could be reinterpreted to illustrate features of the organizing model, that seems to be less crucial than putting in place a set of ideas and ways of seeing that may generate additional findings and different styles of finding.

As presented in this volume the organizing formulation is not intended to be an exhaustive description of entire organizations and all of their complexities.

The formulation is best thought of as a preliminary effort to develop an organizational epistomology. The concern throughout has been with the nature, origins, and limits of organizational knowledge. This book has been about how organizations understand their environments and themselves, with less attention being paid to what organizations do on the basis of this understanding. A large portion of the analysis has been concerned with ideas, metaphors, imagination, and thinking in the belief that organizations spend much of their time elaborating legends, developing myths, telling stories about their past, and generally embellishing the episodes that they single out from their experience for greater attention.

Although our focus throughout has been on processes and on the ways in which organizations unfold, it is possible for us to state where the organiza*tion* resides. The organization consists of plans, recipes, rules, instructions, and programs for generating, interpreting, and governing behavior that are jointly managed by two or more people. If you want to find an organization and its static properties, then in terms of the organizing formulation you look at the contents of the retention process, you identify the dominant assembly rules, you pinpoint the interpersonal cycles that tend to be most salient and incorporated into the largest number of processes, and you try to articulate the cause maps that recur in an organization's description of itself. These several properties constitute the stability, continuity, and repetition that produces the impression of similarity across time in the processes that occur.

ORGANIZING AS METATHEORY

One of the more useful ways to think about the organizing formulation is to view it as a metatheory. In this sense the organizing formulation is a general set of prescriptions for anyone developing his own theory of organizations. The organizing formulation, for example, suggests that anyone who wants to think about organizations should spend some time identifying specific rules by which organizations assemble themselves. Having specified such rules, the analyst inserts them into the generic category of *assembly rules*. The formulation also says an analyst can insert his own ideas about organizational action into the category of *enactment* and his own ideas about perception into the category of *selection*. The retention process further directs the analyst to make explicit his assumptions about organizational memory and his assumptions about how and where memory is a constraint.

What happens is that the organizing formulation takes the analyst's several thoughts about rules, ambiguity, perceptions, actions, memory, and choice, and weaves them together so that the analyst can see the consequences. The formulation also provides hints as to what should be singled out for deeper theoretical comment when organizations are addressed. The formulation also suggests that retention has an effect on actions and interpretations and that the analyst should work out for himself the nature of those effects. The formulation finally says, whatever you have formulated and in whatever way it interacts, be sure that it doesn't fly apart due to deviation-amplifying loops. Pay particular attention to locations where there are an odd number of negative signs.

ORGANIZING AND LOOSE COUPLING

The picture of organizing that emerges from the formulation is one in which there are numerous enactment-selection-retention (ESR) sequences underway at any moment in time scattered throughout the organization. There is loose coupling among the ESR sequences, and they are most likely to be coupled at the retention process. To visualize this coupling, imagine that you have a handful of cards that are fanned as if you're ready to play them. Right where your thumb rests lies the retention process. Most of the ESR sequences in the organization converge on that thumb, but above the thumb the enactments and the selections diversify, fan out, and have relatively little contact with one another. The image of fanned cards is consistent with the point just mentioned that the contents of the retention system, in particular recurrent cause maps, constitute the major portion of stability within an organization. There may well be as many ESR sequences as there are members in the organization. Those sequences can be coordinated to people, positions, tasks, or whatever. The important thing to realize is that there are numerous ESR sequences going on in an organization, they occur in several places, they are loosely coupled, and it is the total pattern of crediting and discrediting among these several simultaneous sequences that has a strong influence over whether the organization survives or disappears.

The property of loose coupling is emphasized throughout the organizing model. If organizations are loosely coupled, then relatively small units—such as double interacts, dyads, and triads—become eminently sensible as places to understand the major workings of organizations. These elements are tightly coupled, stable, and available for assembly into collectivities that can be more complicated than any one individual can understand (Wallace 1961). It is the combination of loose coupling plus causal loops that amplify the consequences of small actions plus social influence in double interacts that has convinced me that a minimalist approach to understanding organizations is a productive way to start. A surprising variety of organizational phenomena are visible in and perpetuated by surprisingly small units of analysis. Given the survival value of loosely coupled structures, these seem to be useful units of analysis.

ORGANIZING AND SIZE

Organizational size is a major variable in the organizational literature, but as we just noted, the organizing model is built on quite small sizes of groups. The reasoning behind this focus is this: From a social psychological standpoint, size may not be the primary reality for most people operating in organizations. Notice that for any employee of a large organization, most of the organization is probably *environment* rather than *actor* (Indik 1963). Most relationships among variables that are sensitive to size simply become ecological changes for actors or groups.

If you believe that individuals are limited in their abilities to process information and in the number of interpersonal relationships that they can manage at any one time (Northway 1971), then size just does not take on that much importance. Size is important because it may create overload (Weick 1970) and it may increase the incidence of role conflicts, but those realities of overload and role conflict can also be produced inside much smaller units (e.g., conflict between job demands and family demands).

It's also clear that size is a difficult point of departure to use in gaining an understanding of organizations (Kimberly 1976). The reason for this is that whenever there is a change in size, *several* things happen. This means that when groups of differing size are compared, one never knows how to interpret the comparison. For example, in a twelve-person group as compared to a three-person group, (1) it is more difficult to communicate to everyone, (2) there is not sufficient time for everyone to talk, (3) there is more need for a leader and greater likelihood that he will control what happens, (4) members are more likely to form into smaller clusters to maintain intimate contact, (5) differences in participation rates become exaggerated, and so forth. Given those differences between such relatively small units as twelve versus three, then even at that level it's not clear what we are to conclude when an investigator asserts that a group of three is more productive than a group of twelve. Conceivably, any one of the five differences by itself or some complex interaction between two or more of these five, could produce the outcome.

As we hinted before, the number of persons in a group may at times be crucial, but this is true mostly of very small numbers (Mills 1965). The crucial transitions are those from one person to two, from two to three, from three to four, from four to seven, and from seven to nine. The justification for these transitions can be stated briefly. The transition from one to two creates the basic unit of social behavior, the dyad. In a dyad there is interdependence, reciprocal behavior, and the necessity for accommodation to another person. Most of the double interacts that have been our unit of analysis start from dyads. The transition from two to three is significant because now there exists the possibility of an alliance between two members against the third one. The phenomena of control, cooperation, competition, and influence are produced by this transition. These phenomena, formerly suppressed, now become more visible, more subject to manipulation and sanction, and unfold with more vigor in a triad in part because a triad is simply less vulnerable than the dyad.

If one person leaves the triad a social unit still remains, which is not true if a person leaves a dyad. The transition from three to four creates the possibility of two equal dyads or alliances, and this may perpetuate both a social unit and the problems of control. The significant feature of four is that an alliance between two members is not sufficient to gain control. The excluded pair may themselves form an alliance, in which case the possibility of a stalemate increases. The jump from four to seven is crucial because just as individuals can form coalitions in the interest of control, so can groups. A seven-person group has the potential of splitting into two dyads and a triad. If the two dyads combine resources, they can gain some control over the larger triad. But if the triad can keep the dyads apart or can persuade one of the dyads to join it, then the triad will be in control. Perfect symmetry with regard to all the processes we have described would be found in the nine-person group. Here there can exist three groups of three. This permits coalitions *within* a specified triad and coalitions *between* a pair of triads. This property of coalitions within and between is not possible in the case of seven.

If we can understand how nine people go about the work of getting organized, producing, dissolving, and restructuring, then we should have some clear idea of what to expect when we watch one thousand people go through the same activities. Size is important largely in terms of the problems of control and affiliation that it raises and the alternative solutions that it provides for solving these problems. Most of these problems are evident in rather small units. Different processes are triggered when different combinations of people are possible, and that's the dynamic we've tried to highlight.

Another way to recast the discussion of size is to say that processes of social influence are of major importance in the organizing formulation (Moscovici 1976). For example, in the situation of a double interact we are interested both in the influence of person A on person B and the influence of person B in turn on what person A finally concludes from the interaction. Conformity, independence, and social pressure are mainstays in any set of concepts about human interaction, and all of the dynamics associated with these processes unfold in the cycles where two or more individuals hammer out their differences concerning what's up in the organization and what should be done about it. The majority of existing scholarship concerning persuasion, such as McGuire's mediational model (1968), converge on the interpersonal cycles and the ways in which these cycles are more or less successful in reducing equivocality.

ORGANIZING AND ORGANIZATIONAL THEORY

Aside from issues of size, it should be apparent that there are numerous places in the formulation where statements of contingency would be welcome. For example, there may be certain environments in which it would be more effective for an organization to bind its retention positively to enactment and negatively to selection, whereas under changed circumstances the opposite pattern might be more sensible. Similarly, the pattern of binding ecological change and enactment might vary as a function of different circumstances or different resources or different dependencies. Also, organizational members obviously can't enact everything. There are constraints, and part of the psychological contract when one joins an organization is that some freedom to enact is traded for wages and benefits. Which constraints on enactment are most intense and under what conditions they are most intense remain to be worked out in specific organizations, but these appear to be questions that provide a pretext for contingency statements.

While the organizing formulation does contain conventional systems imagery, it is not predominantly a formulation about open systems. This is a subtlety that should be mentioned lest the model be misrepresented. The formulation bears kinship to open system models because of the role of ecological change and the fact that exogenous factors influence ecological change. That ecological change affects the organization directly at only one point: the enactments of that organization. If an organization credits its retention in both the selection and enactment process, it can effectively seal itself off from ecological changes for long periods of time. There is a certain amount of autism in the organizations we are describing. Organizations can feed on themselves for long periods of time, and open systems models have directed theoretical energy away from understanding how self-containment can persist. The organizing model suggests that organizations can and do act like closed systems. Enthusiasms for open system models should not divert attention from also understanding the ways in which organizational inertia and organizational attentiveness to one's own past experience can continue unpunished for surprisingly long periods of time.

It also seems important to reiterate the argument that goal consensus is not a precondition of order and regularity in this model. The common assertion that people organize in order to accomplish some agreed-upon end is not essential to an explanation of the orderliness found in concerted action, nor is goal-governed behavior that evident in organizations. Organizational actions at best, seem to be goal-interpreted. Goals are sufficiently diverse, the future is sufficiently uncertain, and the actions on which goal statements could center are sufficiently unclear, that goal statements explain a relatively small portion of the variance in action. It is probable that goals are tied more closely to actual activities than is commonly recognized and that they are more productively understood as summaries of previous actions.

As one final footnote for future thinking, a question that comes out of the organizing arguments is "Where's the heat?" The organizing model is relatively cool. Passion is at a premium in it partly because there's seemingly so small an amount of it. Emotions, searchings, frustrations, heat, fury, joy, delight, depression, and moodiness, all prominent enough parts of organizational life, are hard to find. That's a common shortcoming of many cognitive models, and it leaves us perhaps sadder but not apologetic. The heat is in there; you simply have to look for it (Heider 1960).

Equivocality is arousing (Hunt 1963), and this free-floating arousal sets the stage for emotional labeling (Schachter 1964) and for a narrowing of perception (Easterbrook 1959) and frustration (Kahnemann 1973). Heat is there in the form of ambivalence when people are torn between simultaneous contradictory actions and interpretations. Heat is there in the form of pleasure in the process of clarifying puzzles and producing interesting versions of what's up. Heat is there in the form of a prior definition of a situation that is brought forward and clarifies a contemporary puzzle. Discrepancies can be pleasurable in their own right if they are not too extreme. Interpersonal rewards that flow from stable interpersonal cycles are a potential source of satisfaction. The generation of novelty and variety is there as a potential source of enjoyment.

Thin as that set may seem, it simply points to the argument we are trying to make: specification of emotion is an obvious place where homework is needed. That's not unique to this formulation (see Steinbruner 1974). Understanding is not just left-brain activity (Samples 1976). As we have unfolded it in the preceding pages, understanding is shot through with right-brain activities of intuition and imagination. Feeling and soul are woven sufficiently into each of the processes and sufficiently inseparable from them, so that inserting this artificial separation between cool versus hot processes may be unnecessary.

Implications for Practice

One way to look at this book is as a Swiss Army knife for organizational design. If it's true that sense-making involves seeing what one has said, then it's also true that if we can reword the sentences that people utter about themselves, we can alter the conclusions they arrive at concerning who they are and what they're up to. Our strong impression is that when people in organizations have conversation, those conversations are not particularly instructive, nor are their pauses within those conversations cultivating. We're trying to make it possible for people to have better conversations so that they can see their circumstances more richly (Redfield 1963, pp. 44-57).

Toward this end we have introduced a number of tools to be made part of these converstions. The tools are implied in words such as these:

retrospect	grammars for organizing
assembly rules	recipes for organizing
deviation-amplification	requisite variety
deviation-counteraction	contour gauge
cause map	future perfect thinking
disconfirmed assumptions	consensual validation
double interact	adaptability
ambivalence	means convergence
split decisions	stream of experience
enactable environment	figure-ground
enacted environment	spirit levels
grooved memory surface	uptight variables
artificial selection	mutual equivalence structure
arbitrary	partial inclusion
bracketing	mutual fate control
labeling	loose coupling
puns	self-fulfilling prophecies
equivoques	historicizing
discrediting	perceptual cycle

We've also suggested that you think of your organization as an orchestra, spirit table, set of weakly held assumptions, garbage can, seesaw, organized anarchy, breeding farm, baseball game, display of statues, and so forth.

It's safe to say that in the past your conversations about organizations have not contained many of these images. It's probably safe to say also that you can at least understand by now how the words might be used in conversation to raise questions about the organizations that you deal with. It remains to be seen whether these alternative ways of talking about the organization will alter the way in which you see that organization.

The primary implication of the organizing model for the practictioner is the suggestion that it's possible for an individual to get better at knowing his organization.

If we transform the organizing formulation into a series of diagnostic questions, those questions would include such items as the following:

1 What and where is the retention process?
2 Who ties the retention process to enactment and selection, with what frequency, and with respect to what content?

3   In what direction is retention tied to enactment and selection, positive or negative?

4   If retention can't be discredited, who argues that the current retained content is totally valid and why should the person be that committed to such a position?

5   What other mechanisms are there to alter the content of retained cause maps if the maps are not discredited in practice?

6   Is the supply of variety sufficient in the organization? Is there enough variance in the number of rules available to construct processes containing a highly variable number of cycles? (Notice if you have only two assembly rules, than those two rules can't be very responsive to variations in input. If you're going to have many versus few cycles activated to apply to an input, then in turn you have to have a variable number of rules that will select varying numbers of cycles.)

7   Are the cycles plentiful, varied, and combined into new combinations with some regularity?

8   Are there a sufficient number of negative causal relationships? (People see predominantly variables that move in the same direction: that is, more leads to more or less leads to less. Therefore, they are apt to miss situations in which variables move in the opposite directions, but these are precisely the movements that are crucial for control purposes.)

9   Who judges the equivocality of information and how are these judgments made?

10 Who chooses the assembly rules that will be used to assemble processes, and how is the content of these assembly rules decided on and revised?

11 How active is the organization when it inspects its environment? An organization that is simply registering what goes on outside of it can either stand in a stationary position or can move about in that environment. A mobile existence generates more data than does a sedentary one (G. W. Bateson 1966, p. 415).

12 Who cleans out the files, when, with what decision rules, and with what amount of zeal? (This person is acting like the Allied bombing raids of which Speer was so fond.)

13 When some intervention to improve the organization fails (e.g., Mirvis and Berg 1977), was the failure due to total discrediting or total crediting, misjudgments of the amount of equivocality in inputs, insufficient cycles mobilized for application to the input, the "wrong" cycles being applied, an insufficient number of assembly rules, the "wrong" assembly rules applied to the input, selected inputs not being incorporated into preexisting

material or being incorporated too fully and losing their distinctiveness, or excessively loose coupling among the organizing processes?

One thing a person can learn about his organization is what it looks like when examined in terms of those questions. Answers to those questions in turn will say something about adaptation, adaptability, the availability of resources for adapting to new environments, the richness of sense-making that can occur, and the likelihood that cause maps available within that organization will illuminate rather than obscure what the organization is doing as well as serve up interesting definitions of what it may be up to.

Other pieces of practical advice can be distilled from the arguments of previous chapters, and ten of those pieces of advice are listed below.

1   Don't panic in the face of disorder.
2   You never do one thing all at once.
3   Chaotic action is preferable to orderly inaction.
4   The most important decisions are often the least apparent.
5   There is no solution.
6   Stamp out utility.
7   The map is the territory.
8   Rechart the organizational chart.
9   Visualize organizations as evolutionary systems.
10 Complicate yourself!

DON'T PANIC IN THE FACE OF DISORDER

This truism takes on considerable importance if the preceding arguments have any validity. Organizations are viewed by members and observers as presumably rational, accountable, orderly, predictible units that know what they're doing. Given those presumptions, when disorder occurs it's easy for those same observers to assume that the organization is dissolving. But the preceding arguments suggest that that's not necessarily so. Processes have to become disorderly if the disorder in information is to be registered accurately. Unless the disorder in data *is* registered accurately, only a small portion of that disorder can be removed. And in the case of minimal removal, then problems are likely to persist and increase in severity.

It's easy to assume that adaptation is promoted by consistent acts emitted by a tightly run organization (Martland 1978). If people make that assumption, then evidence of ambivalence and hypocrisy is treated as a threat to adaptation and survival. The thrust of the preceding arguments has been that precisely the opposite is true. Ambivalence may guarantee adaptation in the short run and surivival in the long run. If some faction of the organization wants to act on the basis of past wisdom and some other faction wants to act in ways that oppose the past, *both* factions are partially correct. More importantly, both factions should act on behalf of their beliefs. What is being observed here is simply another instance of the split decision pattern that allows the organization to retain both flexibility and stability.

YOU NEVER DO ONE THING ALL AT ONCE

One of the practical recommendations that comes from systems theory is that a person can never do one thing (Hardin 1963). In a highly interdependent system, any action ramifies and has far-reaching consequences. What is less commonly asserted is the equally important point that all of these consequences don't happen at the same time. Some of them happen right away, some of them have remote and delayed effects.

The implications of this are substantial. If a system maintains an odd number of negative cycles then any change, no matter what it is, will eventually be controlled, and the system can dissolve its own disruptions. Any artificial intervention to handle a disruption could destroy the controlled relationships within the system. And if these control relationships were destroyed, a host of new disruptions could occur. It is possible that a well-functioning control system could be destroyed in the interest of handling a momentary disruption, a disruption that eventually would be dissolved anyway because of the pattern of relationships within the system.

The danger of inappropriate intervention is especially likely if members mistakenly assume that people, rather than relationships, are the critical control points in an organization. The thrust of the organizing model is that it's easy to overmanage an organization and that it is an excess rather than a deficiency of intervention that lies at the heart of many organizational problems. In the organizing formulation, managing is already accomplished by such means as incentives, norms, deviation-counteracting feedback loops, and people who model their own actions after actions of people who are rewarded by the organization.

One of the misleading metaphors that is often used to describe managers is to argue that they are akin to conductors of orchestras (e.g., Kirkpatrick 1975). Examination of what conductors actually do (e.g., Rubin 1974; Faulkner 1971, 1973; Arian 1971) suggests that contrary to popular folklore, conducting is most effective when it is tacit, unobtrusive, noninterfering, and takes into consideration control processes already woven into the orchestra.

As a perfect example of this reformulated way of thinking about orchestra conducting, consider the problem of the leader of a jazz orchestra trying to decide on the tempo at which a number should be played. If the leader sets the tempo too slow, the tune sounds dead and lacks brilliance; if he sets it too fast, the musicians can't execute the notes. So typically the leader announces a tune, imagines how it sounds and at what tempo it sounds best, snaps his fingers to capture that correct tempo, communicates this tempo to the orchestra, gives the downbeat, and everyone starts. If the leader has guessed wrong, it's possible to speed up or slow down the tempo slightly while it's being played, but the changes you can make during execution are not very big. And that's what the manager of any organization presumably does. He gets a promotion or he gets fired depending on the soundness of the tempos that he sets.

Given that obvious state of the world, now consider the interesting solution to tempo-setting that has been adopted by Buddy Rich on occasion. He starts playing a tempo either by snapping his fingers or by playing his drums; he then quietly asks the members of his orchestra, "What tune would sound good at that tempo?" They give him some suggestions, he chooses one, the musicians pull out the music while the tempo continues, and when everybody has their music in place Rich signals the start of the tune.

The fascinating thing is that Rich stands the conductor metaphor, as well as rationality, on its ear. He doesn't plan and then execute what he planned to do. He reverses things. He starts executing something before he knows what it is he's executing. He starts playing some tune, except that he doesn't know what tune he's playing. He learns what tune he's been playing only after he's played it for awhile and gets suggestions from his musicians as to what the tune was.

CHAOTIC ACTION IS PREFERABLE TO ORDERLY INACTION

The discussions of the enacted environment have emphasized that meaning is retrospective and only elapsed experience is available for meaningful interpretation. The practical implication of this is that an organization would be in a better position to improve its efficiency if the elapsed experience were filled with action rather than inaction. Action, when viewed retrospectively, clarifies what the organization is doing, what business it is in, and what its projects may be. Inaction, viewed retrospectively, is more puzzling and more senseless: there is a greater likelihood for bizarre meanings to be attached and for an unhealthy amount of autism to be introduced. Actions, in other words, provide tangible items that can be attended to.

In the absence of actions, any act of reflection is directed toward relatively unfilled periods of lived experience. This means that to find a filled period of action that can be made sensible, the reflection pushes farther back in time and fixates on more dated experience. Since that experience is even farther out of touch with current happenings, the likelihood of misinterpretation is increased.

When a group is without a project and is confused, the emission of actions that can be viewed reflectively increases the chances that the group may discover what it is doing. Thus, when there is confusion and some member of a group asks, "What should I do?" and some other member says, "I don't know, just do something," that's probably a much better piece of advice than you might realize. It's better for the simple reason that it increases the likelihood that something will be generated which can then be made meaningful. It's okay not to know where you're going as long as you're going somewhere. Sooner or later, you'll find out where that somewhere is.

THE MOST IMPORTANT DECISIONS ARE OFTEN THE LEAST APPARENT

This point is a restatement of the idea that decisions made in the selection process have less to do with the fate of a system than do the decisions made concerning retention. This means that the retention process and the persons who mediate between it and selection and enactment are the most crucial points in terms of organizing.

The person who makes decisions about what the goal of the company should be next year is less important to continued functioning than are the persons who decide what is known by the company, what should be done next in terms of selection and enactment, and whether opposing decisions are made for selection and enactment. The company historian in a very real sense is also the company prophet (or profit?). Knowing what will be done about the company history, he can state with some accuracy what the fate of the system will be; for unless one of the processes within the company is permitted to counteract history and the other to preserve it, destruction is likely.

THERE IS NO SOLUTION

One thing that's apparent in the preceding analyses is that there are no simple answers and there is no simple finite set of causes for anything that happens in an organization (see Steinbeck 1941, chap. 14, on nonteleology). Furthermore, origins are often impossible to discover, because they usually lie at some distance from the symptom and they have usually grown all out of proportion to their beginnings through deviation-amplifying loops. People may show a strong tendency to search in the vicinity of a problem for its cause, but in the case of interdependent systems this form of search is wasteful and typically inaccurate.

We've repeatedly suggested that improvisation, reaccomplishment, and invention are required as substitutes for open-ended analyses. Puns and dilemmas are typically managed rather than solved, and it's that reality which we have in mind when we try to warn managers away from spending time, energy, and money on finding *the* answer or *the* cause or *the* one lever in the organization which, when moved, will have dramatic results.

The kind of change that is prominent in the organizing model is incremental rather than discontinuous. We've tried to suggest that innovation, imagination, and improvisation can be woven into everyday activities as a chronic component of them. The modifications that are implied by the organizing model are continuous, small-scale modifications that cumulate into a steady updating of the organization. If an organization updates itself on a *daily* basis then it's possible for that organization to maintain a close fit with its surroundings. This is a rather different portrait from the view of organizations which says they move along in a stable, equilibrium condition until they experience some trouble, in which case there is a search for some major change or cure that will reestablish the equilibrium (Hunt 1972, chap. 17). Cures and answers simply aren't available.

There are at least two good reasons why managers should soft-pedal their efforts to find the solution. One way that managers manage trouble is to blame people. Notice that the implication of the organizing model is that in most situations people insert a sizable portion of what that situation sends back to them and this means that *self*-blame as much as *other* blame makes sense. The enactment formulation places substantially more responsibility on the actor than is true of other formulations. And consistent with this shift in responsibility goes a shift in who is an appropriate target for blaming.

Notice also that the quest for *the* solution is unlikely to yield much because of the inherent equivocality of situations. One of the implications of equivocality is that there really is no such thing as the judgment *wrong*. In an equivocal world things are *reasonable* or *unreasonable*. If you take a stream of experience and impose a construction on it, then it's nonsense to say that the construction is wrong or right. The best you can say is simply that there are other ways to interpret that stream and that they raise more interesting possibilities. If situations have that kind of arbitrary quality to them, then they are incapable of solution, especially by any simple means. Instead, they have to be managed and the meanings rearranged and a concern for the solution tabled.

STAMP OUT UTILITY

Whenever people adapt to a particular situation, they lose some of the resources that would enable them to adapt to different situations in the future. They sacrifice future adaptability for current good fit. If they try to beat this trap by cultivating future adaptability and sacrificing current adaptation, they are no better off. They live in an eternal state of readiness and loneliness and are able to handle everything except the next customer who walks through the door.

Some people argue that this dilemma is not crucial because when adaptation falters, people can always borrow the solutions being used by those who are successfully adapting. I think that argument is naive. If responses become standardized when organizations merge, if people generally praise their own groups and downgrade others, and if people fear appearing frivolous, then from whom are they going to borrow all of these elegant solutions? We seem to have plenty of parasites, but where is the host?

If borrowing is not all it is cracked up to be, then we must look elsewhere for adaptations. The main alternative place to look is inside the organization, and what the alert manager looks for is persistent galumphing.

Miller defines *galumphing* as "patterned voluntary elaboration or complication of process, where the pattern is not under the dominant control of goals" (1973, p. 92). He argues that play or galumphing preserves adaptability. "Play is a way of organizing activity, not a particular set of activities; it is a syntax, not a vocabulary" (p. 94). The relevance of galumphing to adaptation is that galumphing provides a way to diversify enactments. Play

> makes us flexible and gives us exercise in the control of means that we are capable of using but that are superfluous right now. . . . [When people play] they may be mastering incidental skills. But more important, they are using their capacity to combine pieces of behavior that would have no basis for juxtaposition in a utilitarian framework. They are creating novelty. . . . It is by doing things that an organism develops combinatorial flexibility (p. 96).

From this standpoint, play is not viewed as a means to an end but rather as a crooked line to the end. It gets around obstacles, but the obstacles were put there by the player in order to complicate the player's life. Deliberate complication, if it gives the person experience in combining elements in novel ways, can be potentially adaptive for dealing with novel problems. Notice that means activities are given much freer sway. They are not dominated by goals. What play basically does is unhook behavior from the demands of real goals. The person gets experience in combining pieces of behavior that would not be juxtaposed in a utilitarian world.

The heart of Miller's argument is that play is important not because it teaches some new skill, but because it takes activities that are already in one's repertoire and gives one practice in recombining those into novel sets. What seems to be implied is a kind of second-order learning. It is not that one learns to recombine a single set of means into a clumsy but passable golf swing; what one may be learning, instead, is that it is possible to recombine the available repertoire of means in novel ways. A person gets repeated practice in doing this whenever he or she intentionally complicates a process.

Several possibilities are implicit in this line of analysis. Less efficient organizations could retain more adaptability than more efficient organizations if the less efficient organizations, which use more complicated means to achieve ends, are actually learning to recombine their repertoire. This would hold true only if they continually reshuffled their modes of inefficiency. Although Miller does not mention it, an additional benefit of galumphing might be that people discover previously unnoticed portions of their repertoires. When people recombine activities, they may clarify retrospectively just what is being recombined. So deliberate complication might yield better knowledge of the elements in an existing repertoire as well as lead to the discovery that a known repertoire can be recombined in novel ways.

Most organizations live in a climate of accountability. Within such climates variability is treated as noise (Klingsporn 1973), mutations are a nuisance, and unjustified variation is prohibited. The unfortunate effects of these practices may be reversed by clumsy acts that provide excuses to redraw boundaries around elements.

One of the major causes of failure in organizations is a shortage of images concerning what they're up to, a shortage of time devoted to producing these images, and a shortage of diverse actions to deal with changed circumstances. If it's the case that believing is seeing, then the person who is bound by the maxim "stamp out utility" is doing everything possible to enrich the believing so that in turn the things that are seen are rich and important as clues for survival.

If an organization is narrow in the images that it directs toward its own actions, then when it examines what it has said, it will see only bland displays. This means in turn that the organization won't be able to make much interesting sense of what's going on or of its place in it. That's not a trivial outcome, because the kind of sense that an organization makes of its thoughts and of itself has an effect on its ability to deal with change. An organization that continually sees itself in novel images, images that are permeated with diverse skills and sensitivities, thereby is equipped to deal with altered surroundings when they appear.

THE MAP IS THE TERRITORY

People often confuse symbols with the thing symbolized. They believe that a Phi Beta Kappa key *is* education, no matter how it is acquired (e.g., by cheating); that a rug on the floor *is* power, no matter who says so; that a Cadillac *is* status, whether the car is a repo, leased, rented, or purchased on time. In each case, the important thing that semanticists emphasize is that the symbol is *not* the thing (Hayakawa 1961), a reality that is signified by the phrase "the map is not the territory."

Maps are not territories for the simple reason that there is a great deal of slippage between symbols and things. Symbols are usually an inaccurate copy of things, and one treats them as tangible and true at some risk. Maps that have no relation to the real world are useless and misleading, which is why people are forewarned to be suspicious of the maps in their heads and chronically to inquire as to the adequacy with which they match things.

That is reasonable advice and constitutes part of the activity that managers should consider when they reflect on how things are going. But there is a limit to the soundess of that advice. When an organization produces a cause map and superimposes it on subsequent occasions, it does in fact create the territories that it inhabits. Given that chain of events, the map does become the territory. The map, however, is itself a simplification, ignores large portions of the stream of experience, and might well produce a more rewarding existence if it were altered. That being the case, an organization that thrives on doubt can routinely treat as certain those things that it doubts and doubt those things that it treats as certain. It either doubts its doubting or doubts its certainty.

Maps that emerge from the organizing process can also be treated as territory because they have received more attention than almost any product the members produce. Organizations are in the business of making sense. If they attend to anything with consistency and regularity, it is to their sense-making activities. Therefore, the outcome of this sense-making, flawed as it may be, nevertheless portrays the territory with some accuracy. These enacted environments are accurate partly because they have been consensually validated and partly because the territory is created by the map-maker, insuring a closer fit between the two activities. Maps constrain enactments, which means that maps constrain territory-building and bracketing. When those enactments are processed it is not surprising that they should resemble former maps and, in the process, be valid and accurate renderings of the territory that people in the organization face. Once again we see a way in which organizations resemble closed rather than open systems and we see why unqualified usage of open systems theory can divert people from some of the crucial means by which organizations persist.

Hard-headed realists (that is, those who lost the ballgame portrayed in Chapter 2) take pride in asserting that organizations are concerned with real things like profit and loss. To label *profit* a thing is to miss much of what is interesting about it. Profit is one way of labeling and making sense of the world; it is a variable in a cause map, it can be an enacted environment, and it can be a symbol. It is one form of sensibleness that can be imposed on an organization's stream of experience, but it is only one form of sensibleness, and it is an arbitrary one at that.

To understand the full force of the arguments that profit, loss, money, and assets are reasonable though arbitrary ways to label and bracket the stream of experience, consider this example related by Watzlawick, Weakland, and Fisch:

> The reality of a banknote does not reside primarily in the fact that it is a rectangular piece of paper with certain markings, but rather in the interpersonal convention that it is to have a certain value. An intriguing example was reported to Bateson by the inhabitants of a certain coastal area of New Guinea who use shell money for small, everyday purchases, but

heavy millstone-shaped rock tokens for larger transactions. One day such a stone was being transported from one village to another across a river estuary when the boat capsized in the rough surf and the "money" disappeared forever in the deep water. Since the incident was known to everybody concerned, the stone continued to be used as legal tender in many subsequent transactions, although strictly speaking its reality now existed only in the minds of a large group of people (1974, p. 96).

RECHART THE ORGANIZATIONAL CHART

Throughout this book we have taken liberties with that sacred organizational trapping, the organizational chart, and we would urge managers to take similar license with that chart.

The one modification of an organizational chart that is most consistent with the arguments in this book is to replace people with variables. A conventional chart would look like the one in Fig. 9.1.

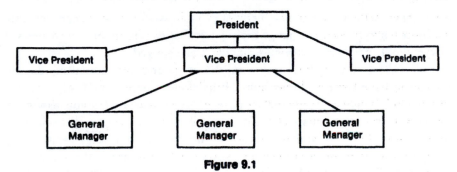

Figure 9.1

A modified chart would look like the one in Fig. 9.2. In Fig. 9.2 people have been represented as variables, a substitution that is consistent with the idea of partial inclusion, and a substitution that highlights what is salient about each of these individuals in the cause map of someone who has to deal with them.

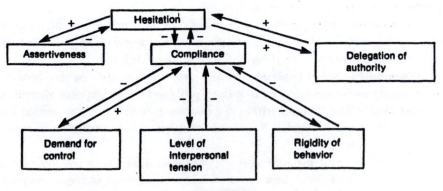

Figure 9.2

Whole persons aren't contained in the boxes on organizational charts. But managers forget that, which is why organizational charts are never the way things work—even though people invest enormous time in drawing, reviewing, pondering, and worrying over them. The essence of organizations is to be found in variables, connections, and positive and negative signs. The variables include recurrent styles, behaviors, and interpretations associated with each position. These variables have a durability because they represent behaviors that are "pulled" from all occupants by the job description for the position, the roles that are sent to it, and the expectations that are imposed on it. People are interchangeable in the sense that similar pulls are imposed on any occupant, usually with some success, and that's why a representation of the organization in the form of a cause map is an informative means to redraw the conventional organizational chart.

VISUALIZE ORGANIZATIONS AS EVOLUTIONARY SYSTEMS

Awareness of the evolutionary features of one's work situation can promote intelligent intervention to change those parts that can be changed and amused resignation to those inevitabilities that can't be changed.

To initiate an evolutionary analysis of your work situation, do the following. Take several photographs of the places, people, and tools that you work with. Be generous in the number of shots and angles you assemble. Enlarge the pictures so that small details are clear. Now take a large number of small gummed labels and write the words *ecological change, enactment, selection,* and *retention* on them. Once you've done that, attach the appropriate label(s) to all of the people and trappings that you work with. Think about your workplace as if it were a self-contained evolutionary system and then proceed to label which features correspond with which evolutionary processes. Ask yourself what there is too much and too little of. Is there retention with no enactments or selection? Do some people now seem more or less important than they did before they were coordinated with evolutionary processes? The questions can go on.

The purpose of this exercise is to make concrete and visible the ways in which your specific work situation resembles the generalized evolutionary work situation that has been described throughout this book.

Intentional usage of evolutionary images can be carried one step farther. An especially useful device to aid in solving problems is the relational algorithm (Crovitz 1967, 1970). This algorithm is a miniature evolutionary system and it is this resemblance that makes it a suitable exhibit of how evolution operates inside the organization.

Evolutionary systems are creative systems, and creativity usually means putting old things into new combinations and new things into old combinations.

In either case, novel relations between pairs of things are the essence of creativity. It was Crovitz's genius to see that there were exactly 42 relational words in Basic English (a word-list of 850 words) that could be used to relate two items.

The prototype sentence for depicting an idea is "Take one thing in relation to another thing." Or, more sparsely, "Take one thing [   ] another thing." One at a time, the 42 relational words (for example, *about, across, after, where, while, with*) are inserted in the brackets to see if they solve the problem. (Table 9.1 lists the complete algorithm.)

TABLE 9.1
Relational Algorithm
(From Crovitz 1970, p. 100.)

about	at	for	of	round	to
across	because	from	off	still	under
after	before	if	on	so	up
against	between	in	opposite	then	when
among	but	near	or	though	where
and	by	not	out	through	while
as	down	now	over	till	with

For example, suppose I am having trouble threading a needle. My two domain or "thing" words are *thread* and *needle*. Perhaps I cannot thread the needle because I have a relational blind spot. The only sentence I can construct is "Take the thread *through* the needle." Now, if I run through the other 41 words, I come up with combinations such as "Take a thread *among* a needle" (which suggests that I should try to thread several needles at once on the outside chance that one of them might accidentally be threaded), "Take a thread *around* a needle" (wrap thread around needle and try to poke it through material), "Take a thread *as* a needle" (sew with raw thread that is toughened and sharpened at the end), "Take a thread *up* a needle" (move the thread from the base to the top, gradually tilting the needle and thereby spearing the hole). The choice of a pair of domain words is undoubtedly crucial. If we had simply reversed the pair, "Take a needle *through* a thread," new possibilities (or no possibilities) might have occurred.

Try your own hand at constructing a relational algorithm. In the space below write down a current problem you are experiencing that has these characteristics:

1   It is a meaningful problem with which you're confronted.

2   You are directly involved in the situation.

3   The problem is presently unresolved.

4 You are dissatisfied with the situation and would like to change it.

5 The problem is important to you.

Some typical work problems that might be listed include:

1 A manager is dissatisfied with the *quality* of his *subordinate's work* and with the person's apparently *negative attitude.*

2 A chief engineer thinks that his plant *superintendent* is not effective in resolving a persistent *conflict* between the *engineering* and *manufacturing* departments.

3 A staff specialist believes that his *services* are being resisted or not adequately used by the *administration.*

4 A subordinate has been unable to convince his *superior* that certain *policy changes* are needed.

5 A marketing manager thinks that the *staff* of which he is a *member* is overly *competitive,* more *interested* in destroying one another than in *collaborating.*

Write the statement of your problem here:

Once you have written your statement of the problem underline all nouns, domain words, and tangible elements in that statement. (Italicized words in the list of "typical work problems" above illustrate the kinds of words you should look for.)

Once you have identified the domain words that are crucial in your problem, write one of these words on each of the blank lines in disc *A*. After you have written all those words on disc *A*, repeat the same list on the blank lines of disc *C*. Then, cut out disc *C* and disc *B* (with the relational words). Put disc *C* on top of the relational disc (disc *B*), and attach both of these discs to the large disc (disc *A*) with a paper fastener.

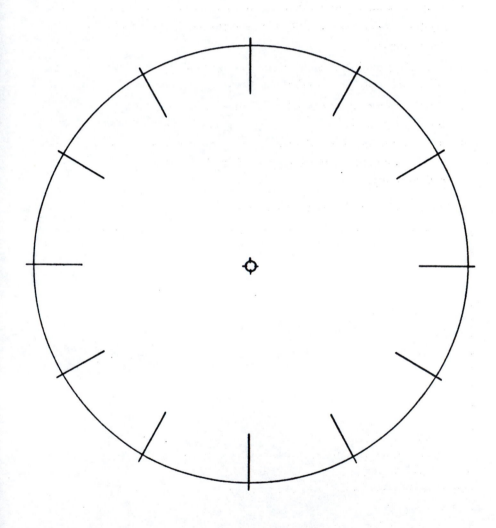

Disc A

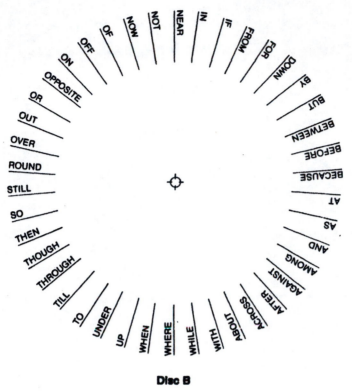

Disc B

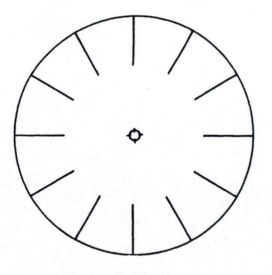

Disc C

Now, by turning either disc *C* or the relational disc (*B*) you can put the old components of your problem into new relationships to discover solutions that had not occurred to you before.

To illustrate the process of idea generation, consider this example. "During one of the many nineteenth-century riots in Paris the commander of an army detachment received orders to clear a city square by firing at the *canaille* (rabble). He commanded his soldiers to take up firing positions, their rifles leveled at the crowd, and as a ghastly silence descended he drew his sword and shouted at the top of his lungs." Now, what could he shout that would allow him to follow orders yet save lives? Among the domain words in this problem are:

1 commander
2 soldiers
3 city square
4 rabble
5 firing positions
6 rifles
7 crowd

The possible combinations are sizable, and the solutions are plentiful. To see what the commander did to solve his problem, work with the domain words *rabble* and *crowd*. Take the rabble about a crowd, across a crowd, after a crowd, and so on. After you've worked your way through that list, you'll see why the commander yelled what he did:

"Mesdames, m'sieurs, I have orders to fire at the *canaille*. But as I see a great number of honest, respectable citizens before me, I request that they leave so that I can safely shoot the *canaille*." The square was empty in a few minutes (Watzlawick, Weakland, and Fisch 1974, p. 81).

The value of these 42 relational words for gaining insight into managing is substantial. Consider the strategies implied by these combinations:

take
managing
{
among organized anarchies
while designing jobs
from incentives
opposite MBO
between unclear goals
as ambivalence
through federal regulations
near retrenchment
where mergers
under dependence on oil
}

Ecological change   ⟶   *Enactment*   ⟶   *Selection*   ⟶   *Retention*

(The statement of a problem)   (Writing words and spinning wheels)   (Interpreting what combinations mean)   (Remembering good ideas, domain words, and relations)

Figure 9.3

Any one of those combinations, when made the object of reflection, can suggest ways of managing that represent doing old things in new ways.

The relevance of the relational algorithm to evolution is diagrammed in Fig. 9.3. The discs produce the variations, a very small number of which survive as meaningful interpretations to be imposed again in the future.

The epistemology that is implicit in evolution is made explicit by means of the relational algorithm. It is just that kind of concretization that is being urged when we say that people should visualize organizations as evolutionary systems.

Relationships with people can also be modeled after the ESR framework. A standard employee interview format goes: (1) What's the problem? (ecological change), (2) What have you done about it? (enactment), (3) What do those actions mean? (selection), and (4) What should we conclude? (retention). Now comes the twist associated with organizing. At the conclusion of this straight-forward interview, when people are discussing what to do, the sensitive manager has to say in effect, "Go ahead and do what we've decided, *but* it may not be the whole story, so be open to the possibility that our conclusion right now is incorrect. And if it's too hard to act and simultaneously doubt what you're doing, then have someone else do your doubting for you."

In this example the conversation between the two people simulates an evolutionary system right down to using ambivalence as the ultimate compromise. Split decisions are the tough part to execute. That's why certainty drives out ambiguity, routine drives out improvisation, and why organizations lag seriously in their responses to changed environments.

Conventional features in work situations readily find their place in an evolutionary model. Productivity is an interpretation imposed on enactments by the selection process. Departments are arbitrary collections of double interacts. A task is a linkage between enactment and ecological change where ecological change consists of the "requireds" in the task, enactment the behaviors of task performance, and the effect of enactment on ecological change representing "task redefinition." Tasks may also be present in interlocked cycles.

Technology can be viewed either as an ecological change or as an enacted environment (machines "remember" an organization's routines). When people talk about job enrichment they are talking about the linkages between enactment and ecological change as well as possible modifications of retention effects on enactment.

The image of an evolutionary system is not just a convenient gimmick for exposition, it coordinates with many aspects of managing and organizing. Effective managing would seem to involve maximizing rather than minimizing these points of contact.

COMPLICATE YOURSELF!

This argument is sufficiently familiar that there's no reason to belabor it. It lies at the heart of the organizing formulation as the overall prescription for adaptation.

At the time of the blackout in New York City there was a lively debate on whether the National Guard should have been called in to help the police control the looting that accompanied the blackout.

> The Guard is not designed for such sophisticated crisis management, and its members, for the most part, are utterly unfamiliar with the technique of ghetto policing. Indeed the spector of a platoon of heavily armed Guardsmen being supervised by a frightened weekend superior officer from the Finger Lakes . . . does not exactly reassure (Plate 1977, p. 31).

Members of the New York Police Department who are familiar with crisis management in ghettos are significantly more complicated with regard to those situations than are people associated with enforcement in other areas.

The importance of complication is difficult to overemphasize. Take cause maps, for example. Any cause map is an oversimplification of situations. In the real world signs on relationships can change, the swiftness with which an effect follows activation of a cause is variable, the magnitude of the change that will occur is variable, insertion of a new variable into a cause map can change the entire set of conclusions that are drawn from it, it is fairly easy to leave out variables, there are exponential relationships that can override apparent deviation counteraction, and in any large system of loops, different loops may be activated a different number of times, which makes prediction difficult.

What that means is that a cause map itself is a simplification, even though it does help to complicate how an individual examines his organization. If you ask an individual to describe his organization you'll get a fairly simple answer. If you then press that same individual to develop a cause map of it, new conclusions will be seen, and a more complicated perspective on that organization will emerge. Nevertheless, the cause map omits a large number of characteristics. Whatever additional ways we can find to complicate observers should also be adopted because the primary thrust of organizations is toward simplification, homogeneity, and crude registering of consequential events.

A means of complication implicit in the organizing model itself is for the organization to operate for some period of time while totally discrediting what it has known. The organization operates as shown in Fig. 9.4. This produces

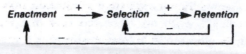

Figure 9.4

intentional complication because the members do and think different things and this stocks the retention system with new images. These newer images, much like the diverse material that filters through the perforated spoon onto jelly (see Chapter 8), create several new gullies along which incoming material may be reorganized. Shuffling past images by means of an interlude of discrediting is helpful because it increases the number of beliefs that are available for seeing the world. This proliferation of relatively independent images means that more of the happenings in that world will be sensed.

Discrediting by means of randomizing (e.g., Schelling 1963, chap. 7) is another way to introduce complication and improve adaptability. The form of this argument can be sketched using Moore's (1957) analysis of divination as practiced by the Naskapi Indians in Labrador. Every day the Naskapi face the question of which direction the hunters should take to locate game. They answer the question by holding dried caribou shoulder bones over a fire. As the bones become heated they develop cracks and smudges that are then "read" by an expert. These cracks indicate the direction in which the hunters should look for game. The Naskapi believe that this practice allows the gods to intervene in their hunting decisions. The interesting feature of these practices is that they work.

To see how these practices work, think about some of the characteristics of this decision procedure. First, the final decision about where to hunt is not a purely personal or group choice. If no game is found, the gods—not the group—are to blame. Second, the final decision is not affected by the outcomes of past hunts. If the Indians were influenced by the outcomes of past hunts, they would run the definite risk of depleting the stock of animals. Their prior success would induce subsequent failure. Third, the final decision is not influenced by the typical human patterning of choice and preferences, which can enable the hunted animals to take evasive action and become sensitized to the presence of human beings. The use of scapulas (bones) is thus a very crude way of complicating human behavior under conditions where avoiding fixed patterns of activity may have an advantage. Restated in Moore's own words, "It seems safe to assume that human beings require a functional equivalent to a table of random numbers if they are to avoid unwitting regularities in their behavior, which can be utilized by adversaries" (1957, p. 73).

Our impression is that using tables of random numbers to make decisions may be effective in a broader range of settings than simply those involving adversaries. For example, one reason why adaptation may preclude adaptability is that people remember only those practices that are currently useful. Memory undercuts innovation. It is conceivable that if groups made greater use of randomizing devices, which let them forget current adaptive practices, they might be in a better position to cope resourcefully with change. If an executive burned caribou bones to decide where to look for new customers or where to relocate his factory, it is not obvious to us that his organization would be any worse off than if he used a highly rational plan to decide these issues.

The use of randomizing procedures such as "reading" cracks in burnt caribou bones has several advantages:

1 The consequences are small if you make a mistake.
2 A decision can be made when there are insufficient facts.
3 A decision can be made when there are insufficient differences among the alternatives.
4 Bottlenecks can be broken.
5 These practices confuse competitors.
6 They create an infinite number of alternatives.
7 The procedure is fun.
8 A decision can be reached swiftly.
9 No skill is required of the user.
10 The technique is inexpensive.
11 There is agreement on the process.
12 No files or storage are required.
13 There are no favorites, all alternatives are weighted equally.
14 The solution is arrived at nonargumentatively.
15 Genuine novelty is introduced.
16 One's luck can be changed by initiating a different pattern of responding.

Finally, to be complicated is to take pleasure in the process rather than pleasure in the outcome. That holds true for the process of theorizing as well as for the process of managing.

To take pleasure in the process is to understand what an Ithaka means.

Ithaka

As you set out for Ithaka
hope your road is a long one,

full of adventure, full of discovery.
Laistrygonians, Cyclops,
angry Poseidon—don't be afraid of them:
you'll never find things like that on your way
as long as you keep your thoughts raised high,
as long as a rare excitement
stirs your spirit and your body.
Laistrygonians, Cyclops,
wild Poseidon—you won't encounter them
unless you bring them along inside your soul,
unless your soul sets them up in front of you.

Hope your road is a long one.
May there be many summer mornings when,
with what pleasure, what joy,
you enter harbors you're seeing for the first time;
may you stop at Phoenician trading stations
to buy fine things,
mother of pearl and coral, amber and ebony,
sensual perfume of every kind—
as many sensual perfumes as you can;
and may you visit many Egyptian cities
to learn and go on learning from their scholars.

Keep Ithaka always in your mind.
Arriving there is what you're destined for.
But don't hurry the journey at all.
Better if it lasts for years,
so you're old by the time you reach the island,
wealthy with all you've gained on the way,
not expecting Ithaka to make you rich.

Ithaka gave you the marvelous journey.
Without her you wouldn't have set out.
She has nothing left to give you now.

And if you find her poor, Ithaka won't have fooled you.
Wise as you will have become, so full of experience,
you'll have understood by then what these Ithakas mean.

—C. P. Cavafy

Organizations keep peoply busy, occasionally entertain them, give them a variety of experiences, keep them off the streets, provide pretexts for story-telling, and allow socializing. They haven't anything else to give.

references

Aldrich, H., and D. Herker. 1977. Boundary spanning roles and organization structure. *Academy of Management Review* 2: 217-230.

Aldrich, H. E., and J. Pfeffer. 1976. Environments of organizations. In A. Inkeles, J. Coleman, and N. Smelser (eds.), *Annual review of sociology* (Vol. 2). Palo Alto, Calif.: Annual Reviews, pp. 79-105.

Alexander, R. D. 1975. The search for a general theory of behavior. *Behavioral Science* 20: 77-100.

Allison, G. T. 1971. *Essence of decision: Explaining the Cuban missile crisis.* Boston: Little, Brown.

Allport, F. H. 1924. *Social psychology.* Cambridge, Mass.: Houghton Mifflin.

———. 1955. *Theories of perception and the concept of structure.* New York: Wiley.

———. 1962. A structuronomic conception of behavior: Individual and collective. *Journal of Abnormal and Social Psychology* 64: 3-30.

Allport, G. W. 1961. *Pattern and growth in personality.* New York: Holt, Rinehart and Winston.

Anderson, N. G. 1974. Science and management techniques. *Science* 183: 726-727.

Aram, J. D. 1976. *Dilemmas of administrative behavior.* Englewood Cliffs, N.J.: Prentice-Hall.

Archibald, W. P. 1974. Alternative explanations for self-fulfilling prophecy. *Psychological Bulletin* 31: 74-84.

Argyris, C. 1964. *Integrating the individual and the organization.* New York: Wiley.

Arian, E. 1971. *Bach, Beethoven, and bureaucracy: The case of the Philadelphia Orchestra.* University, Ala.: University of Alabama Press.

Ascher, W. 1978. *Forecasting.* Baltimore: Johns Hopkins University Press.

Ashton, R. H. 1976. Deviation-amplifying feedback and unintended consequences of management accounting systems. *Accounting, Organizations and Society* 1: 289-300.

Atkinson, J. W., and D. Cartwright. 1964. Some neglected variables in contemporary conceptions of decision and performance. *Psychological Reports* 14: 575-590.

Auden, W. H., and L. Kronenberger. 1966. *The Viking book of aphorisms.* New York: Viking.

Axelrod, R. (ed.). 1976. *Structure of decision: The cognitive maps of political elites.* Princeton, N.J.: Princeton University Press.

Bailey, F. G. 1977. *Morality and expediency: The folklore of academic politics.* Chicago: Aldine.

Bakan, D. 1975. Speculation in psychology. *Journal of Humanistic Psychology* 15, No. 1: 17-25.

Ball, D. W. 1972. "The definition of situation": Some theoretical and methodological consequences of taking W. I. Thomas seriously. *Journal for the Theory of Social Behavior* 2: 61-82.

Barnard, C. I. 1938. *The functions of the executive.* Cambridge, Mass.: Harvard University Press.

————. 1948. *Organization and management.* Cambridge, Mass.: Harvard University Press.

Bartlett, F. C. 1932. *Remembering.* Cambridge: At the University Press.

Bateson, G. W. 1951. Conventions of communications: Where validity depends on belief. In J. Ruesch and G. Bateson (eds.), *Communication, the social matrix of society.* New York: Norton, pp. 212-227.

————. 1966. Information, codification, and metacommunication. In A. G. Smith (ed.), *Communication and culture.* New York: Holt, Rinehart and Winston, pp. 412-426.

————. 1971. The cybernetics of "self": A theory of alcoholism. *Psychiatry* 34: 1-18.

————. 1972. *Steps to an ecology of mind.* New York: Ballantine.

Bateson, M. C. 1972. *Our own metaphor.* New York: Knopf.

Bavelas, J. B. 1973. Effects of temporal context on information. *Psychological Reports* 32: 695-698.

Beer, S. 1975. *Platform for Change.* New York: Wiley.

Behrens, J. C. 1977. *The typewriter guerillas.* Chicago: Nelson-Hall.

Bell, G. D. 1967. Formality versus flexibility in complex organizations. In G. D. Bell (ed.), *Organizations and human behavior.* Englewood Cliffs, N.J.: Prentice-Hall, pp. 97-106.

Bem, D. J. 1967. Self-perception: The dependent variable of human performance. *Organizational Behavior and Human Performance* 2: 105-121.

————. 1974. Cognitive alteration of feeling states: A discussion. In H. London and R. E. Nisbett (eds.), *Thought and feeling.* Chicago: Aldine, pp. 211-233.

Bennett, J. W. 1976. Anticipation, adaptation, and the concept of culture in anthropology. *Science* 192: 847-853.

Berger, P. L., and T. Luckman. 1967. *The social construction of reality.* Garden City, N.Y.: Doubleday, Anchor Books.

Berk, R. A. 1974. A gaming approach to crowd behavior. *American Sociological Review* 39: 355-373.

Berkowitz, L. 1956. Personality and group position. *Sociometry* 19: 210-222.

Bernard, H. R., and P. D. Killworth. 1973. On the social structure of an ocean-going research vessel and other important things. *Social Science Research* 2: 145-184.

Bidwell, C. E. 1965. The school as a formal organization. In J. G. March (ed.), *Handbook of organizations.* Chicago: Rand, pp. 972-1022.

Bierce, A. 1946. *The collected writings of Ambrose Bierce.* New York: Citadel.

Bigelow, J. D. 1978. Evolution in organizations. Unpublished doctoral dissertation, Case Western Reserve University, 1978.

Bill. 1957. Why Alcoholics Anonymous is anonymous. In *Alcoholics Anonymous comes of age.* New York: AA World Services, pp. 286-294.

Billow, R. M. 1977. Metaphor: A review of the psychological literature. *Psychological Bulletin* 84: 81-92.

Blau, P. M. 1954. Patterns of interaction among a group of officials in a government agency. *Human Relations* 7: 337-348.

Blauner, R. 1960. Work satisfaction and industrial trends in modern society. In W. Galenson and S. M. Lipset (eds.), *Labor and trade unionism.* New York: Wiley, pp. 339-360.

Bonini, C. P. 1963. *Simulation of information and decision systems in the firm.* Englewood Cliffs, N.J.: Prentice-Hall.

Bonoma, T. V. 1976. Conflict, cooperation and trust in three power systems. *Behavioral Science* 21: 499-514.

Borovits, I., and E. Segev. 1977. Real-time management—An analogy. *Academy of Management Review* 2: 311-316.

Bougon, M., K. E. Weick, and D. Binkhorst. 1977. Cognition in organizations: An analysis of the Utrecht Jazz Orchestra. *Administrative Science Quarterly* 22: 606-639.

Boulding, K. E. 1971. The dodo didn't make it: Survival and betterment. *Bulletin of the Atomic Scientists* 27, No. 2: 19-22.

Bradney, P. 1957. Quasi-familial relationships in industry. *Human Relations* 10: 271-278.

Brand, S. 1975. Caring and clarity: Conversations with Gregory Bateson and Edmund G. Brown, Jr. *CoEvolution Quarterly,* Sept. 23, 1975, pp. 32-47.

Braybrooke, D. 1964. The mystery of executive success re-examined. *Administrative Science Quarterly* 8: 533-560.

Brockett, C. 1975. Toward a clarification of the need hierarchy theory: Some extensions of Maslow's conceptualization. *Interpersonal Development* 6: 77-90.

Bruyn, S. T. 1966. *The human perspective in sociology.* Englewood Cliffs, N.J.: Prentice-Hall.

Buckley, W. 1967. *Sociology and modern systems theory.* Englewood Cliffs, N.J.: Prentice-Hall.

————. 1968. Society as a complex adaptive system. In W. Buckley (ed.), *Modern systems research for the behavioral scientist.* Chicago: Aldine, pp. 490-513.

Burke, K. 1968. *Counter-statement.* Berkeley and Los Angeles: University of California Press.

Burnstein, E. 1969. Interdependence in groups. In J. Mills (ed.), *Experimental social psychology.* New York: Macmillan, pp. 307-405.

Cadwallader, M. 1959. The cybernetic analysis of change in complex organizations. *American Journal of Sociology* 65: 154-157.

Campbell, D. T. 1958. Systematic error on the part of human links in communication systems. *Information and Control* 1: 334-369.

————. 1959. Systematic errors to be expected of the social scientist on the basis of a general psychology of cognitive bias. Paper presented at APA.

————. 1965a. Ethnocentric and other altruistic motives. In D. Levine (ed.), *Nebraska symposium on motivation, 1965*. Lincoln: University of Nebraska Press, pp. 283-311.

———— 1965b. Variation and selective retention in socio-cultural evolution. In H. R. Barringer, G. I. Blanksten, and R. Mack (eds.), *Social change in developing areas*. Cambridge, Mass.: Schenkman, pp. 19-49.

————. 1969. Ethnocentrism of disciplines and the fish-scale model of omniscience. In M. Sherif and C. W. Sherif (eds.), *Interdisciplinary relationships in the social sciences*. Chicago: Aldine, pp. 328-348.

————. 1970. Natural selection as an epistemological model. In R. Naroll and R. Cohen (eds.), *A Handbook of method in cultural anthropology*. Garden City, N.Y.: Natural History Press, pp. 51-85.

————. 1972. On the genetics of altruism and the counter-hedonic components in human culture. *Journal of Social Issues* 28, No. 3: 21-37.

————. 1974a. Evolutionary epistemology. In P. A. Schilpp (ed.). *The philosophy of Karl R. Popper* (Vol. 14-I). LaSalle, Ill.: Open Court, pp. 413-463.

————. 1974b. Unjustified variation and selective retention in scientific discovery. In F. J. Ayala and T. Dobzhansky (eds.), *Studies in the philosophy of biology*. New York: Macmillan, pp. 139-161.

————. 1975a. "Degrees of freedom" and the case study. *Comparative Political Studies* 8: 178-193.

————. 1975b. On the conflicts between biological and social evolution and between psychology and moral tradition. *American Psychologist* 30: 1103-1126.

Cannon, R. 1973. *The Sea of Cortez*. Menlo Park, Calif.: Lane.

Caplow, T. 1964. *Principles of organization*. New York: Harcourt, Brace and World.

Carzo, R., and J. N. Yanouzas. 1967. *Formal organization: A systems approach*. Homewood, Ill.: Irwin-Dorsey.

Chafetz, J. S. 1970. A brief and informal essay in the social-psychology of sociology. *Sociological Focus* 4, No. 2: 53-60.

Child, J. 1972. Organization structure, environment and performance: The role of strategic choice. *Sociology* 6: 1-22.

Cohen, A. M., E. L. Robinson, and J. L. Edwards. 1969. Experiments in organizational embeddedness. *Administrative Science Quarterly* 14: 208-221.

Cohen, M. D., and J. G. March. 1974. *Leadership and ambiguity*. New York: McGraw-Hill.

Cohen, M. D., J. G. March, and J. P. Olsen. 1972. A garbage can model of organizational choice. *Administrative Science Quarterly* 17: 1-25.

Conant, R. C., and R. W. Ashby. 1970. Every good regulator of a system must be a model of that system. *International Journal of Systems Science* 1, No. 2: 89-97.

Conger, L. 1969. Castles in the air. *The Writer* 82, No. 6: 8-9.

Cooley, C. H. 1931. *Life and the student.* New York: Knopf.

Cooney, J. E. 1978. "Marketing warfare" seeks military link for sales campaigns. *Wall Street Journal,* April 28, 1978, p. 25.

Cronbach, L. J. 1975. Beyond the two disciplines of scientific psychology. *American Psychologist* 30: 116-127.

Crosbie, J. S. 1977. *Crosbie's dictionary of puns.* New York: Harmony.

Crovitz, H. F. 1967. The form of logical solutions. *American Journal of Psychology* 80: 461-462.

————. 1970. *Galton's walk.* New York: Harper and Row.

Curtis, J. 1976. When sisterhood turns sour. *New York Times Magazine,* May 30, 1976, pp. 15-16.

Cyert, R. M., and J. G. March. 1963. *A behavioral theory of the firm.* Englewood Cliffs, N.J.: Prentice-Hall.

Dachler, H. P., and B. Wilpert. 1978. Conceptual dimensions and boundaries of participation in organizations: A critical evaluation. *Administrative Science Quarterly* 23: 1-39.

Dailey, C. A. 1971. *Assessment of lives.* San Francisco: Jossey-Bass.

Davis, M. S. 1971. That's interesting: Towards a phenomenology of sociology and a sociology of phenomenology. *Philosophy of Social Science* 1: 309-344.

DeBeer, G. 1958. *Evolution by natural selection.* Cambridge: At the University Press.

deBono, E. 1969. *The mechanism of mind.* Baltimore: Penguin.

Deutsch, K. W. 1963. *The nerves of government.* New York: Free Press.

Diesing, P. 1962. *Reason in society.* Westport, Conn.: Greenwood.

Downey, H. K., and J. W. Slocum. 1975. Uncertainty: Measures, research, and sources of variation. *Academy of Management Journal* 18: 562-578.

Duncan, R. 1972. Characteristics of organizational environments and perceived environmental uncertainty. *Administrative Science Quarterly* 17: 313-327.

Dunn, E. S., Jr. 1971. *Economic and social development.* Baltimore: Johns Hopkins University Press.

Easterbrook, J. A. 1959. The effect of emotion on cue utilization and the organization of behavior. *Psychological Review* 66: 183-201.

Edwards, D. 1978. The trading room: It's not a gentleman's game. *MBA* 12, No. 6: 13-25.

Ehrlich, P. R., A. H. Ehrlich, and J. P. Holdren. 1973. *Human ecology: Problems and solutions.* San Francisco: W. H. Freeman.

Elbow, P. 1973. *Writing without teachers.* London: Oxford.

Emery, F. E., and E. L. Trist. 1973. *Towards a social ecology.* New York: Plenum.

Etzioni, A. 1964. *Modern organizations.* Englewood Cliffs, N.J.: Prentice-Hall.

Evan, W. M. 1963. Indices of the hierarchical structure of industrial organizations. *Management Science* 9: 468-477.

Faulkner, R. R. 1971. *Hollywood studio musicians*. Chicago: Aldine.

―――. 1973. Orchestra interaction: Some features of communication and authority in an artistic organization. *Sociological Quarterly* 14: 147-157.

Fenichel, O. 1945. *The psychoanalytic theory of neuroses*. New York: Norton.

Fernandez, J. W. 1972. Persuasions and performances: Of the beast in everybody . . . and the metaphors of everyman. *Daedalus* 101, No. 1: 39-60.

Festinger, L. 1954. A theory of social comparison processes. *Human Relations* 7: 117-140.

Finlay, D. G. 1978. Alcoholism and systems theory: Building a better mousetrap. *Psychiatry* 41: 272-278.

Forrest, C. R., L. L. Cummings, and A. C. Johnson. 1977. Organizational participation: A critique and model. *Academy of Management Review* 2: 586-601.

Freeman, D. 1974. The evolutionary theories of Charles Darwin and Herbert Spencer. *Current Anthropology* 15: 211-237.

Frick, F. C. 1959. Information theory. In S. Koch (ed.), *Psychology: A study of a science* (Vol. 2). New York: McGraw-Hill, pp. 611-636.

Fromkin, H. L. 1973. The psychology of uniqueness: Avoidance of similarity and seeking of differentness (Krannert Graduate School of Administration, Working Paper 438). Unpublished manuscript, Purdue University.

Gans, H. J. 1972. The positive functions of poverty. *American Journal of Sociology* 78: 275-289.

Garfinkel, H. 1962. Common-sense knowledge of social structures: The documentary method of interpretation. In J. Scher (ed.), *Theories of the mind*. New York: Free Press, pp. 689-712.

―――. 1967. *Studies in ethnomethodology*. Englewood Cliffs, N.J.: Prentice-Hall.

―――. 1974. "Good" organizational reasons for "bad" clinic records. In R. Turner (ed.), *Ethnomethodology*. Baltimore: Penguin, pp. 109-127.

Gass, W. 1965. *On being blue*. Boston: Godine.

Geertz, C. 1973. *The interpretation of cultures*. New York: Basic Books.

Georgiou, P. 1973. The goal paradigm and notes towards a counter paradigm. *Administrative Science Quarterly* 18: 291-310.

Gergen, K. 1974. *Social psychology: Explorations in understanding*. Del Mar, Calif.: CRM.

Ghiselin, M. T. 1969. *The triumph of the Darwinian method*. Berkeley and Los Angeles: University of California Press.

―――. 1974. *The economy of nature and the evolution of sex*. Berkeley and Los Angeles: University of California Press.

Gilfillan, D. P. 1977. Organizational processes in two jazz orchestras: Some evidence regarding the social psychology of organizing. Unpublished doctoral dissertation, University of Minnesota.

Glad you asked. *Depot Dispatch*, January 20, 1975, p. 2.

Glassman, R. B. 1973. Persistence and loose coupling in living systems. *Behavioral Science* 18: 83-98.

Goffman, E. 1969. *Strategic interaction*. Philadelphia: University of Pennsylvania Press.

———. 1974. *Frame analysis*. New York: Harper.

Goldsmith, E. 1971. The limits of growth in natural systems. *General Systems* 16: 69-75.

Gombrich, E. H. 1960. *Art and illusion*. Princeton, N.J.: Princeton University Press.

Gonos, G. 1977. "Situation" versus "frame": The "interactionist" and the "structuralist" analyses of everyday life. *American Sociological Review* 42: 854-867.

Goodell, R. 1977. *The visible scientists*. Boston: Little, Brown.

Goodwin, G. A. 1971. On transcending the absurd: An inquiry in the sociology of meaning. *American Journal of Sociology* 76: 831-846.

Gould, S. J. 1975. A threat to Darwinism. *Natural History* 84 (December): 4, 9.

———. 1977. The continental drift affair. *Natural History* 86 (February): 12-14.

Graen, G. 1976. Role-making processes within complex organizations. In M. D. Dunnette (ed.), *Handbook of industrial and organizational psychology*. Chicago: Rand, pp. 1201-1245.

Graves, R. 1966. *Collected poems*. Garden City, N.Y.: Doubleday, Anchor Books, p. 78.

———. 1970. The human toll of science. *Science* 168: 96.

Grossman, L. 1976. *Fat paper*. New York: McGraw-Hill.

Gruber, H. E., and J. J. Vonèche (eds.). 1977. *The essential Piaget*. New York: Basic Books.

Guetzkow, H. 1961. Organizational leadership in task-oriented groups. In L. Petrullo and B. M. Bass (eds.), *Leadership and interpersonal behavior*. New York: Holt, Rinehart and Winston, pp. 187-200.

Hall, R. H. 1977. *Organizations: Structure and process* (2nd ed.). Englewood Cliffs, N.J.: Prentice-Hall.

Hall, R. L. 1957. Group performance under feedback that confounds responses of group members. *Sociometry* 20: 297-305.

Hardin, G. 1963. The cybernetics of competition: A biologist's view of society. *Perspectives in Biology and Medicine* 7: 61-84.

———. 1971. Nobody ever dies of overpopulation. *Science* 171: 524.

Hardin, G., and J. Baden. 1977. *Managing the commons*. San Francisco: W. H. Freeman.

Hauschildt, J., and W. Hamel. 1978. Methodology of empirical goal research—On its way into a blind alley. *Theory and Decision* 9: 173-186.

Haworth, L. 1959. Do organizations act? *Ethics* 70: 59-63.

Hayakawa, S. I. 1961. The word is not the thing. In P. R. Lawrence, J. C. Bailey, R. L. Katz, J. A. Seiler, C. D. Orth III, J. V. Clark, L. B. Barnes, and A. N. Turner, *Organizational behavior and administration*. Homewood, Ill.: Dorsey, pp. 397-400.

Hedberg, B. L. T., P. C. Nystrom, and W. H. Starbuck. 1976. Camping on seesaws: Prescriptions for a self-designing organization. *Administrative Science Quarterly* 21: 41-65.

Hedgpeth, J. W. 1971. Philosophy on Cannery Row. In R. Astro and T. Hayaski (eds.), *Steinbeck: The man and his work.* Corvallis: Oregon State University Press, pp. 89-129.

Heider, F. 1958. *The psychology of interpersonal relations.* New York: Wiley.

————. 1959. Thing and medium. *Psychological Issues* 1, No. 3: 1-34.

————. 1960. The Gestalt theory of motivation. In M. R. Jones (ed.), *Nebraska symposium on motivation, 1960.* Lincoln: University of Nebraska Press, pp. 145-172.

Hein, P. 1966. *Grooks.* Cambridge, Mass.: MIT Press.

————. 1968. *Grooks II.* Cambridge, Mass.: MIT Press (Borgens Billigböger).

Heiskanen, I. 1967. *Theoretical approaches and scientific strategies in administrative and organizational research. A methodological study.* Helsinki: Helsingbors.

Henshel, R. L., and L. W. Kennedy. 1973. Self-altering prophecies: Consequences for the feasibility of social prediction. *General Systems Yearbook* 18: 119-126.

Hermann, C. F. 1963. Some consequences of crisis which limit the viability of organizations. *Administrative Science Quarterly* 8: 61-82.

Herndon, J. 1971. *How to survive in your native land.* New York: Simon and Schuster.

Hexter, J. H. 1962. *Reappraisals in history.* Evanston, Ill.: Northwestern University Press.

Hirschman, A. O. 1970. *Exit, voice, and loyalty.* Cambridge, Mass.: Harvard University Press.

Hirschman, A. O., and C. E. Lindblom. 1962. Economic development, research and development, policy making: Some converging views. *Behavioral Science* 7: 211-222.

Hollander, E. P. 1976. Leadership and social exchange processes. Unpublished manuscript, State University of New York at Buffalo.

Hollander, E. P., and R. H. Willis. 1967. Some current issues in the psychology of conformity and nonconformity. *Psychological Bulletin* 68: 62-76.

Holton, G. 1965. Introduction to the issue "science and culture." *Daedalus* 94: v-xxix.

Hunt, J. McV. 1963. Motivation inherent in information processing and action. In O. J. Harvey (ed.), *Motivation and social interaction.* New York: Ronald, pp. 35-94.

Hunt, J. W. 1972. *The restless organization.* Sydney: Wiley and Sons Australasia Pty. Ltd.

Indik, B. P. 1963. Some effects of organization size on member attitudes and behavior. *Human Relations* 16: 369-384.

Israel, J. 1972. Stipulations and construction in the social sciences. In J. Israel and H. Tajfel (eds.), *The context of social psychology.* New York: Academic, pp. 123-211.

Jacob, F. 1977. Evolution and tinkering. *Science* 196: 1161-1166.

Jacobs, D. 1974. Dependency and vulnerability: An exchange approach to the control of organizations. *Administrative Science Quarterly* 19: 45-59.

James, W. 1950. *The principles of psychology* (Vols. 1 and 2). New York: Dover.

————. 1956. Is life worth living? In W. James, *The will to believe*. New York: Dover, pp. 32-62.

Janis, I. R. 1972. *Victims of groupthink*. Boston: Houghton Mifflin.

Jantsch, E., and C. H. Waddington (eds.). 1976. *Evolution and consciousness*. Reading, Mass.: Addison-Wesley.

Jencks, C., and N. Silver. 1973. *Adhocism*. Garden City, N.Y.: Doubleday, Anchor Books.

Jennings, L. M. 1978. *Secretarial and administrative procedures*. Englewood Cliffs, N.J.: Prentice-Hall.

Johnson, A. W. 1978. *Quantification in cultural anthropology*. Stanford, Calif.: Stanford University Press.

Johnson, B. Mc. 1977. *Communication: The process of organizing*. Boston: Allyn and Bacon.

Jones, E. E., and H. B. Gerard. 1967. *Foundations of social psychology*. New York: Wiley. .

Jones, R. A. 1977. *Self-fulfilling prophecies*. Hillsdale, N.J.: Erlbaum.

Jones, R. A., and R. A. Day. 1977. Social psychology as symbolic interaction. In C. Hendrick (ed.), *Perspectives on social psychology*. Hillsdale, N.J.: Erlbaum, pp. 75-136.

Jordan, N. 1968. *Themes in speculative psychology*. London: Tavistock.

Kahneman, D. 1973. *Attention and effort*. Englewood Cliffs, N.J.: Prentice-Hall.

Kaman: How to bring aerospace knowhow to the guitar industry. *Business Week*, June 26, 1978, p. 74.

Katz, D. 1964. The motivational basis of organizational behavior. *Behavioral Science 9*: 131-146.

Katz, D., and R. L. Kahn. 1966. *The social psychology of organizations*. New York: Wiley.

Kaufman, H. 1975. The natural history of organizations. *Administration and Society 7*: 131-149.

Keese, P. 1975. Fog clouds NHL expansion. *New York Times*, May 22, 1975, pp. 47, 50.

Kelley, H. H. 1967. Attribution theory in social psychology. In D. Levine (ed.), *Nebraska symposium on motivation, 1967*. Lincoln: University of Nebraska Press, pp. 192-238.

————. 1968. Interpersonal accommodation. *American Psychologist 23*: 399-410.

Kelley, H. H., and A. J. Stahelski. 1970. Social interaction basis of cooperators' and competitors' beliefs about others. *Journal of Personality and Social Psychology 16*, No. 1: 66-91.

Kelley, H. H., and J. W. Thibaut. 1969. Group problem solving. In G. Lindzey and E. Aronson (eds.), *The handbook of social psychology* (2nd ed., Vol. 4). Reading, Mass.: Addison-Wesley, pp. 1-101.

Kelley, H. H., J. W. Thibaut, R. Radloff, and O. Mundy. 1962. The development of cooperation in the "minimal social situation." *Psychological Monographs 76*, No. 19 (Whole No. 538).

Kiesler, C. A. 1971. *The psychology of commitment.* New York: Academic.

Kimberly, J. R. 1976. Organizational size and the structuralist perspective: A review, critique, and proposal. *Administrative Science Quarterly* 21: 571-597.

Kimble, G. A. 1978. *How to use (and misuse) statistics.* Englewood Cliffs, N.J.: Prentice-Hall.

Kirkpatrick, D. L. 1975. The orchestra conductor and the manager. *Training and Development Journal* 29: 24-28.

Klein, L. 1976. *A social scientist in industry.* New York: Wiley.

Klingsporn, M. J. 1973. The significance of variability. *Behavioral Science* 18: 441-447.

Koestler, A. 1970. Literature and the law of diminishing returns. *Encounter* 34, No. 5: 39-45.

————. 1978. *Janus.* New York: Random.

Komorita, S. S., and J. M. Chertkoff. 1973. A bargaining theory of coalition formation. *Psychological Review* 80: 149-162.

Krech, D. 1968. Titchener on experimental psychology. *American Psychologist* 23: 367-368.

Krippendorf, K. 1971. Communication and the genesis of structure. *General Systems* 16: 171-185.

————. 1975. Some principles of information storage and retrieval in society. *General Systems* 20: 15-35.

Kursh, C. O. 1971. The benefits of poor communication. *Psychoanalytic Review* 58, No. 2: 189-208.

Laing, R. D. 1970. *Knots.* New York: Pantheon.

Lana, R. E. 1969. *Assumptions of social psychology.* New York: Appleton-Century-Crofts.

Lave, C. A., and J. G. March. 1975. *An introduction to models in the social sciences.* New York: Harper and Row.

Lazarus, R. S. 1966. *Psychological stress and the coping process.* New York: McGraw-Hill.

Leach, E. R. 1967. An anthropologist's reflections on a social survey. In D. G. Jongmans and P. C. Gutkins (eds.), *Anthropologists in the field.* Atlantic Highlands, N.J.: Humanities Press, pp. 75-88.

Leifer, R., and A. Delbecq. 1978. Organizational/environmental interchange: A model of boundary spanning activity. *Academy of Management Review* 3: 40-50.

Leonard, J. 1977. The anarchy of blab. *New York Times Book Review,* May 1, 1977, pp. 3, 50-51.

Lerner, A. W. 1976. On ambiguity and decisionmaker relations in organizations. Unpublished manuscript, Lehman College, City University of New York.

LeShan, L. 1976. *Alternate realities.* New York: Evans.

LeVine, R. A., and D. T. Campbell. 1972. *Ethnocentrism.* New York: Wiley.

Levinson, H. 1972. *Organizational diagnosis.* Cambridge, Mass.: Harvard University Press.

Lewontin, R. E. 1968. The concept of evolution. In D. L. Sills (ed.), *International encyclopedia of the social sciences* (Vol. 5). New York: Macmillan, pp. 202-210.

Lichtenstein, P. E. 1971. Genius as productive neurosis. *Psychological Record* 21: 151-164.

Likert, R. 1961. *New patterns of management.* New York: McGraw-Hill.

Lindblom, C. 1959. The science of muddling through. *Public Administration Review* 19: 79-88.

Linder, S. B. 1970. *The harried leisure class.* New York: Columbia University Press.

Low, A. 1976. *Zen and creative management.* Garden City, N.Y.: Doubleday, Anchor Books.

Lowin, A., and J. R. Craig. 1968. The influence of level of performance on managerial style: An experimental object-lesson in the ambiguity of correlational data. *Organizational Behavior and Human Performance* 3: 440-458.

Luchins, A. S., and E. H. Luchins. 1965. *Logical foundations of mathematics for behavioral scientists.* New York: Holt, Rinehart and Winston.

Lumsden, J. 1973. On criticism. *Australian Psychologist* 8, No. 3: 186-192.

Lyon, H. C., Jr. 1977. *Tenderness is strength.* New York: Harper and Row.

Mandler, G. 1964. The interruption of behavior. In D. Levine (ed.), *Nebraska symposium on motivation.* Lincoln: University of Nebraska Press, pp. 163-219.

Manning, P. K. 1977. *Police work: The social organization of policing.* Cambridge, Mass.: MIT Press.

March, J. G. 1972. Model bias in social action. *Review of Educational Research* 42: 413-429.

————. 1976. Susan Sontag and heteroscedasticity. Paper presented at the Annual Meeting of the American Educational Research Association, San Francisco, April 19, 1976.

March, J. G., and J. P. Olsen. 1976. *Ambiguity and choice in organizations.* Bergen, Norway: Universitetsforlaget.

March, J. G., and H. A. Simon. 1958. *Organizations.* New York: Wiley.

Marrow, A. J. 1975. Management by participation. In E. L. Cass and F. G. Zimmer (eds.), *Man and work in society.* New York: Van Nostrand Reinhold, pp. 33-48.

Martin, M. 1977. The philosophical importance of the Rosenthal effect. *Journal for the Theory of Social Behavior* 7: 81-97.

Martland, T. H. 1978. Costly schools that do not educate. *Business Week,* January 30, 1978, p. 9.

Maruyama, M. 1963. The second cybernetics: Deviation-amplifying mutual causal processes. *American Scientist* 51: 164-179.

————. 1974. Paradigms and communication. *Technological Forecasting and Social Change* 6: 3-32.

Maugham, S. 1967. *A writer's notebook.* London: Penguin.

McAdams, R. 1976. Letter concerning Donald Campbell's presidential address. *American Psychologist* 31: 351-352.

McCall, M. W., Jr. 1977. Making sense with nonsense: Helping frames of reference clash. *TIMS Studies in Management Sciences* 5: 111-123.

McCarl, R. S., Jr. 1976. Smokejumper initiation. *Journal of American Folklore* 89: 49-66.

McCulloch, W. S. 1965. Why the mind is in the head. In W. S. McCulloch, *Embodiments of mind.* Cambridge, Mass.: MIT Press, pp. 72-141.

McDonough, J. 1978. Review of *The King James Version* by Harry James. *Downbeat,* June 15, 1978, pp. 28-29.

McGlashan, A. 1967. *The savage and beautiful country.* Boston: Houghton Mifflin.

McGregor, D. 1960. *The human side of enterprise.* New York: McGraw-Hill.

McGuire, W. J. 1968. Personality and susceptibility to social influence. In E. F. Borgatta and W. W. Lambert (eds.), *Handbook of personality theory and research.* Chicago: Rand, pp. 1130-1187.

McKelvey, B. In press. Organizational speciation. In C. Pinder and L. Moore (eds.), *Middle range theory and the study of organizations.* Boston: Martinus Nijhoff.

McLeod, J., and S. H. Chaffee. 1972. The construction of social reality. In J. T. Tedeschi (ed.), *The social influence processes.* Chicago: Aldine, pp. 50-99.

Mead, G. H. 1956. A. Strauss (ed.), *Social psychology.* Chicago: University of Chicago Press.

Mechanic, D. 1964. Sources of power of lower participants in complex organizations. In W. W. Cooper, H. J. Leavitt, and M. W. Shelly (eds.), *New perspectives in organization research.* New York: Wiley, pp. 136-149.

Mehan, H., and H. Wood. 1975. *The reality of ethnomethodology.* New York: Wiley.

Merton, R. K. 1940. Bureaucratic structure and personality. *Social Forces* 18: 560-568.

————. 1948. The self-fulfilling prophecy. *Antioch Review* 8: 193-210.

————. 1963. Basic research and potentials of relevance. *American Behavioral Scientist* 6, No. 9: 86-90.

————. 1969. Behavior patterns of scientists. *American Scientist* 57: 1-23.

Metz, T. 1968. Look who's running the show after Kennecott bought Carborundum. *Wall Street Journal,* July 28, 1978, pp. 1, 31.

Meyer, L. B. 1956. *Emotion and meaning in music.* Chicago: University of Chicago Press.

Milgram, S., and H. Toch. 1969. Collective behavior: Crowds and social movements. In G. Lindzey and E. Aronson (eds.), *The handbook of social psychology* (2nd ed., Vol. 4). Reading, Mass.: Addison-Wesley, pp. 507-610.

Miller, G. A., and R. Buckhout. 1973. *Psychology: The science of mental life* (2nd ed.). New York: Harper and Row.

Miller, I. 1969. Business has a war to win. *Harvard Business Review* 47 (March-April): 4.

Miller, J. G. 1971. Living systems: The group. *Behavioral Science* 16: 302-398.

Miller, M. K. 1977. Potentials and pitfalls of path analysis: A tutorial summary. *Quality and Quantity* 11: 329-346.

Miller, S. 1973. Ends, means, galumphing: Some leitmotifs of play. *American Anthropologist* 75: 87-98.

Mills, T. M. 1965. Some hypotheses on small groups from Simmel. In L. Coser (ed.), *Georg Simmel*. Englewood Cliffs, N.J.: Prentice-Hall.

Minogue, K. R. 1973. *The concept of a university*. Berkeley and Los Angeles: University of California Press.

Mintzberg, H. 1975. The manager's job: Folklore and fact. *Harvard Business Review* 53, No. 4: 49-61.

————. 1978. Patterns in strategy formation. *Management Science* 24: 934-948.

Mirvis, P. H., and D. N. Berg. 1977. *Failures in organization development and change*. New York: Wiley.

Mithaug, D. E., and R. L. Burgess. 1968. The effects of differential reinforcement contingencies in the development of social cooperation. *Journal of Experimental Child Psychology* 5: 441-454.

Mitroff, I. I. 1974. Norms and counter-norms in a select group of the Apollo moon scientists: A case study of the ambivalence of scientists. *American Sociological Review* 39: 579-595.

Mol, H. 1971. The dysfunction of sociological knowledge. *American Sociologist* 6: 221-223.

Moore, O. K. 1957. Divination—A new perspective. *American Anthropologist* 59: 69-74.

Moore, W. E. 1964. Predicting discontinuities in social change. *American Sociological Review* 29: 331-338.

Morison, R. S. 1965. Toward a common scale of measurement. *Daedalus* 94: 245-262.

Moscovici, S. 1972. Society and theory in social psychology. In J. Israel and H. Tajfel (eds.), *The context of social psychology*. New York: Academic, pp. 17-68.

————. 1976. *Social influence and social change*. New York: Academic.

Munroe, R. L. 1955. *Schools of psychoanalytic thought*. New York: Holt.

Murdy, W. H. 1975. Anthropocentrism: A modern version. *Science* 187: 1168-1172.

Neisser, U. 1976. *Cognition and reality*. San Francisco: W. H. Freeman.

Nevins, A., and F. E. Hill. 1963. *Ford: Decline and rebirth, 1933-1962*. New York: Scribner.

Nisbett, R. E., and T. D. Wilson. 1977. Telling more than we can know: Verbal reports on mental processes. *Psychological Review* 84: 231-259.

Nord, W. R. 1976. *Concepts and controversy in organizational behavior*. Pacific Palisades, Calif.: Goodyear.

Northway, M. L. 1971. The sociometry of society: Some facts and fancies. *Canadian Journal of Behavioral Science* 3, No. 1: 18-36.

Nystrom, P. C., and W. H. Starbuck. 1977. Why prescription is prescribed. *TIMS Studies in the Management Sciences* 5: 1-5.

Ortony, A. 1975. Why metaphors are necessary and not just nice. *Educational Theory* 25, No. 1: 45-53.

Osofsky, J. D. 1971. Children's influence upon parental behavior: An attempt to define the relationship with the use of laboratory tasks. *Genetic Psychology Monographs* 83: 147-169.

Partridge, B. 1978. The process of leadership on the shopfloor. In B. King, S. Streufert, and F. E. Fiedler (eds.), *Managerial control and organizational democracy*. Washington, D.C.: V. H. Winston, pp. 187-200.

Pearce, J. C. 1973. *The crack in the cosmic egg*. New York: Pocket Books.

———. 1975. *Exploring the crack in the cosmic egg*. New York: Pocket Books.

Percy, W. 1975. *The message in the bottle*. New York: Farrar, Straus, and Giroux.

Plate, T. 1977. Why the cops didn't shoot. *New York*, August 1, 1977, pp. 29-31.

Porter, L. W., and E. E. Lawler. 1965. Properties of organization structure in relation to job attitudes and job behavior. *Psychological Bulletin* 64: 23-51.

Pugh, D. S. 1966. Modern organization theory. *Psychological Bulletin* 66: 235-251.

Rabinowitz, L., H. H. Kelley, and R. M. Rosenblatt. 1966. Effects of different types of interdependence and response conditions in the minimal social situation. *Journal of Experimental Social Psychology* 2: 169-197.

Rainey, H. G., R. W. Backoff, and C. H. Levine. 1976. Comparing public and private organizations. *Public Administration Review* 36: 233-244.

Raven, B. H., and H. T. Eachus. 1963. Cooperation and competition in means-interdependent triads. *Journal of Abnormal and Social Psychology* 67: 307-316.

Ravetz, J. R. 1971. *Scientific knowledge and its social problems*. New York: Oxford University Press.

Redfield, R. 1963. *The social uses of social science*. Chicago: University of Chicago Press.

Reed, R. 1975. Farmers angry over doubling of machinery costs. *New York Times*, August 31, 1975, pp. 33.

Reynolds, W. E. 1974. The analysis of complex behavior: A qualitative systems approach. *General Systems* 19: 73-89.

Rickards, T., and B. L. Freedman. 1978. Procedures for managers in idea-deficient situations: Examination of brainstorming approaches. *Journal of Management Studies* 15: 43-55.

Roby, T. B. 1966. Self-enacting response sequences and reinforcement: Conjecture. *Psychological Reports* 19: 19-31.

Rohde, K. J. 1967. Effect of early experience on the child: Possible solutions to controversy. *Psychological Reports* 20: 134.

Rosenthal, R., and L. Jacobson,. 1968. *Pygmalion in the classroom: Teacher expectation and pupils' intellectual development*. New York: Holt, Rinehart and Winston.

Ross, L. 1977. The intuitive psychologist and his shortcomings: Distortions in the attribution process. In L. Berkowitz (ed.), *Advances in experimental social psychology* (Vol. 10). New York: Academic, pp. 173-220.

Rothenberg, A. 1971. The process of Janusian thinking in creativity. *Archives of General Psychiatry* 24: 195-205.

————. 1976. Janusian thinking and creativity. *Psychoanalytic Study of Society* 7: 1-30.

Rowan, J. 1974. Research as intervention. In N. Armistead (ed.), *Reconstructing social psychology*. Baltimore: Penguin, pp. 86-100.

Rubin, S. E. 1974. What is a maestro? *New York Times Magazine*, September 29, 1974, pp. 32-36, 42-47, 50-54.

Ruse, M. 1974. Cultural evolution. *Theory and Decision* 5: 413-440.

Sahlins, M. D., and E. R. Service (eds.). 1960. *Evolution and culture*. Ann Arbor: University of Michigan Press.

Salaman, G. 1971. Two occupational communities: Examples of a remarkable convergence of work and non-work. *Sociological Review* 19: 389-407.

Salancik, G. R. 1977. Commitment and the control of organizational behavior and belief. In B. M. Staw and G. R. Salanick (eds.), *New directions in organizational behavior*. Chicago: St. Clair Press, pp. 1-54.

Salancik, G. R., and J. Pfeffer. 1977. An examination of need-satisfaction models of job attitudes. *Administrative Science Quarterly* 22: 427-456.

Samples, B. 1976. *The metaphoric mind*. Reading, Mass.: Addison-Wesley.

Sampson, E. E. 1977. Psychology and the American ideal. *Journal of Personality and Social Psychology* 35: 767-782.

Sapolsky, H. M. 1972. *The Polaris system development*. Cambridge, Mass.: Harvard University Press.

Sashkin, M. 1976. Changing toward participative management approaches: A model and methods. *Academy of Management Review* 1, No. 3: 75-86.

Schachter, S. 1964. The interaction of cognitive and physiological determinants of emotional state. In L. Berkowitz (ed.), *Advances in experimental social psychology* (Vol. 1). New York: Academic, pp. 49-80.

Scheff, T. J. 1965. Decision rules, types of error, and their consequences in medical diagnosis. In F. Massarik and P. Ratoosh (eds.), *Mathematical explorations in behavioral science*. Homewood, Ill.: Dorsey, pp. 66-83.

Schein, E. H. 1965. *Organizational psychology*. Englewood Cliffs, N.J.: Prentice-Hall.

Schelling, T. C. 1963. *The strategy of conflict*. New York: Oxford University Press.

Scher, J. M. 1962. Mind as participation. In J. M. Scher (ed.), *Theories of the mind*. New York: Free Press, pp. 354-375.

Schneider, L. 1962. The role of the category of ignorance in sociological theory: An exploratory statement. *American Sociological Review* 27: 492-508.

Schutz, A. 1964. The problem of rationality in the social world. In A. Broderson (ed.), *Alfred Schutz: Collected papers* (Vol. 2). The Hague, Netherlands: Martinus Nijhoff, pp. 64-88.

————. 1967. *The phenomenology of the social world*. Evanston, Ill.: Northwestern University Press.

Scott, R. A. 1967. The factory as a social service organization: Goal displacement in workshops for the blind. *Social Problems* 15: 160-175.

Scott, W. R., S. M. Dornbusch, B. C. Busching, and J. D. Laing. 1967. Organizational evaluation and authority. *Administrative Science Quarterly* 12: 93-117.

Seiko's smash. *Business Week,* June 5, 1978, pp. 86-97.

Shaffer, L. S. 1977. The golden fleece: Anti-intellectualism and social science. *American Psychologist* 32: 814-823.

Shaw, M. E., and J. M. Blum. 1965. Group performance as a function of task difficulty and the group's awareness of member satisfaction. *Journal of Applied Psychology* 49: 151-154.

Sherif, M., and O. J. Harvey. 1952. A study in ego functioning: Elimination of stable anchorages in individual and group situations. *Sociometry* 15: 272-305.

Sherif, M., and C. W. Sherif. 1969. *Social psychology.* New York: Harper and Row.

Shibutani, T. 1971. On sentiments and social control. In H. Turk and R. L. Simpson (eds.), *Institutions and social exchange.* Indianapolis: Bobbs-Merrill, pp. 147-162.

Sidowski, J. B. 1957. Reward and punishment in a minimal social situation. *Journal of Experimental Psychology* 54: 318-326.

Silverman, D. 1971. *The theory of organisations.* New York: Basic Books.

———. 1975. *Reading Castenada.* London: Routledge and Kegan Paul.

Silverman, I. 1977. Why social psychology fails. *Canadian Psychological Review* 18: 353-358.

Simmel, G. 1959. On the nature of philosophy. In K. H. Wolff (ed.), *Essays on sociology, philosophy, and aesthetics.* New York: Harper, pp. 282-309.

———. 1971. Group expansion and the development of individuality. In D. N. Levine (ed.), *Georg Simmel on individuality and social forms.* Chicago: University of Chicago Press, pp. 251-293.

Simon, H. A. 1957. *Administrative behavior.* New York: Free Press.

———. 1962. The architecture of complexity. *Proceedings of the American Philosophical Society* 106, No. 6: 467-482.

Simons, H. W. 1976. *Persuasion.* Reading, Mass.: Addison-Wesley.

Singer, E. A., and L. M. Wooton. 1976. The triumph and failure of Albert Speer's administrative genius: Implications for current management theory and practice. *Journal of Applied Behavioral Science* 12: 79-103.

Siu, R. G. H. 1968. *The man of many qualities.* Cambridge, Mass.: MIT Press.

———. 1974. *Ch'i: A neo-Taoist approach to life.* Cambridge, Mass.: MIT Press.

Skinner, B. F. 1966. The phylogeny and ontogeny of behavior. *Science* 153: 1205-1213.

Slack, C. W. 1955. Feedback theory and the reflex arc concept. *Psychological Review* 62: 263-267.

Smith, D. 1978. Control and orientations to work in a business organization. *Journal of Management Studies* 15: 211-222.

Smith, E. R., and F. D. Miller. 1978. Limits on perception of cognitive processes: A reply to Nisbett and Wilson. *Psychological Review* 85: 355-362.

Smith, L. M., and P. A. Pohland. Grounded theory and educational ethnography: A methodological analysis and critique. In J. Roberts and S. Akinsanya (eds.), *Educational patterns and cultural configurations*. New York: McKay, pp. 264-279.

Starbuck, W. H. 1976. Organizations and their environments. In M. D. Dunnette (ed.), *Handbook of industrial and organizational psychology*. Chicago: Rand, pp. 1069-1123.

Staw, B. M., and G. R. Salancik. 1977. *New directions in organizational behavior*. Chicago: St. Clair Press.

Stebbins, G. L. 1965. Pitfalls and guideposts in comparing organic and social evolution. *Pacific Sociological Review* 8, No. 1: 3-10.

Steinbeck, J. 1941. *The log from the Sea of Cortez*. New York: Viking.

Steinbruner, J. D. 1974. *The cybernetic theory of decision*. Princeton, N.J.: Princeton University Press.

Steiner, I. D. 1955. Interpersonal behavior as influenced by accuracy of social perception. *Psychological Review* 62: 268-274.

Stern, J. P. 1963. *Lichtenberg: A doctrine of scattered occasions*. London: Thames and Hudson.

Stewart, R. 1976. *Contrasts in management*. New York: McGraw-Hill.

Stieglitz, H. 1975. What's not on the organization chart. In J. H. Donnelly, Jr., J. L. Gibson, and J. M. Ivancevich (eds.), *Fundamentals of management*. Dallas: Business Publications, pp. 113-119.

Sudnow, D. 1978. *Ways of the hand*. Cambridge, Mass.: Harvard University Press.

Suicide attempts? *Ithaca New Times*, April 10, 1975, p. 2.

Swanson, G. E. 1970. Toward corporate action: A reconstruction of elementary collective processes. In T. Shibutani (ed.), *Human nature and collective behavior*. Englewood Cliffs, N.J.: Prentice-Hall, pp. 124-144.

Tannenbaum, A. S. 1968. *Control in organizations*. New York: McGraw-Hill.

TenHouten, W. D., and C. D. Kaplan. 1973. *Science and its mirror image*. New York: Harper.

Teuber, M. L. 1974. Sources of ambiguity in the prints of Maurits C. Escher. *Scientific American*, July 1974, pp. 90-104.

Thibaut, J., and H. H. Kelley. 1959. *Social psychology of groups*. New York: Wiley.

Thompson, J. D. 1967. *Organizations in action*. New York: McGraw-Hill.

Thorngate, W. 1976. "In general" vs. "it depends": Some comments on the Gergen-Schlenker debate. *Personality and Social Psychology Bulletin* 2: 404-410.

Treadwell, A. C. 1975. The characteristics and content of educational administration: An exploratory study. Unpublished manuscript, Cornell University.

Tukey, J. W. 1977. *Exploratory data analysis*. Reading, Mass.: Addison-Wesley.

Tullar, W. L., and G. V. Barrett. 1976. The future of autobiography as a predictor of sales success. *Journal of Applied Psychology* 61: 371-373.

Turner, S. R. 1977. Complex organizations as savage tribes. *Journal for the Theory of Social Behaviour* 7: 99-125.

Upton, A. 1961. *Design for thinking.* Palo Alto, Calif.: Pacific Books.

VanFleet, D. D., and A. G. Bedeian. 1977. A history of the span of management. *Academy of Management Review* 2: 356-372.

Vickers, G. 1967. *Towards a sociology of management.* New York: Basic Books.

Vinacke, W. E., D. C. Crowell, D. Dren, and V. Young. 1966. The effect of information about strategy on a three-person game. *Behavioral Science* 11: 180-189.

Von Foerster, H. 1967. Time and memory. *Annals of the New York Academy of Sciences* 138 (Article 2): 866-873.

Vonnegut, K., Jr. 1975. *Wampeters, foma and granfalloons.* New York: Delta.

Waddington, C. H. 1977. *Tools for thought.* New York: Basic Books.

Wade, N. 1972. Fischer-Spassky charges: What did the Russians have in mind? *Science* 177: 778.

Wager, L. W. 1972. Organizational linking pins. *Human Relations* 25: 307-326.

Wallace, A. F. C. 1961. *Culture and personality.* New York: Random House.

Wallerstein, R. S., and H. Sampson. Issues in research in the psychoanalytic process. *International Journal of Psycho-Analysis* 52, No. 11: 11-50.

Warwick, Donald P. 1975. *A theory of public bureaucracy: Politics, personality, and organization in the State Department.* Cambridge, Mass.: Harvard University Press.

Watzlawick, P. 1976. *How real is real?* New York: Random House, Vintage Books.

Watzlawick, P., J. H. Beavin, and D. D. Jackson. 1967. *Pragmatics of human communication.* New York: Norton.

Watzlawick, P., J. Weakland, and R. Fisch. 1974. *Change.* New York: Norton.

Webb, E. J., and G. E. Watzke. The future as prologue: Methods for predicting the future. Unpublished manuscript, Stanford University.

Weick, K. E. 1970. The twigging of overload. In H. B. Pepinsky (ed.), *People and information.* New York: Pergamon, pp. 67-129.

————. 1976a. Careers as eccentric predicates. *Executive* 2, No. 2: 6-10.

————. 1976b. Educational organizations as loosely coupled systems. *Administrative Science Quarterly* 21: 1-19.

————. 1977a. On repunctuating the problem of organizational effectiveness. In H. Pennings and P. Goodman (eds.), *Organizational effectiveness.* San Francisco: Jossey-Bass, pp. 193-225.

————. 1977b. Organization design: Organizations as self-designing systems. *Organizational Dynamics* 6, No. 2: 30-46.

————. 1978. The spines of leaders. In M. W. McCall, Jr., and M. M. Lombardo (eds.), *Leadership: Where else can we go?* Durham, N.C.: Duke University Press, pp. 37-61.

Weick, K. E., and D. P. Gilfillan. 1971. Fate of arbitrary traditions in a laboratory microculture. *Journal of Personality and Social Psychology* 17: 179-191.

Weick, K. E., D. P. Gilfillan, and T. Keith. 1973. The effect of composer credibility on orchestra performance. *Sociometry* 36: 435-462.

Weiner, S. S. 1976. Participation, deadlines, and choice. In J. G. March and J. P. Olsen, *Ambiguity and choice in organizations.* Bergen, Norway: Universitetsforlaget, pp. 225-250.

Weisskopf-Joelson, E. 1971. Some comments on the psychology of the psychologist. *Journal of Psychology* 78: 95-113.

Wender, P. H. 1968. Vicious and·virtuous circles: The role of deviation-amplifying feedback in the origin and perpetuation of behavior. *Psychiatry* 31: 309-324.

White, J. H. 1964. The Janus: A locomotive's history revisited. *Journal of Transport History* 6, No. 3: 175-181.

Whyte, W. F. 1959. *Man and organization.* Homewood, Ill.: Irwin.

Wicklund, R. A., and J. W. Brehm. *Perspectives on cognitive dissonance.* Hillsdale, N.J.: Erlbaum.

Wiener, L. 1930. *Articulated locomotives.* New York: Richard R. Smith.

Wilson, E. O. 1975. *Sociobiology: The new synthesis.* Cambridge, Mass.: Belknap.

Wimsatt, W. K. 1976. *Day of the leopards.* New Haven, Conn.: Yale University Press.

Withuhn, B. 1975. A primer for coal shovelers. *Trainline,* Spring 1975, No. 6, pp. 5-6.

Wolf, W. B. 1974. *The basic Barnard.* Ithaca, N.Y.: New York State School of Industrial and Labor Relations. Cornell University.

Wolff, K. H. 1950. *The sociology of Georg Simmel.* New York: Free Press.

Zander, A., and D. Wolfe. 1964. Administrative rewards and coordination among committee members. *Administrative Science Quarterly* 9: 50-69.

Zaret, D. 1978. Sociological theory and historical scholarship. *American Sociologist* 13: 114-121.

Ziman, J. M. 1970. Some pathologies of the scientific life. *Advancement of Science* 27: 1-10.

Zimbardo, P. G. 1969. *The cognitive control of motivation.* Glenview, Ill.: Scott, Foresman.

Zimmerman, D. H. 1974. Fact as a practical accomplishment. In R. Turner (ed.), *Ethnomethodology.* Baltimore: Penguin, pp. 128-143.

index